X Rubicon

Crossing Life, Sex, Love, & Killing in CIA Proxy Wars

An indictment of US Citizens:
ignorantia non excusat

Editor: Jules Bond

Cover Art: *Life Begets Life*, Sophia Rose, 2020

Table of Contents

You've got to be taught

To hate and fear,
You've got to be taught
From year to year,
It's got to be drummed
In your dear little ear
You've got to be carefully taught.

You've got to be taught to be afraid
Of people whose eyes are oddly made,
And people whose skin is a diff'rent shade,
You've got to be carefully taught.

You've got to be taught before it's too late,
Before you are six or seven or eight,
To hate all the people your relatives hate,
You've got to be carefully taught.

You've got to be carefully taught
– South Pacific
– Rogers & Hammerstein

Dedication

and

Acknowledgments

This work is dedicated to **Julie**. This work would never have been possible without her understanding, love, and support, or without her tireless and watchful eye keeping the protagonist alive. There is no amount of thanks that can possibly make up for the pain and suffering this has caused her, but, ***Thank You***.

This work draws heavily upon the works of Abraham Joshua Heschel, especially <u>A Passion For Truth</u> (1973, 1986; New York; Farrar, Strauss and Giroux). He is reminiscent of a Jewish Socrates, who was always willing to bear his soul, and to question and seek the Truth, no matter where he found it.

A deep gratitude is owed to Professor Martin Van Creveld for his scholarly historical account of the privileges of women throughout history (<u>The Privileged Sex</u>, 2013, DVLC Enterprises), especially as related to war. He provided invaluable insight into understanding our own observations and making sense of them. Professor Creveld also was invaluable in assisting in our own understanding of the expendable nature of men, and accepting this Truth even through the pain it caused.

Thank you to Kris H for helping Julie process these things. The protagonist owes you an apology and much more.

Thank you to Ron J for pushing so hard for this to be written. It may be more than you bargained for, but you did push.

Thank you to Dee S, a Friend who is Truly a Friend. You are owed an apology for never having been told these things, but we think you'll understand.

Thank you to both Ted C and Jamie T for listening.

A *special thank you* and *acknowledgment* to Kellie J, a patient therapist who has given freely of her own time to help this couple survive late into life, to understand each other better. She has "mad skillz" and a sneaky bag of tricks, and she sees the cows clogging up the river.

Thank you to Alison Weir and IfAmericansKnew.org for their extensive work detailing the Israeli Apartheid Regime's fascist illegal occupation of Palestine. We encourage everyone to read Alison's historical work, Against Our Better Judgment: *The hidden history of how the U.S. was used to create Israel* (2014, Alison Weir; IfAmericansKnew.org). Run, don't walk, to find out more.

Foreward

Or The Vanguard

by Julie

People will do anything, no matter
how absurd, in order to avoid facing
their own souls. One does not
become enlightened by imagining
figures of light, but by making the
darkness conscious.

Psychology and Alchemy – Carl Jung

Each and every life is pronounced and accented by
suffering. Some suffering is so delirious and fraught with evil it
is unfathomable. We turn away from it whether it be our own
torment or that of another. Is there really any 'other'? Suffering
is as varied and variegated as every human who has or will ever
walk this earth. Regardless of the package in which our suffering
is wrapped, we all experience pain, guilt, shame, fear,
abandonment, loss. Underneath our individual agony there lies a
shared innate desire to understand what has caused our suffering
and the suffering we experience in others especially those whom
we love. I have been on a very intimate journey of suffering with
Rubicon, my husband, my Beloved.

Humans don't like pain, it hurts us. We have become very
adept at avoiding it, denying it, medicating it, cloistering it from
ourselves and from others. An experience so very human in its
commonality (which genuinely connects us so intimately) has

grown into a thick tangle of deceit which only compounds our suffering by separating us from one another. As I write this Foreward, anxiety disorder with debilitating panic attacks, and depression with suicidal ideation are on an ever increasing rampage worldwide. Their mission is to convince us of the treacherous thought that our suffering is unique unto us individually. Yet in no other time have we as a species been so connected in our human brokenness and suffering.

This book is laden with suffering. So why read it? Simply because one human's suffering is all of our suffering. There is no separation. When one of us suffers we all suffer. When we can arrive at a place of acceptance of this basic truth, if allowed to be acknowledged, felt, released, expressed, and integrated, suffering is an extremely wise teacher. By suffering consciously, we are given the freedom to be complete human beings; to stay grounded in humanity despite the yuckiness it contains. I am by no means a tormentor, nor a victim of suffering for suffering's sake. However, something as ubiquitous in human beings, as suffering is, has the power to be experienced in a conscious way and lead us to a deeper understanding of what it means to be a human being and to bring greater healing individually and thus to the whole of humanity. Working through our aversion of suffering and befriending it, accepting its transformational power and wisdom, is essential to any life worth living. The paradox of something so excruciating becoming a portal to peace, compassion, deserves to be examined in all its complexity.

Consideration and contemplation of things, especially atrocious things, is a helpful albeit challenging process. Step one is to acknowledge the truth that something has gone terribly wrong and correction needs to be sought. It requires contrast and choices, pondering events which we have experienced, deciphering how this painful thing has affected us. In contemplation we can start to separate our true selves from the atrocity and come to a beautiful space where we realize the pain/depression/anxiety – is not who we are but rather what we are witnessing within our human form. Step two is to feel the atrocity; truly feel it as it arises. Do not shrink from it. Do not deny its power to transform you from the inside out. Do not abandon yourself. This work can be excruciating but is nonetheless necessary. There is a sweet spot where we chew things over, examine how we got where we are without falling into the abyss of rumination and self doubt or self hatred. This journey is craggy terrain and most of us have not been given a map; we are not taught how to cope and heal from suffering. As is pointed out by Rubicon's experience in the following pages, the journey becomes even more mountainous and steep, twisty and circuitous when the suffering is compounded by being the perpetrator of pain. Suffering will either lead us to be a victim or a creator of healing and to becoming a wiser, more compassionate human being. It brings me no end of joy to declare that my Beloved Rubicon has been led to be the latter.

I am a witness to Rubicon's journey through devastating suffering. I have witnessed the darkness that has imprisoned him for most of his life. He was stuck in a vortex of extreme pain and felt no freedom to share it with anyone. The mere thought of how very alone he felt, fearfully believing I would bolt if he told me what he did in the military or the truth of his sexuality, breaks my heart. He was so full of self loathing. He was suffocating from suffering; poisoning himself on misconceptions of who he was. I would be lying beside him in our bed talking to him, touching him and know he was not there in his body. His mind, crowded with memories, had captured him and kidnapped him far away from my presence. I was totally lost to how to reach him. How I would have loved to have a Fulton Recovery System to extract him from those haunting memories, experiences of which at the time, I had no knowledge! How I yearned to retrieve him from

9

whatever it was that took his presence away! His pain was palpable, visual, I referred to it as the light-less mask of depression; I could taste its bitterness and it felt ever so cruel.

For the longest time I thought his bouts of despair and complete anguish were caused by the neglect he experienced as a child, being brought up by an alcoholic father and an emotionally inaccessible mother. He was physically abused by one of his older brothers, who would punch him into unconsciousness. This trauma surely was enough to cause continued pain. And yet, I felt there were other causes he was hiding from me. I am an extremely curious creature by nature, and I asked many questions only to be blocked by cagey answers and anger if I pried too forcibly. Knowing what I know now, I realize how unpleasant and daunting my questions must have felt to him. Rubicon has often shared with me his mantra: "Keep your fuckin mouth shut". How very isolating. How very poignant that he was able to find his voice and write this book.

I would wonder if I was the cause of his dismal melancholy and rage. I would get hit with a lightning bolt of his hot white fury and be left wondering what I did to elicit such overkill. Afterward he would become riddled with guilt. All the while I felt his deep love and devotion for me. Rubicon is my best friend.

The melancholy I had observed in Rubicon from the very first day I met him, would wax and wane like the passages of the moon. Back and forth, up and down the emotion would fluctuate. He has a wicked sense of humor. His laugh is inviting and contagious. We shared laughter. We shared singing. We shared running highs. We shared literature. As our love for one another was declared we shared every inch of our physical form with each other in ecstasy. And yet, for some inexplicable reason, he would dive so deep into the muck of hopelessness and crippling fear, I

10

was bewildered as to how to pull him back up to the surface to breathe fresh air.

As the melancholy locked him into full blown suicidal ideation prison, I became very fearful of losing him. I was hypervigilant. I hid knives, ropes, his antidepressants, his antipsychotics. I prayed and prayed for protection for him and for relief from his overwhelming pain. I did Reiki on him. I did tonglen meditation. I did these things without his knowledge because it angered him. I would watch him finally succumb to sheer exhaustion and find fitful sleep. I thankfully listened to each breath he took. I would hold him all night on high alert in case he got out of bed. On the nights he didn't come to bed because his mind was choking him with devastating thoughts and fear, I would sleep with one eye open as a mother sleeps lightly listening for her newborn's cry. I would hear him go to the coffeepot at 2:30 am as he evaded the nightmares (I had no idea of their torture at the time) I would strain my ears in case he tried to leave the house.

When I had to leave him alone, I made him promise me he would be breathing when I came back. I was in panic mode anytime I was away from him. I made my trips as short as possible. I timed how long I could be gone before an overdose may kick in if he found his pills or walked to the store down the street for alcohol and sleeping pills. I checked and double checked all possible means of death in the house. Razor blades were stashed out of sight (or so I hoped which wasn't the case one awful day). Sometimes I left our oldest son who was 8-10 years old at the time with him as a guardian. This made me feel extremely guilty and frightened, but I had to work to bring money in and I trusted Rubicon with our son. I trusted he would never leave our son with the responsibility of saving him nor the memory of watching his daddy die. And he never attempted suicide when our son was with him. I am incredibly thankful for

Rubicon's love of our children which often was his only thin thread to life.

As you will read in the coming pages, making love has been an essential connection for Rubicon (isn't it for us all?). It has kept him grounded when he was totally unconnected to life itself. During these depressive episodes his libido was adversely affected first by the depression then the psychological drugs which were necessary to keep him alive. This was a very challenging time for both of us. When he was able to make love to me, I often cried afterward wondering if it would be the last time we ever would. Would he be alive tomorrow? While this was a huge challenge at the time, it taught me to stay very present. My sense perceptions were acutely tuned in to him. We were together. I felt the warmth of his body alive. I felt his heart beating. I felt his breath hasten and his life force as it joined mine.

I so desperately wanted to talk to someone about what this experience was like for me, for our little son, for my Beloved. During this time I witnessed how uncomfortable and uneasy mental illness, especially attempted suicide, makes humans. My friends would bring us food while Rubicon was hospitalized several times. They brought me gas cards to travel to and from the hospital which was 45 miles away, they said they were praying for us, but they would recoil if I tried to share with them the tortuous existence in which we found ourselves. I tried to be very candid with them at first because I felt it honored Rubicon and I wanted to eradicate the fucking false stigma of mental illness. I do not blame them for their fear. They helped me very much in practical ways. I am still very thankful for their aid. But I really needed someone to listen and show us pure understanding and compassion. My husband was/is a beautiful human being who was in excruciating pain. He was/is NOT something to be feared, but uplifted by LOVE. I am still grieving the emotional isolation in which we tried to survive. That was 23 years ago.

A low point came for me one day after Rubicon had returned home from being hospitalized following his second suicide attempt (there were 3 during these dark years). He was feeling better and I was so very, very thankful to have him home. We were at the grocery store. I saw one of my friends there and we approached her to say hi. She had brought us food. She had kept us in her thoughts and prayers during Rubicon's hospitalization. I walked up to her and greeted her with a smile. She froze. When she saw my husband behind me, she actually backed away in horror. I tried to down play her reaction to protect my Beloved from her extremely unchristian treatment. When we got home I went in the bathroom and wept bitter tears.

There was/is never any doubt that my husband would/will always protect me and care for me. Nevertheless, the torment inside of him often saw me as a threat and I became the target of his rage. He was helpless to protect me from his own pain, fear, and rage. How could it be otherwise? He was helpless to protect himself from his own buried pain, fear, and rage. He was reminded nightly of the atrocities he had caused. I would awaken in the middle of the night to his punching me or kicking me as he was engulfed in a nightmarish flashback. I would block his blows and yell at him to wake up. He would never tell me the content nor cause of these nightmares. I asked repeatedly for him to please tell me. Not until 20 months ago, did I know the extent of his anguish. I did not know why, but I did know his suffering became my suffering.

The voice of this narrative is ferocious. It is also prophetic in its plea to open our eyes to the harsh reality of the military, repentance, and redeeming ourselves. Just as I had to block Rubicon's nightmare attacks and shout at him to stop, the author representing my Beloved's voice, shouts at us to wake up and stop the needless killing of our imaginary enemies, the veterans we disrespectively send to slaughter, and the families who then are left to cope with the chaos. Sean's voice is as sharp as Rubicon's experience is cutting. Rubicon is a very passionate and intense person, as you will see as you read on. Sean matches this passion and intensity beautifully. In order to face the intensity of this suffering, we need a very ferocious voice to beckon us swiftly and forcibly to the truth of what is happening. We need this because we have been entangled sooo very long in the deceit and there is so much at stake.

As I continue to process the suffering my Beloved has caused and the suffering he has endured, it is like walking through a raging inferno. Fire has two capacities. Fire can just burn and destroy leaving only destruction and ashes. Fire can also purify and open a space for new life to thrive. For 40 years Rubicon has been engulfed within an inextinguishable fiery hell. It is only by Grace and fortitude that it did not leave him as a pile of ashes. In allowing himself to become vulnerable enough to tell me the truth of his experience, purification began. Working on this book has given him a double dose of vulnerability. He has had to relive each mission and heartbreak again as he retells his story. This book is raw in its honesty and vulnerability. Please treat it with the same honesty and openness in which it is offered to you. You will be transformed in your understanding of humanity. Respect it and invite it to burn up any resistance in you which obstructs you from receiving its truth to purify you.

Can we honor the suffering? Can we honor the despair? Can we honor truth? Can we honor forgiveness? Can we cast aside our judgment and our desperate attempts to freeze and back away? TRUTH and LOVE are our only hope. To be completely truthful - it is our only hope, yes? – I would feel angry at my husband for his hopelessness and despair. My anger did nothing

14

whatsoever to help. I tried to use my anger as motivation to remedy the depression. Nope. It only came across as cold heartedness and self-righteousness. Frustration would arise in me. What am I doing wrong? Why can't I help him out of this unrelenting negativity and sadness? I'm pissed. It's not supposed to be like this. I am very sorry I got caught up in this loop. I have to forgive myself for placing more pain upon him. I don't need to forgive him for anything. Acceptance is the golden practice here.

I had to accept Rubicon's suffering. When I did I could look past the external challenges. I clearly see the incredibly strong and vital man I love beyond measure.

A very amazing event I witnessed in my Beloved was his release (for himself and ultimately for our children) from alcoholism. His father was raised by an alcoholic mother. His mother was the classic enabler and many of her siblings were alcoholics. All of Rubicon's siblings are alcoholic to this day. Rubicon went with what he was taught. He binged on alcohol when the demons of his past became too raucous. This frightened me very much. I knew how much destructive damage this had caused my husband and I did not want this perpetuated onto my children. I was an enabler I confess. Then I woke up and had to act.

Rubicon was in the middle of Electroconvulsive Therapy (ECT). His diagnosis of Treatment Resistant Depression was true to its name and his depression was proving to be very stubborn. Initially the kind and gentle psychiatrist who performed the therapy said Rubicon would undergo 4, possibly 6 sessions. It took 17 before the effect stuck with him. This experience in itself caused frustration and pain. He usually had 2 sessions a week. Sometimes the depression was so pronounced I had to physically coax him into the car to make the 45 minute drive to the hospital. He fought me physically. He yelled at me to leave him the fuck alone! "Just let me die!" he screamed in my face. He would be defiant and angry with me the whole time while the nurses prepared him for the procedure. He would not look me in the eye. He barely answered the nurses questions. I would fill the gap. I would tell the nurses this was not really what he was like with my eyes swelling with tears. After the therapy, it was like night and day. The nurses would invite me back to sit with him as he recovered. He would look at me and whisper a sweet 'Hi'. He would hold my hand. While he often refused to wear his seat belt on the way to the hospital (no matter how much I begged – at this point I had to pick my battles), on our return drive home he would buckle up without a word.

Rubicon has little to no memory of this savage time. I am thankful he does not. But I do remember it and I share with you here to help you better understand the drowning effects of PTSD. We must not freeze and back away from suffering. We must befriend it and build bridges to cross it.

In the following days between the sessions the depression would creep back up and pull him back down into the abyss. And so he began to drink more. After the 9th ECT session, it was a Friday, we were invited to a party at one of his good time buddies. (I cannot call him a friend to Rubicon because he never was in my opinion.) Rubicon was advised after every single ECT session not to consume alcohol for 24 hours after the procedure. He did not follow theses instructions. On the night of the party he got plastered. I was so worried he was screwing up his mind. Our son went with us to the party (we take our kids with us everywhere). I abhorred him seeing his daddy so drunk. He had to help me get him to the car. Rubicon collapsed in the front yard and we couldn't get him up. I asked one of the guys to help me get him in the car. When we got home, we got him as far as the couch, and I gave him a bucket to throw up in and got our son to bed. I apologized to our son for what he had been exposed to and told him it would NOT continue. I slept very little that night, arising several times to make sure Rubicon was okay.

Something very egregious was happening within our family and I knew I had to take action. The next day after he had recovered from the hangover, while he was out in the garage, I went out to talk to him. I told him I would stand by him through the psychological challenges, through poverty, through pretty much anything that was thrown on our path together, but I could not abide with alcoholism. While I do believe it is a very strong addiction, I knew he was stronger. I told him when he picked up a bottle of Jameson's or several beers at a sitting, he was making a choice. He would have to decide if he wanted to continue choosing alcohol or me. I strongly felt I needed to protect our son from what his daddy had experienced growing up in an alcoholic family. And I believed Rubicon would make the same decision had it been me using alcohol to self medicate. He was not pleased with me, but I can't remember if it was that same day or the following day, he took down the Jameson whiskey bottle and emptied it down the sink. He told me he would stop drinking. He has kept his promise. This was not easy for him. I know the emotional pain he was feeling was intense and he was often overwrought, but he didn't reach for alcohol to numb himself again. The pride I feel for his resolve and strength is very profound. He has changed the course of our children and our grandchildren by deep self examination and being very honest with his own suffering. He suffered consciously so that he would not perpetuate the dysfunction of alcoholism onto our family. I am ever so thankful for his resolve and his love and devotion to us.

I have had to make room for Rubicon's ghosts and his past sexual partners. They are still roaming around within him. In all honesty, I felt threatened by how very present they have remained for him. While I was in the here and now trying to find him and

17

anchor him in the present with me, he was reliving a lifetime packed into less that 3 years. As we continue to share the traumas we have both experienced, our understanding for one another broadens and expands. Trauma is contracting and stifling. As we open to one another and bathe each other in grace, our vulnerability cracks our protective shells, gentle expansion occurs.

Just as suffering is a very human experience, so is sexuality. You may find the following descriptions of Rubicon's sexual experiences intense. Again, I ask you to dispense judgment and not get trapped in your own opinions of what is right or wrong about sexuality. I hope you don't miss the beautiful vulnerability Rubicon expresses and how sex was about the only connection he had with life rather than death. I dare say it kept my Beloved alive when everything else was warring against him. Sean gives you graphic images of sex in this work. Without sex there is no life. Humanity would cease to exist. It is one of the strongest human desires. We have done a great disservice to ourselves and our progeny by not honoring it and celebrating it because of religious baggage. If you have an understanding of a Divine Creator, then you cannot deny that that Creator created this very pleasurable experience for us. We need to stop living small when it comes to this most precious gift. Objectification of another for the sake of power or lustful gratification is not acceptable. But the very human experience of sex is vital to our conversation as a species. I hope we will do better. "Thinking is difficult, that's why most people judge." (Carl Jung)

I invite you, the reader, not to get trapped in the intensity and overwhelming nature of this narrative. If you get snared in personal shock, judgments, and opinions, you will miss the truth of the message which ultimately can bring about understanding, and radical change. This writing has the potential to shake you to your core and inspire you to open your heart and find compassion. Please allow it to touch you deeply and do its healing work. We are all in this together. You WILL be shocked. This experience is extremely shocking. Some of you will be shocked, because you won't want to believe such evil demands were placed on a young man at the tender age of 18 years and that he did such evil deeds in the name of "freedom and liberty". And you won't want to even entertain the notion that this is not just one veteran's story. There are thousands of stories akin to this one.

I understand this shock. When Rubicon first opened up to me I was incredulous to what he had done. It did not affect my love for him in the least, but it utterly shattered my heart. I am still grieving all the dark lost years of torment it caused him – us. But grief is an essential path to complete healing. We are on our way. The two of us. Through reading this book you are also with us on this journey of truth.

Julie
May 2022

Statement of the Author

Included in this work is a letter from the ODNI requesting that this work *appear* to be fiction. With that in mind, the following shall suffice to meet that requirement:

It is impossible to load this account with lies to further an immoral agenda. THIS WORK IS FICTION in the sense of the lies, corruption, propaganda, and false agendas which made it possible. To suggest that the truth must become a lie, or that truth become subservient to a false and egregious cause is unacceptable and impossible. That said, THIS WORK IS NOT FICTION. Some people will believe nothing. Some will refuse to believe that which they know to be true. Some will readily believe that which they know to be untrue. Some will make excuses for lying and corruption. Rarely will a person believe anything without question – there's ALWAYS motivation.

Many years ago a great man, Abraham Joshua Heschel, wrote a great book, A Passion For Truth. I am an atheist, yet this philosophic Jewish scholar touched my heart. He wrote about his life long endeavor struggling to come to terms with Love and Mendacity existing simultaneously. He gave the mythic account of Truth being despised by its fellows, Mercy and Righteousness – and Truth was buried in the ground (by God – imagine that):

"Mercy and Truth collided;
Righteousness and Peace engaged in a clash"

"Truth wants to emerge, but man does not want its appearance… They think they dance, yet they are paralyzed. Delusion holds them enraptured. They feel so comfortable in

20

the clutches of their self-deception that when
Satan himself embraces them, they think he is
in love with them."

This then, is what we are facing here. The Mendacity of
the United States Government and its agent of destruction, the
CIA, and its Citizenry – unchecked and unbalanced, thinking
Satan is in love with them. The colonial powers in the world still
run amok creating evil for profit.

Names have been changed to comply with the
requirements. Some names have been changed to protect those
who need protection. Some have been changed to that which fits
the individual's real or pretended character. Some names are so
well known it doesn't matter what the fuck we call them (just
don't call them late for feeding on the government teats), so we
leave their names as they exist because they deserve it and
because their words and deeds have already become part of a vast
public record.

> "The challenge we face is a test of our
> integrity. We are all on trial, we are all under
> judgment. The issue is not political or social
> expediency. The issue is whether we are
> morally strong, whether we are… worthy to
> answer… Shall we continue to be deaf, shall
> we continue to be sensitive only when our
> own needs and interests are involved?
> "We have attained a high standard of
> living. We must seek to attain a high standard
> of thinking… There is nothing in the world
> that may be regarded as holy as eliminating
> anguish, as alleviating pain."
>
> *The Insecurity Of Freedom* – Abraham Joshua Heschel

21

Rubicon's Statement

Once you had gold,
Once you had silver,
Then came the rains
Out of the blue.
Ever and always.
Always and ever.
Time gave both darkness and
dreams to you.

Once You Had Gold – Enya

How it happened he did not know.
But all at once something seemed to
seize him and fling him at her feet.
He wept and threw himself around
her knees. For the first instant she
was terribly frightened and she
turned pale. She jumped up and
looked at him trembling. But at the
same moment she understood, and a
light of infinite happiness came into
her eyes. She knew and had no
doubt that he loved her beyond
everything and that at last the
moment had come...

Epilogue – Crime & Punishment
– Fyodor Dostoyevski
Translation: Constance Garnett

For over forty years I have dragged around the corpses that haunt my existence. I do not believe in ghosts, yet there they are, constantly in my head, my dreams. On hot summer days I see blood on my hands. I know it's not there, yet I see it, and smell it. Smelling iron (or copper) fills my nostrils with the stench of human blood and guts.

I made the decision, right or wrong 38 years ago, not to tell my wife these things. I've held on to these events, closely and deeply guarded for over forty years. I'm getting later in life, and a serious reflection occurred which brought these events forward with a vengeance. Part of this recognition was a realization that the most profound effect I've had in life was the success I had killing and destroying – "If you've got a job to do you've got to do it well, you've got to give the other fella Hell" (*Live And Let Die* – Wings). These events had caused marital problems. They had caused pain to others – victims and their families, my wife, my sons, and daughters – as well as to myself, so a year and a half ago I told my wife. Among other feelings, she was relieved to finally know why I kicked, ran, hit, and stabbed in my sleep – and what had caused years of depression and anger. I sat down with the three oldest children and told them the whole truth. I apologized especially to my wife and oldest son. By not telling them sooner, I had allowed them to grow up believing they had caused my problems. But my son had always been one to try and outdo anything I did, and earlier in life the words stuck hard in my throat and choked me; I didn't want him attempting to try and outdo me in this. But now, we cried and he said he felt relieved that I was finally telling him.

I was encouraged by my wife, the author, and therapist to write these things down. Upon commencing, it immediately became urgent; not just for the sake of spreading out my life

23

before me to better understand what had happened, but also to relay these things to others, especially young men who hold dreams of military glory, for such a thing *does not exist*; and, to indict the American public for its lack of oversight upon its government, military, and the secret death and destruction meted out in their name. Writing these things has brought back intense pain.

Within 2-1/2 years I became guilty of planning and assisting in the slaughter of thousands, and was directly responsible for the killing of >300, from a distance, close up, and personal. I had become everything I despised. If you are a young man or woman thinking of joining the military, think again. Recruiters are salesmen selling you a false narrative in exchange for your soul. You are nothing to the military except expendable. No matter what any fool tells you, you will regret killing for false beliefs, lies, and corruption. Don't believe any idiot flying service flags in front of their house, or those claiming how great the military treated them, for they have never seen nor participated in what you are about to read. Don't believe any cunt walking around with semi-automatic weapons or a 9mm pistol on their belt. Every military hawk is simply a little bitch named *Rolf,* with no experience, yet dreaming of the glory of patriotic killing.

A mind is a terrible thing to waste, and the military and PTSD will waste your mind. As far as PTSD goes, it's one thing to be the witness and/or victim of violence, it's quite another thing to be the perpetrator of violence. In the end, you will suffer for it, and the military and the VA, and the Congress, and the Presidents couldn't give a rat's ass whether you receive treatment or not. The VA treats a fraction of PTSD cases, and has programming in place to drive vets away, to deny claims for help. Money runs the system, not the need to take care of veterans with legs and arms intact, yet with shattered minds straining to come to terms with what they have done and experienced, and many times give up on life.

This writing is a *mea culpa*, an admittance of guilt. It is the repentance that making amends demands. I AM guilty of the evil I have committed and in which I've participated. To get you started, I admit your guilt for you, so that you spend less time asking why. Read on and you'll understand what this means.

Preface

He said, "I was just a child then. Now I'm only a man."

...By the cold and religious we were taken in hand,
Shown how to feel good and told to feel bad.
Tongue tied and terrified we learned how to pray,
Now our feelings run deep and cold as the clay;
And strung out behind us the banners and flags
Of our possible pasts lie in tatters and rags.

Your Possible Pasts – The Final Cut
– Pink Floyd

Hello, Darkness, my old friend
I've come to talk with you again
Because a vision softly creeping
Left its seeds while I was sleeping
And the vision that was planted in my brain
Still remains
Within the Sound of Silence

The Sound of Silence
– Simon & Garfunkel
Performed by Disturbed

Wherever you are today, stop, and look all around you. Chances are you're looking at a veteran of combat. In his head may be relative peace and calm, but more likely in his head is pain, anger, sadness, and depression. I don't mean the "Fortunate Son" of a Senator or President, and I don't mean the guilded and insulated experience of an officer (no doubt there are officers who know these experiences, but the vast majority do not and tell tales of bullshit); I mean the unheralded unfortunate enlisted man or NCO who has faced something beyond your experience, beyond your immediate ability to comprehend. This man may be ready to blow his brains out, cut his own throat, or drink cyanide just to stop that pain. He is a veteran of killing, for *you*, in *your* name, for *your* cause(s). He may have seen so much death and destruction within a relatively short period of time... experiences that would make your head spin or your heart stop if you felt his pain. Yet, he attempts to live still and survive.

From the beginning through now, millions of veterans have had to deal with PTSD; millions of veterans still living strive to live with memories of killing, with dreams of blood, with guilt pounded into our heads on a nightly basis by those ghosts of our dead entreating us, attempting to kill us, and questioning us throughout our attempts to sleep. We smell diesel and our mind flies backward. We smell iron and our mind flies backward into pools of blood. We feel temperatures and stickiness and see blood on our hands.

When I joined the military, I was barely past being a large boy. 2-1/2 years became a lifetime for me, and when I extricated myself from that environment, you were not there to help me recover, just like you have not been there to help other vets recover. The VA was certainly not there to help me recover, nor have they been there to help the overwhelming majority of vets recover. Neither the VA nor the civilian mental health system takes combat PTSD seriously. Congress certainly doesn't take it seriously. Recent estimates concerning the VA's treatment of vets with PTSD state that the VA only treats 30% of PTSD cases at most. This is by Congressional, Presidential, and VA design – they don't want to spend the money, and they reject vets for treatment based upon *set up to fail criteria* – and this in a time when Congress openly speaks of attaining a trillion dollar military budget, gives away military equipment to police departments, sells and gives away weapons all over the world, and gives *billions* every year to the Israeli apartheid regime to inflict genocide and apartheid. Beyond this, recent research points out that VA treatment fails the majority of the time – even when they declare a vet "cured" many have their symptoms return within months or a few years, and these vets give up on the system, and often give up on life.

This work is an attempt to enlighten you as to how a boy becomes a man and attaches himself to humanity, as well as the combat veteran's situation – why he is like he is – and your part in causing this situation. *You are as guilty as a lying President, Congress, and CIA in causing and allowing outrages and atrocities to be committed in your name.* You may believe that a vet's voluntary military service contract absolves you, but it does not!

If you fail in your responsibility as a Citizen, you fail your fellow Citizens, your country, and the world. You allow the corruption which will bring this country to its knees, and you allow your country to be beheaded by special and foreign corrupt interests. If you fail to stand witness and take heed of your own part, and you fail to correct and to push hard to take care of that veteran and his PTSD, you fail as a human. If you're reading this, you must be an intelligent person (so-called). Ignorance for lack of information is understandable and normal, though still unacceptable; however, choosing ignorance when you have the information readily accessible or in hand only points to failing in yourself. By choosing ignorance you disallow yourself the chance to change and grow, to become wiser. By choosing ignorance you fail your children and grand-children. Your daughter may fall in love with a vet and not know how to help him; your son may never recover. You would like to think yourself intelligent enough to discern facts and outwit the scurrilous politicians, wouldn't you? This work will help you do that.

> An unexamined life is not worth living…
> Most people, including ourselves, live in a
> world of relative ignorance. We are even
> comfortable with that ignorance, because it
> is all we know. When we first start facing
> truth, the process may be frightening, and
> many people run back to their old lives. But
> if you continue to seek truth, you will
> eventually be able to handle it better. In
> fact, you want more! It's true that many
> people around you now may think you are
> weird or even a danger to society, but you
> don't care. Once you've tasted the truth, you
> won't ever want to go back to being
> ignorant.
>
> > Socrates

"Thank you for your service" won't cut it, won't even satisfy a basic need for these combat vets; primarily because *you* haven't got a clue as to what "service" *you* are referring. It's a statement you would make to your food server, gas station mechanic, etc… Military personnel such as swim instructors, clerks, generals, cooks, officers off the battlefield, etc… all love this attention, but they don't deserve it, and every combat veteran knows this. The combat veteran not only places his life on the line, he places his entire mind and his entire future life on the line. There ARE worse things than dying. The veteran who has been involved in what has been termed "dark atrocities" (a *growing* special ops trend) may smile at you, but in his head he's more likely thinking, "You haven't got a fucking clue halfwit!" He truly believes you've neither the guts nor the intelligence to listen and discern, nor the emotional wherewithal to deal with the truth of what has been done, in *your* name. The fact that you say this phrase with such blind fawning may be even more offensive. Service to him means not only facing death, but facing the death and pain he has inflicted, in *your* name under *your* orders.

In this work I'll not discuss others vets' experiences, as I expect them to empower themselves to start speaking without fear, because ***you have <u>no</u> right to be spared these details or uncomfortable feelings,* because you *are* responsible**. I had to grow from a boy into "only a man"; now *you* must grow into a man or woman with a conscience (no matter your age). I'll discuss the 18 missions I was sent on, and I do hope you feel the pain and deal with it responsibly, because you *are* responsible.

Crossing Rubicons

All folks who pretend to religion and grace,
Allow there's a *hell*, but dispute of the place:
But, if *hell* may by logical rules be defined
The place of the damn'd – I'll tell you my mind.
Wherever the damn'd do chiefly abound,
Most certainly there is *hell* to be found:
Damn'd poets, damn'd critics, damn'd blockheads, damn'd
knaves,
Damn'd senators bribed, damn'd prostitute slaves;
Damn'd lawyers and judges, damn'd lords and damn'd squires;
Damn'd spies and informers, damn'd friends and damn'd liars;
Damn'd villains, corrupted in every station;
Damn'd time-serving priests all over the nation;
And into the bargain I'll readily give ye
Damn'd ignorant prelates, and counsellors privy.
Then let us no longer by parsons be flamm'd,
For we know by these marks the place of the damn'd:
And *HELL* to be sure is at Paris or Rome.
How happy for us that it is not at home!

The Place of the Damned
– Jonathan Swift

When you're very young, you are *so* in search of knowing, yet naive, and will believe almost anything adults tell you. Later on you begin to discern falsehoods and lies, hypocrisy and duplicity; yet, you are still naive. To make matters even worse, you have no fully functional braking system in your brain until

~25, yet you are required at 17-19 to make major decisions about your life and future, about life and death. I don't know if this is a joke, a way for nature to get you making moves and engaged in something before you realize how much it sucks, or if its a way to weed out the idiots, or, it's a combination of all of these things, and more. So at 18 (and it has happened sooner), you are able to be trained to kill, expected to kill, yet you are still treated as sub-adult. You slowly learn how Presidents lie, Senators and Congressmen are bribed, and your country is involved in killing and supporting apartheid and right-wing dictators and oligarchy all over the globe. You learn the astounding quantity and depth of the lies, denials, and obfuscations that come out of Washington. But first, you are forced to cross rubicons and participate without real knowledge.

A rubicon is a line, a choice, decision, or forced, made consciously or unconsciously, that is irrevocable once crossed. It is a word based upon Caesar crossing the Rubicon River (a small creek usually) into Rome with his army – it was highly symbolic and something which was forbidden. Once crossed, he could not undo what he had done (even if he had wanted to). People have many rubicons in their life. Some rubicons, like sex, are forced upon everyone regardless.

We are indoctrinated in certain ways and certain things. While these are not rubicon crossings, beliefs, propaganda, and/or political beliefs can cause crossings. When young, we were taught Communists were an evil godless horde that needed to be eradicated from the Earth. All Communists were Stalin and Mao, and Socialist equaled Communist… and did I mention they had no god?!? They wanted desperately to destroy *our way of life* and turn us all into government slaves. Even if Nixon did meet with the Chinese, he was just putting it over on them for "our way of life", Capitalism, endorsed by God AND Jesus himself (according to the zealots). Vietnam was wrong, yet no one really detailed the

32

history on why. Kennedy, Johnson, Nixon (even if he did get caught doing something), sunny Jimmy Carter, 'Merican! Ronald Reagan, George (Read My Lips) Bush Sr, Billy Clinton (and Hillary and Newt), George (We Need To Torture) Bush Jr, Barack (More Secrets Than Anyone) Obama, Donald (just a moron) Trump, and, *a thread through all of Nixon through now,* Joe (I never met a war I didn't like) Biden (*faux* FDR) – *they* would never lie to *me*, would *they*? Hell was/is always everywhere else. We'll discuss the problem with these later, but when young, you generally accept because you simply are ignorant of facts and *they* wouldn't lie to *you (would they?).*

This book is not explicitly about sex, but sex is legitimately a huge part of life, forever and always (no matter what lying celibates or feminists may tell you). Sex is a grounding in humanity; whereas, except for psychopaths or sociopaths, killing disrupts and destroys this grounding. The need for this grounding force goes beyond simple humanity for combat veterans; it becomes a way of connecting with humanity to be drawn back into life, rather than death. It's necessary to discuss sex in relationship to war and killing, because it has been theorized by certain psychologists and feminists that war and killing "is a man's thing", toxic-masculinity, and that killing is akin to sexual assault. This is beyond stupidity, it is egregiously false and hypocritical, especially when spewed from non-experienced promoters, who fit the description of the age-old combat veterans' description of non-experienced people that are like "virgins talking about sex". Catherine the Great, Caligula's mother, the widow who dominated Papal policy in ancient Rome, Bloody Mary burning humans alive to satisfy religious zealotry, Queen Victoria and her ilk, Golda (Apartheid Groupie and Palestinian Butcher) Meir, Margaret Thatcher, Madeleine Albright, etc… all knew how to kill or throw countless soldiers into war and conflict and pathologically disregard the deaths of

33

soldiers and civilians – war is every bit a woman's thing as well as a man's.

If you start honestly sharing about a life, you are going to run into sex, and it shouldn't be ignored. Sex and Love are powerful psychological grounding forces.

Young men entering life in this country, and countries around the world, *know* that they *will be required* to fight and die if demand is made, without choice or much chance at reprieve, and most often for lies and corruption that make up the worst part of *every* government or movement. Men of limited means or connections soon learn how expendable they are. In this book, a young man enters the military and ends up losing his life, without physically dying in the military, and must learn to live with himself and recover some peace of mind. This book contains graphic depictions of sex, sexual thoughts, death, and killing. **You have been forewarned. If you are not stable or adult enough to handle these things, and choose not to read further, consider yourself part of the problem which allows atrocities to take place – you are a co-conspirator in government sanctioned murder. Remember, in a conspiracy, it is not necessary to show that the right hand knows what the left hand is doing.**

I, like many of you, learned at a young age to fend for myself, to be a self-advocate, and an autodidact. When very young, I wanted to be an astronaut, but soon realized I didn't have the drive for science, at least in that field. Then, as I was always joyfully part of the choirs at school, I thought experiencing the high achieved singing in these groups would be the ultimate life. The look of terror on my father's face when I bought the Mormon Tabernacle Choir Christmas Album, listened in ecstasy, and announced that I (Catholic at the time) wanted to join that choir. Then I thought being a cartoon voice and/or writing cartoon

34

dialogue would be most satisfactory and fun, and this would require living in California.

When young, I loved nothing more than music… then sex and music. I took Boston (the band) to heart and I didn't want anything but peace of mind and honesty over hypocrisy. When I graduated I wanted nothing more than to work, earn some money, and move to California. But the economy then was a sunken shit-hole with double digit unemployment, inflation, and every US corporation screwing Americans to manufacture products overseas in order to increase profits. Styx sang of that unemployment line, and Kansas told me to Carry On… But no work is no work and I began to wonder what the hell I was going to do on the Telegraph Road (Dire Straits). While attending a polka fest (beer, bratwurst, dancing with pretty girls), I spoke with a just enlisted young man in the Air Force, and after much conversation thought I'd try it.

After this rubicon, I began to unlearn (learn?) every bullshit thing I had ever been taught (propagandized) about the US government and its' military operations. When young, I knew more than anything that I never, *ever*, wanted to be a Nazi or Fascist – we had fought a devastating global war to stop it – yet that's exactly what I became under military training and CIA functioning. To learn that everything you had been taught concerning the US, justice, fair play, etc… was a lie is debilitating enough, even though *most* people experience this loss of innocence, a rubicon all its own; but through operant conditioning and lies to become a participant in what one military psychologist terms "dark atrocity" is to become a psychiatric casualty. Such a thing requires years to overcome enough to function relatively normal.

The vast majority of Americans are unaware of the activities of the US in foreign nations. We know about major wars and conflicts – those that are declared or at least discussed. We don't know about American history when it comes to interventions based upon corporate needs, or those conflicts based upon politics, ideology, or corporate need tied to ideology. These are termed *Undeclared Actions* or *Undeclared Conflicts*. They are undeclared for a simple reason: they are shameful displays of which most Americans would not approve. The vast majority of Americans, believing that no military conflicts exist outside of Congress' say so, are totally unaware that the US has been involved in Undeclared Conflicts and Actions almost non-stop since the supposed end of WW2. This ignorance must end. Congress has given in law the authority to the CIA to start any conflict it deems appropriate. In theory, the State Department could put the kabash on these operations, but the President gets what the President wants (and Israel, at US expense, gets what nobody but Zionists want). On any given day around the globe, US Special Forces are engaged in death and destruction directly, or indirectly as trainers and accessories, including assisting organizations and groups labeled as terrorists by the US itself. The US, trained the Mujaheddin and became friends with the Taliban, caused a coup (via CIA operations) in 2014 in Ukraine to bring neo-Nazis to power in order to poke the Bear and start a quagmire for the Russians (those same neo-Nazi militias supported by the CIA were fully absorbed into the Ukrainian armed forces), and trains terrorists and arms them, and imports them into Syria. The United States has Special Forces operating in ~85% of the countries around the world. We train and assist dictators, right-wing death squads, and Fascists everywhere, *ad nauseam*. The CIA has covert field operators in 100% of the countries of the world, including the United States (regardless of the law).

This then is the story of how a normal (so-called) young man is transformed in life, by normal (so-called) choices, but ultimately by crossing the military rubicon into dark atrocities

36

ordered by the US government and its' Citizens, in the process eerily being labeled with the code name Rubicon.

"Then let us no longer by [Presidents] be flamm'd, for we know by these marks the placed of the damn'd: And *HELL* to be sure, is at Paris or Rome. How happy for us that it is not at home!"

Let's see how how a young man, myself, got there, and became a full-fledged US Government Fascist Fuck, and changed for the...

Learning To Fly

Well, I started out,
down a dirty road;
Started out, all alone…
I'm learning to fly,
But I ain't got wings;
Coming down,
Is the hardest thing.

Tom Petty & The Heartbreakers

Why is Sex important to this narrative? As previously stated, Sex and Love are the ground force of humanity. We start life being immersed by Nature into Sex. Two humans, or more, can share love through sex and bond, grounding themselves in love and humanity. Sure, there are those (Donald Trump, Bill Clinton, Joe Biden), *playas*, who care nothing for humanity or grounding, and they steal sex, as they prefer assuming power to fly high. That is not the normal man or woman. Sex is also important to this narrative as *faux* experience and analysis by an Army psychologist has stated that killing is akin to sex. Nothing could be further from the truth. *Killing is the opposite of Sex and Love.* Killing and Rape are the taking of life. Sex and Love are the giving and sharing of life.

Our base brains contain programming. We all have the same base programming, unless brain damage or genetic problems are present. Attempts are made to override that programming by upper brain functioning, based on false beliefs and hurts, but the programming remains the same. Breathing and bodily functions are automatic. Your base brain has just four *need* commands on a regular day to day basis which require your actions: Food & Water, Shelter, Clothing (if necessary), and Sex. Of these, Sex will ALWAYS take priority. The only thing that can quash Sex is the threat of violence or death (yet even in death ejaculation may occur). Women can be turned off in a second; men's dicks, unless they are psychopaths (rapists), will become useless under the application of too much adrenaline (it's called Stim Dick, and it most certainly happens). But on a daily peaceful basis… it may be raining ice water, you have no clothes, no food, no shelter, but if Sex presents itself that's what's going to happen. Why, because it's *that* important to life. It's important to our health and brains to engage in Sex, it is not important to our health and brains to kill.

How do we know these things? A man's sexual organ has been known. A woman's sexual organ has not been known in full until relatively recently in time. The similarities are astounding. The function of the clitoris is a gift from nature, just like sex and love. Dr Helen O'Connell first rendered the entire structure of the clitoris, for the first time in the late '90s. It's a work of art. The shaft starting at the exposed nub and going back into the body up to 5 inches! Tendrils extend from the shaft into the upper vagina. Tendril bulbs extend from the shaft down the sides behind the labia. A woman doctoral student then mapped the entire connection of nerves feeding the clitoris. The most astounding part is the nerve bundle coming from the clitoris to the spinal cord. The size of this nerve bundle is approximately the size your pinky finger. According to this researcher, the size of this nerve bundle is almost unprecedented, which reveals the importance of this organ to the brain and body. She has stated outright that the sole (only) function of the clitoris is pleasure – and that pleasure can be achieved multiple times in a session.

Many have argued that there is such a thing as sex addiction. But the opposite would seem to be the truer state of things. The upper brain can come up with many addictions: ego, religion, money, prudishness as power, power, etc… Humans are animals (mammals). If your programming, physical structure, and nerve production are all motivating an active natural drive for sex that is so powerful and important, then the addictions of life (ego, religion, prudishness, power, etc…) that interfere with normal sexual functioning are the true addictions by definition – and they are the problem. Forget your house, your car, your cellphone, and all the facade of the modern world. You were born in the wild, you were naked and may have remained that way. Your only concerns are Food & Water, Shelter, Clothing (if necessary), and SEX. We should be living and fucking constantly. *Killing is part of the upper brain activities of justification and addictions to power and deviance.*

Because I'm a man, I can only speak with surety on how boys grow up. Not that girls wouldn't experience some of the exact same events and feelings, but differences in hormone levels and physicality do exist that is best left to a woman to elaborate. DHEA begins to swell at about 6-8 years for both sexes (forget "gender" for now) to levels that will be the highest in a lifetime, even exceeding teenage levels. This DHEA is not converted at this age into the testosterone levels seen later, but it does have the effect of having you look at others sexually and warmly, even if you have no idea what sex is. For some, the new feelings are too scary; for some, the new feelings are fantastic and exciting. This book is going to treat sex as it existed for me: scary, fantastic, and exciting. Some will think this gratuitous, but to the contrary, it will paint for all to see what almost every boy faces as he grows and learns to fly, and I'm positive that almost all girls experience the same. Further, it gives insight into a boy then young man as he enters the world without road map or complete knowledge;

how he learns to love and stay alive. A boy becomes a man learning to deal with the opposites of life: Sex and Love, Hate (including Lying and Manipulations) and Death.

At an average age of 13 DHEA starts being converted to testosterone in massive amounts. Boys and girls learn to masturbate and orgasm well before this time. My first orgasm occurred in 2nd grade while climbing up the jungle gym pole. I just wanted to reach the top, but with the top 6 inches from my grasp, a funny feeling welled up from deep in my groin and a warm melting excitement spread and enveloped my whole body, leaving me with a tell-tale melted face. This feeling was so delicious and wonderful that I did it again, and again, and again. Every recess I went straight for the pole. I had no idea what this was, and at one point I wondered if something inside was rupturing, but I didn't care. I wanted it, needed it, and wasn't ever going to stop. I finally realized what caused the sensations. I began to wonder if teachers or other kids could tell what was going on, but I didn't care… it was too delicious.

This led to masturbation, anywhere and everywhere all the time. Frank McCourt wasn't kidding when he gave his account. I masturbated in my room, my parent's room, the bathroom, the basement, the neighbors' bathrooms, the woods, the ponds, the parks, and every Sunday at church, and many places I've forgotten. In church I would say I had to go to the bathroom; I would rub a couple out and return to the pew to get serious looks from my parents about my being gone so long. Later, when testosterone was raging, and I was wearing the polyester pants that some asshole invented, my boners would be sticking out straight every time we stood up (multiple times in a Catholic service)… and the bathroom was required. Just imagine a teenage boy, wearing polyester slacks, walking down the side isle in the church with a tent pole holding out his pants in the crotch, and the ONLY way to make it go away was to wank it away until it was tired.

For a long time, I didn't produce any cum. Then one day as I wanked on my brother's bed and I orgasmed, a load of thick white fluid emerged, and I thought I had really broken something or had a disease. I stopped for a few days to "let it heal", but when I wanked again, there it was, and it didn't hurt and it didn't smell. So I would continue, sometimes wanking 4-5 times in a row, but now, after so many wanks the fluid dried up and it seemed like my system was exhausted. In a nutshell, that's how sex began for me. There was no information from school, and the church had a filmstrip which made it clear that I was going to Hell.

I had been having constant dreams of being a bee searching for a target, and once finding it (yes, an actual bee colored target) I would fly up to it and rub my lower abdomen against it and… delight. I had never even really thought about the birds and the bees and their relation to sex – it just wasn't in my conscious thought. Years later when watching the Billy's Buzzing Off skit on Saturday Night Live, I was sure someone must have had the same kind of dreams… and *that* is some deep programming.

Freud was right, if adults in kids' lives are not forthcoming with information, kids will seek information about sex on their own, either through their peers and/or any source they can get their hands on. At the time, information and/or porn available to most kids was in magazine or book form. My first encounter with this media was a Penthouse that someone had thrown in a trash barrel at the park. I thought I had found GOLD. I squirreled away with that mag to a far part of the park and examined every page in detail. I was soooo happy! Somehow, I developed radar for finding these magazines. I learned that many adults, even those who acted the most prudish, had them in their bathrooms and under their beds. This sexual era would be the first Rubicon that I crossed (a years long process), and there would be no turning back.

When 6 or 7, a girl my age lived down the street. She always wanted to play house, and she would set up our house under a sheet tent in her dining room. She liked kissing her husband. Across from her house was an old train depot that had been turned into a store and barber shop. The back of the building was protected by a wedge shape of railroad ties in case a train derailed. She had the idea to climb inside and we did. She asked if I would show her my "thing" and she would show me hers. We undressed and began touching each other wherever our curiosity went, and we kissed.

She and her mom eventually moved, and I began to play with a boy down another street. There was an old feed mill kitty corner to our house, and he and I played there quite often. One day he asked me if I ever played "*caca*", and I told him I didn't and didn't know what it was. He explained, and by his explanation I understood him to be talking about masturbation. I assured him I knew what he was talking about and he wanted to know if I wanted to do it together, and I did. We pulled off our clothes and began wanking, and we'd talk about the lovely feeling from orgasm (a word we didn't know yet). In time, we began to wank each other. In time, I'm sure we would have been sucking each other off, but then I moved.

In the summer of my 14th year, we had a swim meet at our local pool, with girls and boys from 4 teams competing. About half way through the meet a girl of my age approached me and began a conversation. She was pretty with breast buds and I started to get nervous, but she asked about me, laughed at my jokes, and held my hand. She asked if I wanted to walk in the

43

park (it was large and surrounded the pool), and I said, "Sure."
We went out the back gate and walked across the creek to a picnic
pavilion that was rarely used. She asked me if I had ever made
love, which I hadn't, and I believe I just mumbled. She asked me
if I'd like to try, and I shook my head yes. The pavilion was
blocked almost completely by shrubs and trees, and she removed
her suit. She untied my suit and pulled it down and began licking
my cock. When I was hard in an instant, she lay on the bench of a
picnic table and guided me into her. I had never felt such warmth.
I began thrusting and she began breathing hard and moaning, but
she told me I mustn't cum inside her; but I was so nervous, even
though it felt so good I didn't think I would ever cum. She began
pushing into me hard, spasm'd, and was done. I pulled out and
she began sucking my cock until I came. She put on her suit and I
put on mine, and she kissed me. We walked back to the swim
meet, separated with a hug, and I never saw her again. In a way,
this was my 2nd Rubicon crossing.

After this, sex occurred rather frequently with any girl
willing. There was the moving van hayride, where total darkness
allowed high school teenagers to explore each other. There was
also a masturbation session with guys in the storage weight room
area behind the gym in high school. I believe this to be as normal
as apple pie. Young people learn early to ground themselves in
other people… to be part of the human race… to feel the deepest
connection with another.

Killing on the other hand is a disconnection from
humanity. Rarely is it really necessary, yet it becomes the abuse
and control mechanism rendered by psychopaths and those
addicted to power. Donald Trump, Bill Clinton, and Joe Biden
don't represent normality or manliness, they represent power
psychopathy. Monica Lewinski admittedly went to Washington
with joy in her heart to give head, for power and prestige.

Further on, sex for me became my ultimate grounding back into humanity. The touch of skin and sharing of love through the act of sex became a saving grace for me. I needed, like all humans, to feel skin, warmth, the meshing of souls. As we continue, we'll look at some of those actions which led to a better understanding of myself and others.

I'll leave this for now starting a great poem by Girl On The Net:

Fucking

I met a guy from Battersea
Who wanted to make love to me
I told him "Love? It cannot be:
Dude, what I like is fucking.
Though 'shagging' seems a decent word
And 'banging's very often heard,
'Making love' is quite absurd
So please let's call it fucking.
By 'fucking' I don't mean that thing
Where you just stick your penis in
And out and in and out and in
I mean a *proper* rutting.
All grabby hands and grunts and moans,
That's what I wank to on my own.
Here, watch this porn to set the tone:
That's what I mean by fucking…

Fucking, A Poem – Girl On The Net

Origin of the Scout Program

Scout Program Commander & His Flunky; the Men Who Actually Performed the Work; and How I Got In This Mess

In the late '70's AFSOC (Air Force Special Operations Command) desperately wanted to get into the special operations glory, but that glory was in firm control of the still rising star, Navy SEALS, and the older orders of Army Rangers and Green Berets. They knew they could not compete on the ground level with teams, especially given the love affair with the air combat role and officer pilots; however, they did feel that AF Scouts could act as commandos performing tasks where larger teams could not operate so well or at all. The Air Force, unlike the Army, Navy, or Marines, would *never* send an officer purposefully into ground combat. It was (is) a class system and AF officers were (are) deemed too valuable. Enlisted men and NCOs (Non-Commissioned Officers – Sergeants) on the other hand, were expendable and easier to produce and obtain.

The idea for the Scout program being formed high within AFSOC (why they chose the name Scout, I can only guess someone older watched a lot of Wagon Train), they needed someone with connections to be the "Commander" of this program. Enter Major Ian Fleming (not his real name, but his pretended character). Major Fleming had entered the AF Academy and graduated in the early '70's. He was immediately stationed at a base in Oregon, and was immediately unhappy with that location and his duties. Being a friend of a few generals and Congressmen, he petitioned to open a search & rescue outfit at a base in Texas... petition granted. Then he opened another in North Carolina, and another, etc...

Hurlburt Field (Eglin Field #9) had a storied past. Jimmy Doolittle's Raiders practiced there. The Enola Gay practiced there. Hurlburt was then home to the 1st Special Operations Wing (1st SOW) and the 834th Combat Support Group (834th CSG), which were part of the Tactical Air Command. Commando training and activities related with forward observers and forward air combat controllers was not a new thing for Hurlburt. Hurlburt is right on the Gulf (just across the highway), with thousands of square miles of forest, swamp, bombing range, etc... The Wing had support helicopters, transports, and MC-130-E Combat Talons (transports with retractable whiskers for grabbing Fulton Recovery System lines), and AC-130-H Spectre Gunships. These gunships were marvels of ingenuity (just like the Lockheed C-130 itself). All weapons sticking out the left side -- A 105mm Howitzer, a 40mm rapid fire Bofors gun, and twin 20mm Vulcan electric motor Gatling guns side by side. The front hatch was removed to hold a pod of multiple cameras and sensor array (the planes flew unpressurized). In a search and rescue operation the 20mm guns (one or both) could be removed and replaced with search light(s). Now, you can see videos of the inside of these gunships in and out of action, but back then, the electronics, cameras, and the Electronic Warfare booth were considered highly classified. The Talons and Gunships were kept behind wide painted red lines with few entrance/exit points, and MP's with M16s constantly patrolled. If you were to attempt to cross outside the checkpoints, you could expect to be shot or thrown into a dark hole. Cameras were absolutely forbidden.

There was no better place for this Scout Program to land. Major Fleming was recruited to command and be a salesman for the program to those in Washington who made decisions. At first, there was no Executive Officer under the Major. Planning and execution was practically automatic within AFSOC, 1ˢᵗ SOW, CSG, CIA, and the Scout. Later, Lieutenant Weasel (not his real name but his character) appeared as on-site second in command. The Lt was practically fresh from college and still smelled of ROTC, and completely full of himself and shit. He looked like Don Knotts, talked with a high-pitched squeaky voice, and believed he knew everything about rules and warfare that could possibly be known, and barked at people like an annoying terrier. It should be noted here that neither the Major nor Lt had any field or combat experience, anywhere, at anytime. The Major was a foppish character who believed himself to be like James Bond, even though he had never participated in anything at all. Later in his life he would write a book claiming (poorly) to have performed what his underlings had actually performed.

The NCOs for the program were not hard to find. Forward Observers and Air Combat Controllers who had been active in Vietnam were still around, and though older, they could oversee training and impart advice. One of those, who would become my trainer, and eventually my mentor, was Bill. Bill had been quite active in Vietnam, and he knew exactly what we would be facing. He had risen to the rank of Senior Master Sergeant (7 stripes), but after punching a Lt in 1978, he was busted to Technical Sergeant (5 stripes). They offered him a role in the Scout Program and promised him if he completed three years with it they would restore his rank and time in rank, and he would perhaps get another stripe making him a Chief.

In 1979 memos were circulated, including to AFEES (Armed Forces Examining and Entrance Station) induction centers, to search for recruits with certain skills sets. I had no intention of joining the military initially. Like any sane person growing up where I did, I wanted to earn money and move to California. However, the economy at that time was an empty turd. Everything had closed down, offered less, and unemployment went double digits, while inflation picked our pockets. One night at a Polka Fest (pretty girls, polka music, beer, and bratwurst) I met a guy on AF leave. I asked him how he liked it, and he said he did (but he was new to it). After talking for quite awhile, I thought, what the fuck, I'll try it.

The first time (yes first) I attempted to join, was in the state in which I was then living. The recruiter sent me to an AFEES station in that state. After testing and a physical exam, I was asked certain questions, one of which was, "Have you ever smoked pot?" Well, of course I had. I knew this was going to be a sticking point, but I wanted to be honest, so I said, "Yes, but I'm not smoking now." And that was it… I was gone. I even had to find my own ride back (4 hours).

Not knowing what to do, I went to live with my parents in another state (they had moved), and I went to see a local recruiter in the city in which they lived. I told him I wanted to join, and felt him out on the pot issue. He caught my drift and told me, "If they ask you, only say 'I don't smoke pot'; and if they persist with depth of time, still just reply, 'I don't smoke pot'." I had also told this recruiter that I really wanted to fly, but that I understood that required a college degree and officer status. He told me in his best car salesman voice that it would be easy for me to get in, apply to Officer Training School (OTS), and I'd be flying in no-time (sales propaganda). That settled, he filled out my paperwork and sent me off to an AFEES station in this state in July 1979. Testing, physical, and questions. I stuck with what he told me to say, and it worked. We were then given a list of jobs and general locations to choose from. I chose aircraft mechanic and warm climates…

I was called into the AFEES' Major's office. He had noticed on my record from a background check that I had expunged records. He demanded to know what was expunged. I refused. He said, "You have to tell me." I said, "With all due respect, I don't. A Judge reviewed those records, found them to be faulty, and wiped them out. I don't have to tell you." He was quite irate and went to speak with the Colonel in charge. I was sent to the Colonel's office.

To this day, I don't know if what transpired was a setup, but nevertheless… The Colonel was more soft spoken. He told me he understood my position, and wanted time to consider the situation. He put me up another night in the hotel, and had me return the next day. When I arrived I was immediately given another special test to take. It seemed to be mostly about decision making and taking actions. Unbeknownst to me, the Major had spent his time contacting the local police where I had lived and had police records and notes faxed to him. When I arrived I sat in the Colonel's office listening to the Major berate me as unworthy of the Air Force. He warned the Colonel if he let me in, he (the Major) would object vociferously. When he left, the Colonel sat reading the material that had been sent. It was not anything bad. No murders, robberies, etc… It was a bunch of things that the police wish they could have gotten me for, even things which I had never done, and had even started court proceedings, but couldn't make anything work for them.

The Colonel put down the papers and stared at me with a warm and knowing smile. He said he thought I showed ingenuity and I had skill at deception ("not in a bad way!") and a knack for stealth. He told me he would like to sign a waiver for me, and I started thinking Great! Then his countenance changed and he looked sad, and he said the Major could make a lot of trouble for him, but he thought he had a way for both of us to get what we wanted and the Major be damned. He pulled another sheet from a folder lying on the top left corner of his desk. He handed it to me to read. It was a "Classified" memo from AFSOC describing the Scout Program in terms that were rich but not really clear, but I got the gist. The Colonel proceeded to tell me they were very urgently trying to find the "right" people for these positions, and he thought I would be a perfect fit. He said my test scores were exactly what they needed. I realized that this would normally be a dangerous position, but I thought out loud, "How much danger could there be, we're not at war." The Colonel chimed in, "Exactly." He was being so nice to me and I stupidly felt pride that he had let me read the "Classified" memo. I said OK, and he immediately pulled out the waiver and he signed it (he had it all typed up already). The Major was beside himself and attached a letter of objection to the waiver that would be brought up by Major Ian Fleming 2-1/2 years later in order to explain to me what a low-life I really was.

Beside Bill, three other senior NCOs participated. One as trainer to Jim, a field Scout who would end up spending much of his time in Africa (I believe). That trainer and the other two NCOs would go on to participate in training foreign troops (the other great function of special forces).

I have a Love/Hate relationship with Bill. He wore me into submission. He ran me into the ground. At times he seemed like *such* a sadistic fuck. He taught me to kill and accept it as, not right, but necessary. He taught me to subdue my panic, my feelings, etc… He taught me to stay alive under impossible circumstances. He cared whether I lived or died. He died in 1981 in a car crash.

When I quit, Jim was dropped into his first mission in Central America. He died on that mission. Jim *had* been one of the sweetest persons you could ever meet. Over time he gradually became paranoid and Rambo-like. I visited him at his dwelling once off base. He had guns stationed in key locations around rooms and even had his large knife in a sheath on the inside of his entrance door. It was sad to see a man so turned and twisted.

Major Fleming spent most of his time in Washington with his buddies. I'd be surprised if they never thought, "Don't you have any work to do?" In 2-1/2 years I talked with him a total of six times – four of those were when I wanted to quit. Yet, when the hostages were taken by Iranian students, and it was decided to run a rescue operation, he was Johnny on the spot and begged his general friend for Scout participation, and it was granted. *My life was to change forever*. I was crossing a Rubicon. Oddly enough, later when they assigned a code moniker to me, it was Rubicon.

The Scout Program actively ran for approximately 3 years, later to be reborn under other command as Joint Special Operations Command (JSOC) support, later becoming part of SOCOM (Special Operations Command). With these things in mind, let's take a short look at the training and programming necessary to produce Special Forces in general, and a Scout in particular...

Training

I learned how to laugh,
I learned how to cry,
I learned how to live,
I learned how to die,
I learned to stay still,
I learned how to hide,
I learned how to kill,
I learned how to die,
I learned how to Love,
I learned about hope.
What didn't I learn?
How to cope.

"You've got to be carefully taught"
[based on R&H South Pacific]
– Rubicon

Basic training was the same for everyone. Basic took place in beautiful San Antonio. Physical fitness and learning to obey. Other activities included the bar/disco hall. Most bases have an enlisted and/or NCO club bar and dance hall, but the one in San Antonio could have rivaled Studio 51. Atmosphere, cheap drinks, powerful music, and sex. As long as you learned to obey, you got rewarded.

Yet things tend not to get interesting until you move on to your next training station. For me, this was another base in Texas. At this base I would learn to jump – from towers, planes, and helicopters. Jump high, jump low, and rappel. I had to be able to

53

dislodge myself from restraint belts and debris, while blind folded, inside a helicopter body overturned in water. I learned map reading, imaging techniques and reading those images. There was endless physical training and self-defense exercises. There was field training that consisted of killing life-like targets in every manner possible. Shooting and knifing from every angle, strangling with cord, and strangling with garroting wire. There were classrooms for field first-aid, weapons, and lectures on tactics. There was a hard focus on mind development to think in a stealthy manner, and to subdue feelings and release yourself from hesitation. You learn to view your target as, well… a target or an enemy. You don't think about reducing the humanity of your victim, you simply reduce your awareness of their humanity to the point of ignoring it, and focus on them as a target. It is serious operant programming. Part of you thinks, this will come in handy when the Nazis start WW3, because you are too naive and ignorant to realize that WW2 never really ended. Again, obeying leads to trust and rewards… like going off base.

This base had quite a large city beside it and endless diversions. There was the NCO club on base, again with atmosphere, cheap drinks, dancing, and sex. Immediately across from the base was a whole line of bars, strip clubs, etc… completely at the service of service men and women. Sex becomes necessary to uncoil the spring inside that had been almost over-wound, and relieve the tension that builds quickly under such pressure. But sex with other service members is usually blind to passion. I chose to enter a large, open floor, dance bar… well lit with a live band. I sat at the bar and a beautiful woman with strawberry blond hair and light blue eyes sat down beside me. She spoke with a local accent, and asked if I would dance. I obliged (even though I suck at dancing), and we sat at the bar drinking beer and talking. She asked me if I'd like to go someplace else, and I asked where. She thought and said she'd like to take me to her house, and guaranteed I'd like it. She said someone else may show up, and asked if that would bother me. I assumed I understood what she meant. She didn't strike me as crazy or harmful, but sincere. I agreed and she drove us in her car to her house in a high hilly suburb.

She had an enclosed back porch on the second level on the far side. It looked out on a beautiful view of the city. There was also a queen size bed on this porch, making it a perfect place to sleep in hotter weather. We began eagerly kissing and exploring each others' body. I asked her about using a condom, but she said she was on the pill. We removed our clothing, and I saw the beauty of her body, the friendliness of her smile, and the eagerness of her touch. We fell on the bed and I began licking her clit and vulva. I love touching and feeling skin, its electricity, its lines and curves, and the muscles underneath. As I ran my hands all over her she moaned, then pushed me over and sat on my chest with her clit in front of my mouth. She rubbed it forward over my lips and tongue.

About then a man appeared in the doorway, naked and stroking his cock. I asked who he was and she replied it was her cousin. I didn't believe that at all, but felt totally unthreatened. He came over to the bed and sat on his heals between my legs. He felt my hard cock and caressed my balls in his hand, and began to lick and suck. I moaned deep and she became very excited and doubled her pushing and rubbing into my lips and tongue. She came hard, then told me to fuck her hard. She lay on her back and I slid in. It was so warm and wet. I started slow while her "cousin" began fucking her mouth. Seeing this was very exciting. As I began thrusting faster she started to lose focus and couldn't continue with his cock. She was approaching another orgasm, but he was looking so forlorn and sad from lack of touch. The look on his face was pained excitement, and his cock was throbbing with anticipation of participating, and long drools of precum hung from the tip. As I thrust I bent forward and began licking and sucking his throbbing cock. She watched this with wide electric eyes and began to shake. I reached over and grabbed his balls and squeezed them while I sucked, and he grunted, "I'm gonna cum!" He blew his load all over my face and her tits, and she came so hard she shook and became senseless, and this made me cum hard inside her. We kissed and she licked the cum from my face.

At this point in my life prolactin was not a problem and refractory down time was a matter of minutes. We made love four more times that night. Afterward we sat down to talk and eat. I told them I knew he wasn't her cousin. They admitted they were committed boyfriend/girlfriend, but that they wanted, needed, more to explore and experience together. They saw themselves as one, making love with another, and I saw the sense and richness in this. In a sense, I was a sexual tool for them, yet I felt loved and appreciated. I liked being part of this kind of relationship, so we continued for the six weeks I had left at the base. They were satisfied and showed me love and respect, and I respected their special relationship and allowed myself to feel and appreciate the love and respect they showed me. They were getting fulfillment and closer to each other, and they felt good; and this liberated me on so many levels and I felt very good. I had not really faced the fact that I was bisexual. Women were always paramount to me, and they still are, but enjoying love with a man is electric, especially with a woman. But this was 1979, and given the atmosphere regarding this topic, I knew I would be able to tell *no one*, ever, unless the circumstances were obviously altered. The military made it very clear that this behavior was not to be tolerated, and that participation in such activities made one a punishable security threat. I would definitely keep this to myself.

The late nights would take a toll on me, on my sleep, and eventually lead to training trouble. One day, during a lecture on stealth tactics, I fell asleep. I awoke to a large arm around my throat, barely able to breath, and the other students were looking on with grave concern. I realized it was the instructor trying to make a point, and the word point led me to think of my chair leg foot as being tiny enough to point some damage. I could look down enough to see his foot, so I picked up the sides of the chair while pushing a squat, and slammed the foot of the chair onto the middle bones of his foot. He howled and several of the students held him back while I regained my breath. I thought for sure I was going to be kicked out. But even though he couldn't walk (I had broken a few of the bones), he sat down and said, "Good job. That was quick thinking." I never fell asleep in class again.

Hurlburt

When finished with this training I was transferred to my destination base, Hurlburt Field (Eglin Field #9). Upon arrival I met Bill, my trainer then mentor. Hurlburt is surrounded by thousands of acres of forest, swamp, rivers, bombing range, the Gulf, etc… Bill immediately had me running, eating, and lifting weights. He had me hiking double time in every environment. He tracked me through every environment, and had me tracking him. When Navy SEALS visited the base, which was often, he had them track me in every environment. We flew to North Carolina and he had Army Rangers track me. Bill is the only person who ever caught me.

Bill made quite clear to me that when I went into the field as a Scout, normally there would be no team. There would be no backup or help. If I was out of touch too long, they *may* send in a search and rescue team, but that was not a certainty. Special ops go in without identification or uniform patches, and I needed to learn to evade and protect myself because I would most likely be dead before S&R arrived. The gunships would provide some safety, if they were above, but they were only tools I was to direct; and many times they would not be there. Scouts were to be loners and I needed to get into that mindset now.

Utilizing realistic targets with movement, Bill taught me to see and read the person, yet still mentally think of them as targets. In December 1979 some of the Spectre Gunships, newly retrofitted with in-flight refueling capability, embarked on a non-stop distance flight to Guam in order to fully test the in-flight refueling system. Bill and I tagged along with the extra flight teams because we were then to end up in the Philippines.

Philippines

Training in the Philippines doubled. Day and night and day and night. Constant shooting, knifing, and strangling realistic targets, and destroying targets with explosives. I began to call Bill every expletive I could think of and called him a sadistic fuck many times. He told me I would thank him for this training – he knew where I was going to end up, while I still had no clue. But I was wound too tight and became argumentative, and he told Marines that he trusted to take me to a "good" whorehouse. The quotes on good are no comment upon the profession. But sex with a prostitute, while the equivalent of a pressure cooker release valve, does not provide the intimacy required to find satisfaction. Don't get me wrong, Filipino women are beautiful and skilled, but prostitutes are professionals, much like the professionals at a doctor's office. The problem is presented, addressed, and you're out the door. If need be, make a followup appointment at the desk. Followups were absolutely necessary as the training doubled again in intensity. I had become so attuned to killing practices in every manner possible, it became a second nature.

Marine units had been engaged to track me through the jungle (unsuccessfully). Then they were told to defend various targets from destruction. During the final training session, it was announced that training would be performed with live explosives.

I was dropped with my gear in the jungle the night before by a Huey gunship. A wooden structure made of logs was built in the center of the "enemy" encampment. My task was to blow up that structure guarded by about 20 Marines. Locating the compound I assessed the force and location of personnel and structures. At the far northwest edge of the compound was a tent utilized by the force commander. Making my way behind that tent and hearing nothing within, I made a small cut to peek inside. No one was in the tent, so I cut a larger entrance and entered. There was a map table, a single cot, and a small box table that contained a can of lighter fluid. I squirted the lighter fluid around the base of the tent, grabbed the maps, and exited squirting the rest of the lighter fluid toward the entrance. I lit the fluid and ran through the back jungle toward my waiting explosives pack that I had hidden.

The tent became engulfed in flames and the trees next to it began to burn. Every Marine guarding the target ran toward the tent and tried to help put out the fire. I ran with the pack from the opposite end and entered the target under the bottom log. I placed three charges (overkill) in the corners and exited and ran back to my blind. Marines were starting to head back toward the structure, and I didn't want them hurt, so I blew it right away, and it blew all to hell. A few of the logs had broken trees on the way out of the compound, and large splinters had went everywhere, including into one of the legs of one of the returning Marines.

Having completed the mission, I shot my rescue mini-flare (a small flare shell launched from a spring-loaded wand) and Bill arrived in the compound via the helicopter. Bill debriefed me and some of the Marines passed and said good job and patted me on the back. Then, my lights went out. When I regained

59

consciousness I was hit in the face with cold water. At first I grabbed for my knife, but found two Marines holding me tight, and Bill was flashing fingers (how many?) and asking questions to see if I could answer. When he asked me who was President, I said, "An asshole", and he laughed and said, "He's fine" and told the Marines to load me in the back of a truck. When we started moving I asked one of the Marines what the hell happened. He said that one of the men didn't like losing to an AF man, so he came up behind my sight and hit me in the head with his rifle butt. Bill wasted no time in taking the guy down and thoroughly beating him to a pulp until they dragged him off. The Marine was taken to the infirmary with the other Marine with the leg wound. This was graduation day, and we went to the whorehouse one last time.

Preparation for Eagle Claw

Upon return to Hurlburt new orders were received and we were on our way to the Arizona & California desert, White Sands Missile Range. Bill filled me in as we traveled. Iranian students had previously taken the US Embassy and several Embassy employees hostage. A rescue operation was being mobilized and a Scout would be part of that team. AFSOC did not want the Scout role compromised, so I would train for my part with Bill and follow orders from Delta Force personnel later on. We practiced low level and skid drops in a matching terrain, and made practice runs avoiding detection. Target markers were placed in various locations mimicking targets in Iran, and the gunships would destroy these.

Before leaving White Sands, we visited the old territorial prison at Yuma. These blockhouse cells were open to the environment, and you could easily see how many prisoners went insane, baking all day and freezing at night. The Colorado River right beside it is nothing but a giant yellow/brown mud stream. Even the site of fresh water eluded them. We went to a California bar that night and I met a beautiful Native American girl. She was fascinated with my blue eyes, and I was fascinated with her black eyes. Her skin was brownish red and she had long straight black hair. She took me to her apartment and we fucked over and over – she would whimper and cum over and over. Her breasts were small but extremely sensitive. The contrast between her skin and the dark color of her areolas and nipples amazed me like art. When she became excited her nipples would stick out long and hard, begging to be touched. I loved touching her skin and feeling the curves of her body. I loved watching her arch and squirm as she came. I felt like we touched each other deeply.

In the morning she drove me back to the Range entrance and told me to come back if it ever worked out that way. Bill picked me up in a truck and we drove to the plane and left. We returned to Hurlburt to continue training and briefings regarding the first mission. A few weeks before the mission we traveled to Egypt and then into Saudi Arabia. The Saudi's were in possession of updated terrain maps for the location of Desert 1, and we wanted to check them prior to going into place lights, charges, and markers.

A young Saudi woman, an intelligence analyst, was assigned to assist us. Bill went to get something to eat while I was looking at the maps in the map room. Unbeknownst to me, the intelligence analyst had entered the room, and while I was bent over looking at the map, she reached between my legs and grabbed my balls. I turned around and she asked if that was OK. When I looked at her I saw an extremely beautiful woman with light emerald green eyes and black hair beneath a loosely wrapped head scarf. She had fine milk chocolate skin, and I immediately kissed her and reciprocated her previous hand gesture. She gushed air and pulled up her long dress, wearing

61

boots, and bent over the table. I slid into her so easily, and it was intensely warm and wet. She moaned, and I hiked her dress up farther to expose her breasts. They looked like milk chocolate with dark chocolate centers and were so soft, supple, and inviting, and I grabbed them and squeezed them as I thrust. I started to push harder and harder and she began growling deeply... and then she came, shuddering and shaking. I couldn't take it any more and I pulled out and shot hot cum all over her brown ass and it streamed down her crack into her vulva, like cream on dark chocolate. She told me to rub it in and I obeyed, rubbing cum into the skin on her beautiful ass and vulva until it was dissipated. She pulled her dress down and helped me pull up my pants, and then she kissed me and left the room. We saw her once as we were escorted to our plane. She winked at me and smiled, and I smiled back. Bill never missed a trick and when we got on the plane he demanded to know what the hell all that was about.

Once back at Hurlburt, we planned our next trip back to Egypt for stage one of Eagle Claw. But first, before starting in on the missions, it's necessary to introduce someone important to the learning and growth happening in my life...

Kit

In March 1980, while in preparation for Eagle Claw, Fort Walton Beach was invaded by students on spring break. The training, preparation, and programming were all intensely mind numbing. Bill was a good friend, but the needs of sex and love can leave one feeling alone, especially when performing clandestine work. One night I decided to go with some guys from the base to a bar called the Blind Pig.

Where I'm originally from, bars are required to have high windows or blocked windows and view. When we pulled into the Blind Pig parking lot I was taken aback that you could see right into the place, which made it seem refreshing and clean. It had several full length picture windows and as you walked in, just to the right was a magnificent oak and brass bar with every type and size of glass hanging from a rack overhead. The bar area was well lit and further in were tables and a dance floor. We stopped about center to the bar and a waitress approached and took our drink order.

The music was pleasing to me, rock. After our drinks arrived we stood talking for a minute about where we should sit. Then Pink Floyd's Young Lust started playing loud and a cheer went up around the bar, and they followed this with Run Like Hell. I saw movement to the bass out of the corner of my eye, and there she was, a gorgeous woman with light brown hair bleached by the sun, 5'8" with blue/green eyes, a unique beauty, and fluid movements of enchanting dance flowing to Pink Floyd with meaning in her heart. She was wearing a white button up shirt, light blue jeans, and sandal shoes. Her movements entranced me… and to Pink Floyd, one of my favorite bands.

I watched her as though I were dreaming, and I *so* wanted to meet her. Not being a great talent at seduction, I did what I usually did – I thought of the first true personal compliment that came to mind and approached her. She was with two friends and another woman who was obviously her sister. I said hello (but I could have been babbling for all I know), and told her she moved like a goddess. She blushed and her sister rolled her eyes while her friends tittered. I told her I couldn't dance worth a damn, but I really would love to dance with her. She allowed this and we moved to the dance floor. From then, I had no idea what was playing. I moved, but to what beat I had no clue. All I could do was appreciate her. She took my hands and corrected my movements, and she grabbed my hips to make them go the right way. At one point she said, "You really do suck" and I replied, "Yes I do" and she laughed and continued dancing with me.

When we took a break, she sat with me at a table far from the bar in a darker area by some windows on the far side of the dance floor. We drank and we talked, and we laughed. We were the same age. She was from California and attended USC. She worked at a department store to make her own money and they came to Florida to see a different beach than where they lived. She said her sister was jealous and controlling. She loved her Dad and Mom. Her Dad worked at Occidental Petroleum and was paying for her college education. I told her that I was an AF Scout (trying to explain it to her without giving details). We danced more and talked more and laughed more. We had so much in common. She recognized and loved the same music that I loved, and she talked to me like she enjoyed me and she enjoyed talking with me. Her sister, visibly annoyed, tried to break it up, but Kit told her to go ahead with the others, she was going to stay there with me, and my heart fluttered with joy. We stayed and talked and danced for another hour or more, mutually copping feels on slow dances. I began to feel as though I had known her forever. When she smiled at me my heart melted, and all the tension left my body. When she touched my skin, I almost melted into a puddle. I wanted to be one with her, to share our thoughts and bodies.

She, her friends, and her sister were staying at a hotel on the beach. I drove her there and we walked along the beach. We stopped to look at the waves and began kissing and feeling each other's body. We stripped naked and looked at each other. She was a fit and strong beauty with medium size breasts that stood out perky and inviting. We ran our hands over each other and licked and sniffed, smelling the essence of the other. She smelled like coconut and ocean breeze. We fucked on the sand below the Gulf-side view of every window in the hotel. Then we swam naked and got dressed. She said she wanted me to stay with her, but didn't want to go back to her room that night, so I offered my room on the base. She was as horny as a rabbit, and so was I, and we made love five times that night. In the morning I took her to her hotel and arranged to meet her later. She spent almost her entire break with me. We fucked in her room, my room, on the bombing range, in the hotel elevator, on the beach and in the surf. She loved anal sex and I would watch her become begging and senseless with anal orgasms. She would give me a blow job and ram her finger up my ass and watch me whine like her little bitch as I came.

One night she asked me if I had ever participated in group sex. She was always open and honest so I told her about the couple in Texas, that it was a great and loving experience. She said she had never participated in doing this, but she was quite intrigued and kept asking questions. She loved the idea of two being one and making love to a third, and she said she wanted to do this with me. I told her this was possible, but there were

65

certain traits in a third she needed to search out, and that we as a couple would need to commit to each other while simultaneously committing to total participation – I believe she blushed at the reference to her and I as a couple. But since she was leaving the next day, the conversation seemed moot. She told me however, the conversation wasn't over, and now I was quite intrigued.

Kit told me she really liked me, that she had never met anyone like me, and she insisted she would come back in three months. I told her I really liked her as well, that I saw her as unique in so many ways, that we had much in common, and she was so easy to talk with. My work took me away up to 1-2 times per month, but it would be easy to make time for her. We exchanged phone numbers (I had to use the common phone in the barrack's common room). I told her I would look forward to her returning… but at the time I wouldn't have held my breath for this happening. Her sister was a major problem (a negative pain in the ass) and would no doubt be working on her back home. I was sure her sister would get her dad involved. Kit's sister made it clear that I was not worth the time, being a non-commissioned officer.

She had entered my heart and had started a change in me, but I wasn't sure if I'd ever see her again…

Eagle Claw

#1 – April 1980

On 4 November 1979, Iranian students and rebels, furious over the idiotic US decision not to turn over the deposed dictator (the Shah, which the US and Britain had helped install and prop up), overtook the US embassy in Tehran and held 52 Americans hostage. The National Security Advisor to President Carter, Zbignew Brzezinski, over-road State dept caution and diplomacy and convinced Carter (stinging from being embarrassed in front of the Russians) to enact a military rescue operation... Eagle Claw.

When word leaked around that such an operation was being put together, everyone wanted to take part. The Army would provide Rangers; the Navy would provide support and what was the celebrated special force unit still on the rise, the SEALS. Since no joint special operations command existed at the time, the Pentagon chose a few generals and colonels to oversee what had previously been dubbed Delta Force. Delta Force, a virgin, had no operational experience at all, and this was their first mission.

Since AF gunships, troop planes, helicopters, and cargo tankers would be involved, and because AFSOC had been secretly starting its Scout program in order to play in the special operations glory, my training schedule was doubled in order to get me into desert training so that AFSOC could take part. The Commander of the Scout program, the Major, friends with the general in charge of the operation, and friends with certain congressmen, begged for Scout participation. The request was granted and intense training took place at White Sands proving grounds.

I wasn't allowed to train with the Delta Force personnel, as someone in AFSOC felt that this may change my "lone" operational character. I was assigned specific tasks to complete prior to Desert 1, participate at Desert 1, and would accompany DF north of Tehran to a 2nd field base dubbed Desert 2, and then assist in taking the airport while the main DF force obtained the hostages.

A few days before DF was to first land in Iran, at a field base dubbed Desert 1, I was dropped from a C130 Combat Talon via a low-level skid drop. A pallet was fitted with runners, like a sled, and dropped out the back with the cargo door skid plate on the ground, while I rode on the pile of equipment. The drop took place on the north side of a canyon ~400 yards wide with a dry lake bed. The northern edge was lined by rocks 6-12 feet high extending for miles East and West. The southern edge was lined by large hills and small mountainous outcrops. The canyon was open to the west, and to the east, except for a road passing SSE to NNW approximately 400 yards from the drop point. This was chosen as the landing and refueling area, being secluded from the road and sight, *because* the floor of the canyon was hard and dry lake bed.

I paced off 100 yards toward the middle of the canyon, and using a pack shovel buried a diamond shape of R/C lights into the lake bed, the longer points heading East and West. They were tested quickly and I moved on to my other tasks. Along the road to the north, ~2 miles up, was a small village with a small Iranian Army garrison. ~2 dozen soldiers were stationed there in barracks and they possessed four armored vehicles with mounted machine guns. I placed markers on the vehicles for the gunships, on the barracks, and double markers on a cable entrance to the telephone exchange. The last double marker I placed was on the radio tower.

After returning to my drop location, I buried several charges along the North face of the rock piles, I covered what remained on the pallet with a camo tarp, and put on my Fulton Recovery System harness, called the waiting Talon, and set my beacon. When they were close enough, I sent up the balloon with cable, and they yanked me out of there a few hours before daybreak.

After some sleep, the following day was spent in briefings. Delta Force and its commanders were dubbed Large And In Charge. The commanders, at least one of them, had actual combat experience in Vietnam as a Green Beret. The SEALS were mostly young, like me. The Rangers, the bulk of DF were a haughty bunch... mostly young, inexperienced, and Rambo-like. They gave an overly arrogant air that they could waltz into any place, any time, and control it and take it over. They were about to learn some valuable lessons, *if* they cared to really examine it rather than blame non-existent and/or small logistic problems, like weather or mechanical difficulties.

A gunship and transport arrived at the location first. The gunship loitered about the area and took note of the markers. The first transport landed, with myself, and the lead of DF. Other transports were just behind spaced by minutes. The transports lined up to the south, and the rest of DF and gear were unloaded. Two C130 cargo planes, modified with fuel bladders in the cargo areas landed and took position. Helicopters from US carriers in the Gulf landed. There were two missing due to mechanical problems, but command had left a buffer and we would have been just fine.

DF and SEALS spread out along the north perimeter, middle to right flank, and a SEAL and myself were on the left flank. The DF Commander, for some god-forsaken reason, had the DF prepared to block the road. They acted and performed like bulls in a china shop. This made no sense whatsoever as the planes in stealth mode could not be seen from the road and no distinguishable noise was heard from the road, especially traveling in a vehicle with open windows. Yet, when a car came down the road, they stopped it! They actually fucking stopped it! They held the travelers at the side of the road. Then a bus came down the road, and they stopped that as well! They made the occupants stand along the road as well. Then a small tanker truck and car came down the road. It was suggested the tanker was a black market fuel vehicle. The car sped through as well as the tanker and DF shot the tanker with a rocket. All cover was blown. The fire was enough that the garrison would arrive shortly. The gunship pilot was demanding from the DF Commander whether to hit the markers, but he received no reply (whether the DF Commander heard him I don't know). Knowing that word would get out of the area about our presence if no action was taken immediately, I told the pilot to fire on the radio tower and communication cables, which he did. The garrison's armored vehicles were already on their way. The chattering was that we would still go for D2.

The armored vehicles arrived too close before the gunship could hit them. One went down the road, but three others came East and one stopped center at the rock wall, while two others went further East toward our flank. When the three that I could see had stopped, I detonated the charges on the other side of the wall and began firing. The center vehicle and one of the two on the left were blown apart, killing the troops. The last vehicle on the left began firing it's machine gun in the direction of the SEAL and myself. SEALS farther down and I were firing back and picking them off, but the SEAL next to me panicked. He was shaking and crouched down and said he didn't know where his team was. The troops from the armored vehicle were soon dead. The chatter was still that we would go for D2. Then, human disaster struck.

The US helicopters were refueled via hoses from the bladders in the C130s. Yet, for nonsensical political reasons, someone had promised the British they could participate, and they would bring two transport helicopters. The first British helicopter came, landed, and was being refueled, when the second British helicopter came to land. He was kicking up some dust, but no more than any of the other aircraft that had already landed. But the pilot panicked. Everyone was talking at him to calm down and straighten out. And then, he inexplicably turned on his bright white landing lights and blinded himself. He started going tipsy, and everyone was yelling at him to turn off the fucking lights and stay still. He slid forward at a tilt and his rotor blades started chopping into the tanker, and then… BOOM! The C130 with the fuel bladder was engulfed in flames, as was the British chopper. Crews from both craft died in fiery agony.

I knew there was no going forth now and grabbed the SEAL and began to move toward the transports. Everyone was ordered onto the C130 transports. I helped the SEAL next to me find his team and board. We exited likes bats leaving the cave. We went to Egypt and debriefed. I gave my separate account, but the DF Commander, who sat in on all debriefing sessions, didn't want to hear negative assessment of his operation. I wrote down and stated what I saw and heard, but what came out in official statements was a tailored thread of uncontrollable circumstances that did not address what had happened at all.

An operation which had every chance of success, was ruined by hubris, overkill, and special friendships. What could have, and should have, gone smoothly without detection, fairly quickly turned into a chaotic shit-show. DF should never have blocked the road, or attempted to stop any vehicles. This was supposed to be a *stealth* operation, they should have stayed hidden. They had no fucking business what-so-ever pulling over those vehicles, let alone blowing a fuel tanker on a dark desert road with a fire that could be seen for miles. Who the fuck did they think they were?!? Did they have any clue in their brains where we were?!? When they pulled these shenanigans it led to a cascade of problems that could have gotten everyone killed or captured. People out to make a big name for themselves should never be put in charge.

There is only one realm of explanation as to why British helicopters, not forces, were taking part. The British begged and demanded but the Pentagon thought better. The British felt they gave birth to Delta Force because the DF Commander was friends with SAS personnel and got the idea for DF from them. Political pressure was placed and the helicopter bone was thrown. BIG mistake. It would have been much more helpful to let the US handle all the aircraft and allow SAS force operatives to participate.

Official accounts like to say that a sandstorm had made the visibility too low. Bullshit! It's a fucking dry lake bed, and of course there's going to be dust (it's the fucking desert), but every other aircraft landed without causing a problem. Pilot and/or pilot training error caused the accident. Because of the schmoozery, several good airmen died needlessly, all to satisfy British government ego.

The Pentagon and Congress held reviews of the operation. The aftermath for special forces was mixed, yet led to rapidly expanding growth. Officially, no fault was found with DF or command, but DF was a doomed product after that. The fault, officially, was placed on the weather and mechanical failures (helicopters which failed to leave the ships). But neither of these had anything to do with the failure. A few years later the AF Scout program would be dissolved with the reason being it was "beyond the scope of AF ground personnel", which was untrue, as proven by the fact that the 24th was reinstated for the sole purpose of providing the same specialized support to JSOC in 1987. JSOC was the biggest fix to come out of the debacle. Prior to the reviews, special operations were performed separately via NSOC, Naval Intelligence Service, ASOC, AFSOC, DoDIA, CIA Operations... If joint operations were required, and each fiefdom really didn't want that, new command and operations had to be developed for each mission. The big kids didn't play well together usually. Congress and the Pentagon forced change that had been needed for decades.

Many articles and books have been written speculating on the subject, reiterating the official reasons for failure. The one which made me laugh long and hard was written by an AF Major claiming to have done my setup job. Forgetting that the garrison and communications had to be marked, he claimed to have flown into the valley with two CIA agents in a Cessna carrying a collapsible motorcycle. I laughed so long and hard at this, especially because he forgot a shovel to bury the lights which was the main reason for going, and used his knife to hack away at the ground. If he had started a motorcycle engine in that valley (during a *stealth* operation, mind you) he would have been dead or captured within minutes. After laughing so hard, I then became angry. The AF Major, an Academy graduate (retired later as Lt Colonel), was friends with the General in charge of the operation, and with a Congressman, etc... He could spout falsehoods all he wanted without repercussions. What made me the angriest? When someone, a foppish military clown (officer), usurps your vital input for their own massive ego and glorification, and they have never once, in their entire life, put their life on the line – THAT pisses me off!

All these years later the stupidity of massive ego, macho bullshit, and insane decisions related to *stealth* operations still makes me intensely angry. Good men died, and many more were placed in grave danger, in order to satisfy those onanistic mental masturbations.

Cache Out 1

#2 – June 1980

Guatemala. A country torn by civil war. Corporatists with US backing and military personnel trained by US forces and the School of the Americas (SOA). I was going into a country of which I was ignorant – of political and social forces. "You don't know what you don't know." But I know now. Indigenous people were being executed if they failed in any way to accept and endorse the European/US capitalist agenda. That agenda often included theft of land, murder, mayhem, rape, and torture (all by the government and government forces in league with, and with the blessing of, the US). Whole villages were wiped out because they had socialist leanings (they wanted to keep their land and property and not be forced to hand everything over to oligarchs growing the system. (I know! The nerve!). Why did the US have to do the dirty work for the Guatemalan (Salvadoran, Colombian, Honduran, Panamanian, Mexican…) "super duper supermen", when we had trained them how to butcher? Perhaps, because they didn't have C-130 gunships, but yet, they had great pals in the CIA who could order up gunships for them to be "Any Time, Any Place".

This was chosen as my first solo assignment in my new area of production, Central and South America. I had one other Scout program field mate. He was, I believe, sent to locations in Africa. We had a new 2nd Lieutenant now, Lt Weasel. He looked something like Don Knotts, but had the disposition of a little terrier – always barking and finding fault. The Lt had them assign something without opposition (?) so he could evaluate me and my training from Bill. He had read the reports from Eagle Claw and the training reports, but of course, he knew best. The Lt

75

had no experience other than being a pain in the ass. He had never been in the field, never fired a weapon outside of Officer basic (where he fired at still targets). He had no combat experience whatsoever.

Guatemalan rebels had a hidden weapons and explosives cache. They knew the general area of the cache, but not an exact location. Finding and destroying this cache would be relatively simple, and I could have sabotaged it within a very short time and been extracted. But the Lt demanded that I only be sent in to *mark* the targets, and then the gunship would come in and destroy them. This was both unnecessary and extra risk. Bill tried to dissuade him, but he wouldn't listen, and I kept my mouth shut to please the new Lt (and because Bill told me to keep it shut).

In order to get to this cache, I had to start from government controlled territory and move directly through a swamp ~2km before it dried up. I say dried up, but we're only talking about the ground, and relatively. It kept raining that day non-stop. It was miserable, hotter than fuck, and when I got past the swamp, I had to pull leeches from my clothing and skin. A few kilometers past the swamp I found the buried caches. It would have been so easy to just places charges and go, but I dutifully placed markers instead, intent on pleasing Bill and, fuck-me, even Lt Weasel.

I sooooo wished I could blow up those caches, but, having placed all the markers, I had to go back through the swamp, and stop upon exit to remove more leeches. I was picked up by a Guatemalan military vehicle. They drove me to the airfield, and after changing clothing and boots, I climbed on the gunship (69-6575 – soon to be Wicked Wanda) and we headed for the cache. After speaking with the pilot, I sat in the booth with the EWO (Electronic Warfare Officer) and his team. They located the beacons and began circling at 20,000 feet. The EWO saw the

76

close patterns and turned to me with a smart-ass tone and said, "You couldn't destroy that yourself? Lucky you got us to do your work."

Having marked the positions on screen, they led with 40mm shots on each marked location, then the 105mm howitzer dead center, immediately followed by twin 20mm bursts. It was over in minutes; fires raged in craters below. We returned immediately to Hurlburt, and with the propellers beating the air, I slept the whole way on the cargo ramp floor seats.

Now we get to the worst parts of this mission. No, it wasn't the leeches, mosquitoes, fear of poisonous snakes, waterlogged feet, etc... It was debriefing with Lt Weasel. Upon rolling onto the field debriefing occurred, for the pilot and crew, and then for me. Upon entering the building the pilot was coming down the hall and stopped me. He said, "Look, I know you're new. But I thought you were supposed to take out a target if you could...", and he halted because he could see me getting angry. He said, "Talk to me". I told him about this being the Lt's plan, and I was ordered to only place the markers. He just said, "OK thanks.. don't worry about it" and he patted me on the shoulder and walked out.

Now I had to debrief with Lt Weasel and I was already pissed. Bill knew what was going to happen and told me, "Whatever he says, no matter how wrong, just say yessir." The Lt read what I had written for my report, then he turned to me with his lying eyes and high-pitched squeaky voice, "The pilot tells me you should have destroyed those caches yourself. We just can't have you going around making these decisions on your own. Why didn't you just destroy them?" Bill looked at me and shook his head no, but I just couldn't let Lt Weasel walk on that. So I told him, "You are so right sir! I should have followed your orders to a T." Bill smiled but the Lt just looked at me

77

dumbfounded for about 30 seconds, stood up, said, "Well, OK", and he walked out. I knew this relationship was not going to go well.

Ambush 1

#3 – June 1980

When last we left our intrepid Scout… I was having my
first disagreement with Lt Weasel. I had told the gunship pilot
about who planned the former mission, as there was
disappointment over my not having just destroyed an unguarded
cache while there. As it turned out, after explaining to the pilot,
he returned to tell his Squadron Commander, who in turn
informed the Group Commander, who in turn informed the Wing
Commander. The Wing Commander was not pleased with
inexperienced or untrained personnel planning missions.

The Wing Commander, while not having official
command of the Scout Program, called the Scout Program
Commander, Major Ian Fleming, and read him the riot act. This
phone call was relayed back to the Group Commander, then to the
Squadron Commander, to the pilot, and back to me. The result
was a communique directly from Major Fleming to me, and
copied to Lt Weasel. It stated flatly that I was to plan my own
missions without interference, utilizing the gunships when
necessary (after all, they were very expensive pieces of equipment
with large crews). The Lieutenant was NOT happy, but he had no
idea how the chain of command learned of his ineptitude, so
while he began to hate me, he didn't directly attack me. Bill, my
trainer and mentor, was very pleased with this turn of events, as
was I.

Thus began my first planned ambush of a weapons convoy
in El Salvador. This action was ultimately ordered by the CIA.
They have certain rules of engagement: 1) Don't get caught, and

if you do, you better find a way out of it and destroy all evidence of US involvement; 2) When they say they want everyone dead, *they want everyone dead*; 3) No evidence of US involvement is to be left behind; 4) All deaths are sanctioned as long as the Agenda is not altered and the other rules are obeyed.

These convoy ambushes would take on a routine of their own: Study the photographs, satellite imagery, and terrain maps. From these, intelligence regarding the route, the number of vehicles, and the weather forecast it was fairly easy to choose the proper place for an ambush. Once the plan was set and briefed, I would fly into the country the day before on an MC-130-E Combat Talon. From this point weapons and explosives would be supplied by the CIA or other intelligence agency, and I would be dropped or flown by helicopter to a drop zone in order to set the trap. This particular convoy consisted of ~50 vehicles, mostly heavy trucks, a few jeeps and 4wd trucks with bolt on machine guns, and several hundred personnel mostly riding in the trucks with the weapons. The weapons consisted of M16s, AK47s, machine guns, and a few low-tech shoulder fired rockets. There was also enough ammunition to fight a major conflict.

This particular route led through an open area, but the terrain would allow some attempts at escape. Blowing and blocking the road would be easy enough at each end and along the middle, but the gunships would need to be coordinated differently – there would need to be three of them, and they would have to fly a constant equidistant oblong pattern to make sure both sides of the convoy would always be hit simultaneously. The third gunship would concentrate on the heavy trucks. In the early evening a helicopter dropped me in the clearing. I immediately set about placing road charges. One of these charges was placed on a wide path that a small truck could drive down into a lower area. This low area is where I made my blind, yet it wasn't so low that I couldn't see most of the road clearly.

~0230 the convoy entered the trap and the road charges were set off. The gunships began firing 20mm rounds almost non-stop, and the third gunship was firing 40mm and 105mm rounds almost non-stop. I was firing from my position when one of the 4wd trucks made it through the crater on the path leading down to my position. They saw my flash and began firing bursts all around me. I fired and killed the driver and passenger, but the gunner kept firing. I couldn't stay exposed like this as rounds were whizzing past me side to side and above, so I called up to the gunships to ask for help. 69-6575 returned my request with a burst of 20mm and the truck exploded. I thanked them profusely, and I became very attached to this plane. I know it was the pilot and EWO, but I couldn't help loving that plane. It became my favorite.

In ~30 minutes all the trucks were on fire and there appeared to be no movement of personnel. Clean Up (CIA euphemism) was fairly easy for me on this one. There were a few hiders that attempted to kill me, but it just worked out in my favor. Incendiary grenades were tossed in trucks that still had intact cargo. I took my pictures and retrieved my gear and the helicopter picked me up.

Upon returning to Hurlburt, I was congratulated on a successful plan, by the Wing Commander, the Group Commander, the Squadron Commander, the pilots, and Bill. In debriefing the Lt lived up to his name and criticized everything about the plan. It was obvious at this point that we would never have a close relationship.

At that time it felt good to be congratulated. There was pride in developing and executing such a plan. But I had never seen so many dead bodies, nor had I seen such destruction and gore, and the amount of blood was beyond imagination. The missing legs, arms, heads, and holes the size of softballs to basketballs sticks hard in your brain. The amount of human blood that attaches itself to you while creeping your way through a dead convoy is astounding, and the smell permeates your nostrils, throat, and the inside of your mouth. I'm not against the use of force when necessary, but this really didn't seem necessary; and the slaughter is beyond the pale. When I think about this now, it just makes me cry. I was all of 18 at the time and was already responsible for killing many people directly, and being an accessory to the slaughter of hundreds – all in a single night. At the time I was so indifferent to the slaughter, blocking negative thoughts, just steeling my emotions as I was taught, because I thought I was doing the right thing. Now, knowing what I know about the conflict, I'm filled with regret and shame. The images of the event haunt my dreams and fill me with sadness. I wouldn't realize until much later that, conscious of the act or not, each life taken also took part of my connection with humanity, the dead would visit regularly, and would one day bring my mind to the point of total destruction.

Kit

June 1980

Returning to the barracks one day in June 1980, I found a phone message on my door. A girl named Kit had called and said she would be at the same hotel the second week of June. Since first meeting her I had participated in three missions, with plenty of death, and I wasn't looking forward to discussing my work. But I was *so* excited to see her.

I called her and met her out on the beach where we had previously made love and swam. She hugged me and kissed me, and I returned the compliment. It's funny how fast you can know someone and talk to them so easily. My heart immediately opened further, and I asked if she came by herself. She said she came with one of her friends from before. She got sheepish eyes that told me something was up, so I told her to give. She asked if I remembered our previous conversation that she insisted wasn't over. I did. She told me she thought about what I said about traits to look for, and she felt the friend she brought with her was a good candidate. She had already spoken to her friend about it, and she was all for participating. I asked her what did this mean for the two of us. She said she wanted us to be one, and that we would remain one. I hugged her again and told her I would remain one with her, and yes, she could set it up with her friend. She called up and arranged a time, and came and told me. Then, since there was plenty of time, I took her to a small beach, hidden from the road, on the tide pool across from the base. We swam, and we teased each other to distraction in preparation for later.

We arrived back at Kit's room, took a quick shower, and invited the friend over. She was our same age and went to school

83

with Kit. She had long dark brown hair and a mischievous yet friendly smile. Talking with her, I could see why she and Kit were best friends. They had obviously talked about this and wasted no time getting started. They stood in front of me and began kissing and petting each other. They removed each other's shirt and exposed their breasts. The friend had medium size breasts that were firm, but heavy. Kit started sucking these breasts with gusto which thrilled me to no end, and the friend added to the excitement by reaching down and pulling on Kit's nipples. I'm sometimes slow to catch on, but I could tell by the passion they showed each other, this was not their first time. It hit me immediately that Kit, and her friend, were bisexual (though at the time "go both ways" worked just as well). This was fine with me.

They pulled my shorts and underwear off, and both began sucking my cock and balls. I squirmed and sighed over and over. I had both of them kneel on the bed and I rubbed their hot and wet twats ever so gently while they kissed. I entered her friend from behind, and squeezed her breasts and she grunted, and Kit continued to kiss her. Then I switched and entered Kit from behind, and she moaned. It was so easy to make her erupt, because she took all of the moment within herself.

I lay on the bed and Kit rode my cock while the friend reversed on my face. They rode and squirmed while kissing and caressing each other's breasts. The friend rammed her cunt into my face and yelled she was cumming, Kit exploded in a fit, and I told her I couldn't hold it anymore. She pulled my cock out and jacked it off on her friend with cum flying everywhere. They *made* me lick it off.

Afterward, we ordered a pizza and ate and talked. I asked them right off how long they had been lovers. They laughed and asked how I knew. They weren't aware how obvious it was, so I explained to them what I had observed. Kit said they had been lovers since their sophomore year in high school. Both loved men, but they loved loving each other as well. They both knew they wanted to marry a man and have kids… but life demands love, emotional and sexual, and there is no reason to waste a beautiful love handed to you. Loyalty and devotion would alter things later, but that didn't denigrate the meaning of bonding with another now.

We performed this every night they were there, with variations including an oral daisy chain, which all found to be exciting and satisfying. Kit was ecstatic and told me she had never gotten so excited. She wanted to visit again, but wanted us to share a man the next time. I told her anything's possible, but she would have to recruit the man… and I could see the wheels turning.

We talked about our relationship. Was this long-term? Did we want long-term? We both said this experience brought the other closer. Truth be told, I was falling for her hard. We wanted to continue, and she insisted she would be back at the end of summer. I really wanted this, though I needed to ask about the months we were apart, but she beat me to it and said that she was an extremely horny person, and she knew I was, and that neither of us would make it three months without sex. I agreed and asked what she was proposing. She said that we were looking to be with each other long-term, but until that could happen, we needed to be realistic about who we were. She knew I was traveling out of the country up to two times per month, and she knew my work was dangerous and intense. We agreed that we would continue as we were, still taking sexual opportunities as they presented themselves, until such time that our long distance circumstances changed. We both agreed with this and we both professed that we were feeling we were starting to fall in love. The friend, being totally sincere, thought this was "cute" and said we were a "cute couple".

Ambush 2

#4 – July 1980

Another convoy to destroy in El Salvador. Not having Lt Weasel interfere made planning and execution so much easier. Trusting my life to an inexperienced dweeb on a power trip was not something I needed, or wanted.

~50 heavy trucks loaded with M16s mostly, some AK47, explosives, and ~500 rebel personnel. I began to wonder why the rebels had so many US military M16s, so I asked the CIA officer. He stated it firmly and non-nonchalantly: The US supplies the M16s to the government forces, and the rebels buy them from corrupt officials and steal them. Terrain maps and imagery were provided for a route going through the southern mountains. At a point in the route the road (dirt passage), took a sharp westward turn. This point would receive a large enough charge to destroy the turn. The end of the trap would be the blown road several hundred yards back. The middle of the road would receive incendiary charges. The west side of the road was steep hillside, and the east side of the road was a fantastic drop, not far, but no truck of any kind would make that grade. There was no good position on the eastern side, so I had to set up above the road on the western side. This wasn't ideal because the hillside could still be climbed, yet it afforded ~100 yards of open space and the entire road in my view. As precaution, I laid charges at various spots both on the east and west off the road to deter escape ideas if necessary. I wasn't taking any chances after what happened last time.

The trucks (including 4wd escorts with machine guns) entered the trap ~0130. The moon was full and bright. It had rained hard earlier in the day, and the trucks were sliding a bit in the mud, and they were moving rather slow. When the lead truck reached the turn I blew the road charges. The lead truck was on fire as it started sliding down into a ravine and it exploded with a roar. I started firing immediately throughout the line, and the gunships, Wicked Wanda and Big Ben started pounding them with 40mm and 105mm, and successive bursts of 20mm rounds from their Gatling guns. Some of the personnel in the trucks attempted climbing down, but they were killed either by my fire or 20mm rounds. Some attempted climbing up, but that didn't work either. My flash, even though suppressed, still gave away my position and I received quite a bit of fire, so I had to move position several times. The gunships tracked my position and informed where rebels were ascending the hill too close to me for the gunships to fire, and I would concentrate my fire at those locations. It began to feel too close for comfort, and I blew the charges on both sides of the road, which cleared up opposition a great deal.

In ~45 minutes it was all over except for the Clean Up, which I had already started to hate. Once again, the amount of blood, guts, bone, and death took my breath away. Dead bodies lay everywhere, on the hill, the road, and the slide into the ravine; those that weren't dead soon were by my hand. The effusion of blood that leaked from the bodies onto the ground directly, or from the trucks staggered my senses. At times I found myself crawling through pools of blood and corpses (whole and not) searching for the next live rebel. Pictures were always demanded by the CIA of the death and destruction. At times I found myself forcing my own vomit back down. I was not unaware of, or unfamiliar with, animal death. When younger, I had helped a friend make muskrat traps, helped set and check the lines, and assisted in killing the animals swiftly. Then we would take them to be Cleaned. They would be cut open, the guts removed, and the carcass would be skinned for fashion. But the smell of human blood, at least to me, is unique. It strongly smells of iron and copper. The amount of blood was just unbelievable to me, even though I was standing right there, and knew exactly why it was there. I had learned to steel my emotions at these times, because I knew that panic could mean almost certain death, and I had limited time before government forces would arrive. But I really wasn't prepared for human death on this scale, I never hated the Salvadoran or Guatemalan rebels, or even the Sandinistas, but I thought I was doing the work of my country. I thought I was participating as an adult. I thought there is NO WAY my commanders or my President would lie to *me*. I had just turned 19 and was already starting to lose my life.

After returning to base, I was once again congratulated on forming a successful plan. Although, Lt Weasel, in debriefing, tore into my plan, my actions... He stated he could have done much better. As he said this, Bill was behind him shaking his head that no he couldn't. My biggest mistake was telling the Lt what I have stated above about my reaction. He, a man who was never in the field, never killed a human, told me what a wuss I was, what an overly sensitive boy I was (he was all of four years older). He told me, "Real men don't get excited or down over a *little* blood", to which Bill rolled his eyes. OMG how I started to hate Lt Weasel! I chalked up his tirades to being told to stay out of the planning process; and to the fact he had short-man syndrome.

Bill always tried to make me feel better afterward. He knew what it was to kill close up. He knew what I was feeling and attempting to control. He would tell me he knew the CIA's agenda was not right and that most agents were psychopaths who held no regard for human life at all; he told me several times, "They'd kill their own mother if the President said so."

Wicked Wanda

Wicked Wanda was an AC-130-H Spectre Gunship, 69-6575. It had saved my life on more than one occasion.

But first, Wicked Wanda was a serial porn comic which appeared in the back of Penthouse. She was the head mistress of a brothel which was located in a mountain castle. She kept her dead father, the Baron, on a throne under an emerald case. All the rich and elite politicians and famous frequented Wanda's castle (Nixon, John Wayne, and many others). From time to time, other interesting characters also came to Wanda for assistance with sexual needs, or for her unique brand of correction.

A young man came to Wanda's castle, unaware that it only contained women. Upon questioning the man, Wanda discovered not just that he is homosexual, but that he finds women disgusting. Wanda, of course, felt compelled to show the man how a woman could meet his needs. He agreed to a challenge, but he was sure they would never please him.

She and the girls tied him up and began manipulating him, and he was terrified to see his erection grow hard. He told them they still wouldn't be able to satisfy his needs, and Wanda took offense. She bent him over, and inserted a nightstick, which she used frequently, into his ass and began to ream him with gusto. He became so excited he didn't know what was happening. Wanda doubled her speed, yelling, "Is this want you want?!?", and reached around and jacked his cock until he blew a massive load everywhere. Needless to say, the man became a regular.

One day, while looking at my favorite AC-130-H gunship, the 105mm Howitzer reminded me of Wanda's nightstick. I went immediately to the supply room and made a stencil. Then I painted Wicked Wanda over the front door of the gunship. The maintenance Lt found out I had placed the name on the gunship, and he demanded that I remove it. I refused and lost a stripe for 3

91

months, but the pilots and Squadron Commander liked the moniker, so it stayed, and soon monikers were stenciled on all the gunships. This really makes me chuckle: To this day, that retired gunship sits in honor at Hurlburt Field with the name of a beautiful raven haired mistress ready to ram her nightstick up your ass.

Baby

#5 – July 1980

How could anyone hate you?!?

> – Mrs Seinfeld

With every child born, a new expectation
enters the world.

> *Differences* – <u>A Passion For Truth</u>
> – Abraham Joshua Heschel

You wouldn't think Guatemala would ever feel cold, but
the day was rainy and it felt cold to me, chilling me to my bones.
There was no way to stay dry. The convoys I had been assigned
were not pleasant to understate it. At this point I understood I was
halting weapons shipments to communist rebels and killing the
communist rebels traveling with the weapons. Seems simple
enough, doesn't it? But the Guatemalan Army, though forceful
and vicious when in numbers against no threat whatsoever,
couldn't handle determined rebels with weapons. So even though
they had been trained by commanders who had received the best
training in being egregiously vicious by the US military and the
School Of The Americas, they couldn't take on active rebel units
that would fight back, because they would lose – their lives and
their government. So the fascist right-wing Guatemalan
government did what all such kind do… they kissed the US' ass
and let the CIA do all the work for them (unless of course it's an
unarmed village of 1000 where they killed everyone – man,
woman, and child; or, the family accused of being communist and
they go in the middle of the night to strangle every man, woman,

93

and child – and the dog, the cat, and expose the goldfish to the air).

If the CIA feels *ANY* thing to be a threat to the US, so BROADLY determined, then they have authority to engage US military force strikes. The CIA likes to make its partners feel good, so the US strikes, and the dictators or oligarchs in charge reap the rewards for such devastating decision and action.

So this is what I was doing there on this cold and rainy night, waiting in ambush for a weapons convoy which would have several hundred rebel personnel moving to a new location. I had come in from ~5km south. I planted my road charges and charged a few trees front and back. There was no clearing, with quite a bit of overhang along the route, so I used markers for the front end, the middle, and back, by the road. The gunships would pick up these signals, but I would have to laser paint as many of the large trucks as possible to make sure cargo areas would be hit. Around 0130 the gunships arrived and loitered. They saw headlights and heat signatures coming down the road and dropped to attack altitude and position. I told them to fire when I blew the front and back road and trees.

The lead vehicle was a 4wd truck with a 40cal machine gun mounted in the bed. I blew the road and trees. The lead vehicle flew into the air in flames and the tree crashed down across the road. The gunships fired all weapons unceasingly. I went along the line targeting certain trucks to have them blown apart by 105mm shells and targeting rebels with my rifle and firing on them. The Gatling guns rained 20mm shells up and down the line almost non-stop. 40mm shells exploded randomly here, there, and everywhere.

I believe the gunships emptied there supply of 20mm shells, thousands of rounds, each one with the rough explosive force of a grenade, many of them red phosphorus tracers. Some 105 shells contained white phosphorus which burns with intensity until its chemical reaction is complete. It sticks to skin and clothing and causes a chemical burn beyond the measurement of ordinary pain.

At the end of these, the gunships always say they've gotta go, watch out for those that are living, and say good luck with "Clean Up", the CIA's euphemistic catch phrase for making sure *EVERYONE* is dead. This required walking (crawling, etc...) the convoy line looking for people to kill. It's depressing no matter how you attempt to justify it. I was still relatively new at this task, and I already despised it. But before you understand, you believe that you're doing something toward the right end. You know, *They* are in important positions, and *they* just wouldn't lie to you... would *they*?

I reached the end of the convoy, all weapons destroyed, everyone dead... But I heard a baby cry, yet convinced myself that was crazy. Then I heard it louder and followed it. A baby lay in a sling carrier by the side of the road, under some large foliage. It was a beautiful dark and coppery molasses color with big dark eyes. It had a shrapnel wound in its upper left arm. I cleaned my hands with alcohol, and I felt for any piece of metal and bone damage, and the baby wailed. But there was no damage. I looked around to see who the mother might have been, but there were several women rebels in this convoy and nothing seemed obvious. I re-sanitized the wound and bandaged the arm, and the baby continued to cry. I knew I had to get out of there, and the baby had to come with me.

Leaving the baby was not an option. Government troops, who would be directed to the scene by the CIA, would arrive first to claim a success, and they would kill the "communist" baby. I couldn't take it back with me, as I thought the CIA would kill it or hand it over to Guatemalan governmental authorities who would have it killed; and my Lt Weasel would have conniptions if I brought it back to base.

On my route back to extraction was a side path to a village ~3km off my track. I decided that was the baby's best chance. I put the sling around my shoulder with the baby below my face, placed my rain poncho over it, and we skedaddled. It cried for awhile, and while I did have some penicillin and pain killer, I had no idea what or how much I could give it of anything, so I just let it jiggle and finally when I peeked in, it looked at me and smiled, and I thought I was going to cry.

We reached the side path to the village, but a new problem presented itself. My radio, always on, even when squelched, gave location signals on me. If I turned on this path, they would know it. I decided I had to turn the radio off for the time it took to go 3km, find a place for the baby, and 3km back. I knew if my radio were out too long they might send in a search and rescue team, and then the shit would hit the fan. I turned off the radio and began running on an unfamiliar slippery mud path holding a baby against my chest. A few times I almost tripped or wiped out, which made me panic for the baby. But eventually we arrived at the village. There were no lights, but even through the rain the moon provided some light, and I saw a small church. The front door was deep into the wall, and it had a roof over the entrance, so the baby wouldn't be rained on. I put the bulk of my rain poncho underneath it, wrapped the rest of the poncho over it leaving its face exposed, and told it how brave it was and stroked its cheek. The door had a rope pull for a bell, and I pulled it fast over and over and ran for the path. I could see the church door open, they saw the baby and took it inside.

I ran so hard and so fast to the trail head and switched on my radio but kept it squelched. I really didn't feel like making up my lie just then.   Taking a normal pace back to the extraction point I called for the extraction and was picked up in a Huey gunship and taken back to the airfield and back to Hurlburt. As expected, Lt Weasel was furious about my radio signal. There was no fucking way I would ever tell him what happened, so I told him I dropped it in the mud and it must've gotten too wet (which I knew was a bullshit reason). He yelled, he ranted, he raved, and I let him.

Afterward, Bill approached me and asked, "What the hell was that bullshit?" I told Bill. I told Bill everything because I trusted him to advise me without turning on me. I told him there was no fucking way I could leave that baby there to die. He told me he understood, but that getting involved may carry a heavy price for me at some point. He also was glad I didn't tell the Lt, as he was sure it would have meant the end for me. (If only)

Kit

August 1980

Kit returned alone the last week of August, and she would stay the week. I took her to Arthur Treacher's, because we both liked his fish & chips. I was so glad to see her, and she seemed equally glad to see me and expressed as much.

I loved running my hands over her body, touching and feeling her skin and musculature. My work took me down the opposite road of life toward death, and I needed to touch, to feel, to participate in love with another to regain life, to regain my sense of humanity. We sucked and fucked intensely, exploring each other's body and mind with wonder. On the third day I left the base early to be with her. I took her again to the tidal pool, because it was a beautiful spot hidden from the road, and we would be the only ones there. We listened to music on a boom box, and we sang to each other, and she tried teaching me to dance better. We swam naked and she began edging me and teasing. I asked her what she had in mind, and she reminded me of our previous conversation about recruiting a man. I told her that the recruiting would be up to her, because a man willing to participate would be more receptive to a woman's invitation. I told her it would be important to be honest and up front with the man, and some things to sense and ask about. I told her to reject any man who showed signs or intentions of being part of a cuckold relationship, or anyone seeking power or control, or unable to understand the major factor of sharing, and she agreed. She was sure she would be successful – she was very determined.

While I waited in the room, she went down and staked out the hotel bar. She didn't see or hear what she was looking for among the patrons, but then she realized her server was exactly what she was looking for. She asked him if he could take a break and sit and talk. He took his break and she explained and proposed the event to him. He told her at first he was a bit shocked, but then thought about it and thought why not. He had seen us together there before and all seemed appealing to him. She told him where… and when his shift ended he came up to the room.

I'm going to call him Joe. He was 21, ~5'10" with medium dark brown hair. He wasn't overbuilt, but kept himself in pretty good shape. He had a nice ass. We all started a drink, rum and coke, but didn't finish before Joe and I were feeling each other's bulge and kissing. I swear Kit's clothing disappeared in an instant. She approached us and began unbuckling our pants and pushed them down. She rubbed our cocks together with utter delight in her eyes. Joe's cock was long, straight, and meaty. I knelt down and began to suck it while squeezing his balls, and this made Kit wild with delight. She rubbed her pussy and brought up fingers of gruel and wiped it on Joe's cock and we sucked it together, moving from cock to balls and back again. By this time Kit had gruel oozing steadily from her pussy, and she was so excited she didn't know what to do next. I laid her on the bed and straddled her face, rubbing my boner over her lips. She begged to be fucked, so Joe obliged and she moaned deeply as he entered her. He started moving in and out slowly, and Kit began to lose focus, so I went behind Joe and rubbed my cock lengthwise down the crack of his ass. He began thrusting harder and Kit began non-stop moaning and pushing into him, so I reached down and cradled his balls. I could hear Joe getting very close. I placed my face underneath and licked his shaft as he pulled out and thrust back in, and Kit could sense this and she became ecstatic and told him to give her his cum. I grabbed his balls tight and squeezed and he exploded into her and his cum lathered around her cunt and I licked at it. As he pulled out I licked the cum on his shaft and sucked every last drop from his cock. Kit watched this with wild eyes of love, excitement, and wonder and told me to fuck her. I entered her and the wondrous hot cum acted as the best lube and I pounded her hard and fast. She bucked forward and gave the O face and shook and I blew my load into her and she growled and shuddered again. I licked at the cum on her pussy and rubbed it around her clit until she begged for mercy and I doubled speed and she came again and was exhausted. I looked at Joe and he was still breathing hard and sweating, then he said, "That was so fucking awesome!" We lay on the bed with Joe and I on either side of Kit. We just caressed, touched, and held each other for awhile.

Being hungry, we ordered a pizza and cleaned up. While we sat and ate, Joe said he had never had such an experience, and he was grateful to us for inviting him. He had never had a bisexual experience and he felt his mind had expanded from this. Then he blew my mind by saying the same thing off the cuff that Kit's friend had said, "You guys are a cute couple", and then, "It's obvious you care about each other."

On her second to last night there, we made love with Joe again. The next day Kit told me she *loved* me and she never wanted us to be apart. That went straight to my heart, and I told her I loved her and I hugged her and held her tight in my arms. When I released her, she had tears in her eyes and I asked what was wrong. She said, "Nothing. I'm extremely happy, but I hadn't expected to be hit like this." I admitted that I hadn't either, but that we shouldn't waste something so good. I asked her what her plan with school had been, and what it would become. She told me she really didn't want to go to school. She didn't even have an interest outside of a general liberal education... she just didn't know what else to do at the time, and her dad insisted. She said what she really wanted was a man to love, marriage, and kids. She said she wanted to return in December, and I told her to prepare herself.

Colombian Powder Burn 1

#6 – September 1980

Destroying cocaine processing labs for the CIA and DEA became a priority, especially for the CIA when rival suppliers threatened their illegal livelihood for making money to fund Contra rebels and other right-wing paramilitary outfits and dictators around the world. When I was first approached by AFSOC to help in such an operation, my first response was, "Why? The CIA is running those same drugs for profits for arms exports." I was told to mind my own business and form a plan based upon the supplied maps, images, and intelligence. The CIA runs a Command all its own and it supersedes military commands. They issue orders utilizing the US military as they see fit, and it's just as if the President issued the orders. End of discussion!

At the time, there were two major cartel players in Colombia, and several smaller actors. The CIA (as opposed to the DEA) was not interested in smaller actors, but wished to send a powerful message to the main cartels, such as, their drugs should be always available to the CIA at discounted bulk pricing. What better way to send a powerful message than to have a Spectre Gunship destroy a major processing lab in the jungle in the middle of the night. US forces and equipment were not yet explicitly barred from activity in Colombia, even if the Colombians frowned heavily upon this activity.

The Colombian jungles are full of cocaine labs, big and small, and the explosive chemicals for processing cocaine. Destroying a lab really doesn't take much effort with the right explosives, equipment, and/or stealth. A few are the size of a small city, with all the accouterments to keep workers relatively content while they make the pastes and powders. But to destroy something on such a scale as this requires a little planning and rolling execution.

Since gunships were involved, a load of explosives carried into the area would not be necessary. However, a load of sabotage markers to be picked up by the EWOs on their screens on the gunships was certainly necessary; and only a single heavy charge to signal the beginning of festivities.

Dropped ~7 kilometers from the lab, I immediately headed out for the lab. Finding it wasn't too difficult with the maps and imaging that had been provided. When I arrived at the lab I set up a blind to monitor activities. Upon reconnoitering the area I found the fuel supply tank shown in images. That's where I placed the single large charge. There were a couple dozen buildings and shacks, and several cars and trucks. Each was attached with a marker. The cartel guards, while nothing to mess with or take lightly, seemed *laissez-faire*, like they really would not or could not comprehend anyone interfering in their activities. No doubt a lab this large enjoyed certain government protection. It was rather easy to avoid the guards and place the markers on buildings, supply huts, chemical supplies, vehicles, and even on the latrines.

After placing all markers I notified the loitering gunships to commence firing upon the explosion of the fuel tank. After giving them a few minutes to get into attack elevation and position, I flipped the switch and a massive fireball went into the sky. The gunships immediately starting firing 105s, 40s, and twin 20mm. Everything – people, places, things – exploded into fire and began to disintegrate into parts, pieces, mist, and dust. In ~15 minutes the entire facility was destroyed into fire and rubble. I went through to dispatch whoever was left, then went back to my blind to gather what was there. Getting too comfortable, and not paying proper attention, I turned to leave but twisted my ankle which I had carelessly let settle between some tree roots.

It hurt like hell, and my boot wasn't tight enough to let me walk on it, which I needed to do desperately. FARC guerrillas would soon be combing the area to find out what was happening, and I would have rather avoided them at all costs. I took off my boot and ripped the sleeve from my shirt and cut a wrap. I wrapped the ankle and put my boot back on and tightened the laces hard. It still hurt, but I was able to walk somewhat. I began moving in the direction of extraction, a Huey gunship was to pick me up, but only after I called in.

With the ankle I was moving fairly slow. At times I had to hide and let FARC guerrillas, who were headed in the opposite direction, pass by. I kept moving at a slow but steady pace, using a branch I had picked up and cut into a walking stick. Soon, I heard a party of men behind me. If my ankle hadn't been twisted, I surely could have out-foxed or out-paced them. They followed me for 3 kilometers, and I reached the clearing where the helicopter was to extract me, but I needed to get to the other end (~100 yards further) where it was wider. As I moved through the outer edge of the clearing, they sprang upon me and halted me in my tracks.

They all carried AK-47 rifles. Two of them were older, around 40, and the third was a kid around 17 or so. They took my gear and weapons and made me stand with my hands behind my head. They tied twine around my ankles as a hobble, and tied my wrists behind my head running the twine down to my belt and tying it. The two older men began going through my pack, while the younger one was having fun with my knife. He had taken my pistol and put it in the front of his pants. I was truly hoping it would go off because I kept a round in the chamber and he had pulled back the hammer before putting it in his pants. He then began flashing my knife in my face, and while I couldn't understand his words, I got the idea that he planned on carving me up. He ran the point around my eyes and laughed. He ran the point around my ears and laughed. He pushed the point against my tongue, made it bleed, and laughed. He ran the sharp edge around my throat and laughed. He ran the blade down my front, stopping to poke at my heart, and laughed. He pushed the point, then the blade, into my groin and began chuckling, and ran the length of it around my crotch. He was planning on cutting my balls off. He went behind me and bumped his crotch into my ass while he held the blade at my throat, to tell me he was going to rape me, and he laughed. The older men, behind him 10 feet, laughed in agreement... and then they became engrossed in examining my maps.

The older men turned slightly into the moon to view the maps better and I kept examining the situation looking for an out. The younger man turned slightly to examine my rifle. Seeing my chance, I pulled the T-handle blade I kept in a sheath sewn into the neck of my shirt, cut the twine holding my wrists, and I rammed it into the younger man's neck beneath the back of his skull. Before he dropped I pulled my pistol from his pants and shot the older two in the chest as they turned. Not wanting more noise, I put the suppressor on and shot the two older men in the head. I looked at the younger man and found he was still alive and conscious, but not moving, and I assumed he was paralyzed. Revenge was the first thing on my mind, but getting out of there was a greater concern. I pointed my pistol at his crotch, and his eyes grew wide with panic. Two rounds into his crotch and he gurgled with pain, and the third in his brain, and I called the helicopter for pickup.

I collected my gear and weapons, and continued to the wide area of the clearing and the Huey dropped and pulled me in

105

safely. To this day, I don't feel guilt over killing those bastards. The threats of killing I could take, but the threats of mutilation and rape made me want revenge.

To be honest, I had to fight the urge to be like them. I was so tempted to cut off his balls and stick them in his mouth before shooting him in the head. I said as much to Lt Weasel in debriefing. This was the ONLY time he ever cut me slack and treated me with respect; but when he said that he *would* have done it, I knew I had made the right decision. My trainer, always with me in debrief, told me he was glad I didn't do what I had been thinking.

Am I supposed to feel guilt from this? You tell me. FARC guerrillas were egregiously mean assholes. They were willing to kill anyone and everyone, including their own. Rape, kidnapping, and murder for profit had become the major part of their identity. Am I supposed to feel guilt over that sadistic little fuck?!? And yet, somehow, I do. Or rather, not guilt, or even shame, but sadness that a group of people can go so far astray in their thinking and actions that they lose all sense of any decent humanity.

Guatemalan Funeral Pyre

#7 – November 1980

On a bright yet very cloudy night, with a torrential rain pouring down unceasingly, I dropped into the Guatemalan jungle to destroy a weapons cache. The cache was yet to be hidden away, sitting in crates underneath rain tarps. Because the cache was unhidden, four rebel guards protected the weapons at four corners of the cache. There would be no way to get at the cache without killing the guards, and the gunships couldn't see the cache from their vantage point without markers, but since the guards would be gone, there was no sense involving the gunships at all.

So much rain coming down made sighting almost impossible. The guards were within shouting distance of each other, and my suppressors would not suppress noise enough. It was necessary to kill the guards with a quick knife strike. I normally carried a large knife (10" blackened blade). During training we had practiced these knife strikes repeatedly. This would be my first actual multiple knife strikes outside of training. There's a lot of fear and trepidation to control and swallow preparing for this kind of kill. The subject must be approached quietly from the back, or surprised fast from the front or side.

The only way to approach the first guard, on the SW corner, was from the side. He kept his front to the corner vegetation, which gave him too much front view for my comfort. The south side had closer vegetation in which to creep up slowly and set for a quick kill. I crawled through the thick vegetation until I was ~10 feet away, where I thought I was just behind his

107

peripheral vision. I ratcheted down my feelings and did a quick-time crouch to within a few feet and drove my knife into his lung, pulled it out and drove it into his back with a twist. He gurgled a little as blood flowed from his mouth and nostrils, and his breath left his body as his eyes stared wildly and became dark, and I lay him down.

I hesitated for a few seconds, which I knew was inherently dangerous – but this was a sick feeling moment, that I had just done a terrible thing. Unfortunately, I didn't have the luxury of reflection, and there were three more guards that had to die. The NW corner would be next as he was closest. Now that the first guard was gone, I could easily approach that corner of the cache on a crawl. The rain had turned the entire area into mud, but the noise from the rain made moving about without detection somewhat easier. Once at the cache, I moved under the tarp toward the NW corner. When I reached that corner, I peered out from under the tarp. The guard was standing with his back to me. He was shorter than me. I moved quickly and with arm around his throat pulling up his jaw tight, I drove my knife into his back and twisted. He shook for a few seconds and then went limp. I lay him down on the ground.

The third guard at the NE corner, and the fourth at the SE corner, were done in the same manner. Pictures of the bodies were required, but I don't know how they turned out, as the rain came down in sheets. I pulled the bodies under the tarp, to be destroyed with the weapons. I retrieved my explosives pack and brought it under the tarp. Lids were removed to take pictures of the contents and to place incendiary explosives inside. I knew the rain was going to be a problem, because these containers needed to burn hot, so I had brought along magnesium shavings and small, sealed, waterproof packets of elemental sodium and placed a generous amount in about every other container. I made sure the charges registered and crawled back out toward my exit path.

108

~50 yards down my path I detonated the explosives and the magnesium burned bright and hot, and the rain combined with the sodium to force an unstable chemical burn. No weapon would survive that fire. Taking one last picture, I moved away from the area fast. I dodged Guatemalan military (informed to go to the location by the CIA), and reached my extraction point and was returned to a local airbase where a C-130 waited for me already running. We returned to Hurlburt and debriefing immediately took place in a building just off the flight line.

Lt Weasel, in his usual know-it-all mood, berated my choices, but I really didn't care. His word on planning meant nothing anymore. Then he started digging into me regarding the killings. He told me he was surprised, that he didn't think I would have the guts to go through with it. He told me how he would have done it better, and faster, and never felt sorrow or care. Bill could see me getting agitated and he walked behind me and put both hands on my shoulders and squeezed and pushed me down.

I didn't get sick when I killed those men, but it was an extremely sickening feeling – like you know you've done something seriously wrong. However, you console yourself with accolades and "job well done", and try hard to believe that this killing had a reason based in truth. Lt Col Dave Grossman in On Killing, uses unsubstantiated guess work based upon out of context blathering to assume killing is like sex, that plunging a knife into the body of another is like plunging your dick into another – which it most assuredly is not! I know what sex is Col, even if you don't. And I know what killing is Col, and know for a fact that you don't. You are like "virgins talking about sex". Unless you are a psychopath or sociopath, killing up close is a heinous feeling which you learn to force down and control, at the time.

These killings, even if self-condoned at the time, come back with all the force of vengeance they deserve later, and for the rest of your life. These men, almost 42 years later, continue to remind me what I did to them, and perhaps their families. I am fully aware of what I helped do to their country.

Rebel Commander's Convoy

#8 – November 1980

The CIA field officer came to Hurlburt, so I knew this was considered important. He met with Bill and I (excluding the Lt on purpose, as he had been told by the Wing Commander to leave the Lt out of all planning). I would be planning the destruction of a convoy in El Salvador, but this convoy had a "special package", a rebel commander who seemed pretty important to the CIA. This commander was responsible for several rebel victories against government forces. He had been educated in the US, spoke English, and returned home to help his people, the complete opposite of the government commanders who came to the US to train at the School Of The Americas, and returned home to torture, rape, murder, and plunder their people. It was known that this commander would travel with this convoy, and it was ordered that he must die. The CIA officer made it clear as day that once the convoy was "subdued", Clean Up must include the death and/or recorded death of this commander.

The route for this convoy took it down through a mountain pass into a thickly vegetated valley. Without the road, the area was impassible. The rain had not fallen in days, and the road was dry and hard packed. To the east was a steep hill impossible to climb from the road side, but accessible from behind with a path that wound down to a point south after where the trap would block the front of the convoy. A Huey gunship dropped me with gear on top of this hill. I setup a few weapons here, and proceeded down the path with explosives and pack shovel. This road was fairly steep grade, and it was necessary to completely block the road and prevent escape through the surrounding area in

111

the front. Several trees were charged to make quite the log jamb, and the road was charged at various places going up. Charges were placed close to the road at the front, to be detonated late in order to discourage escape in the frontal direction. Trees were charged at the rear of the trap, I verified the charge signals, and I returned to my roost. In addition to my M16, I had brought a sniper rifle to make sure no one could make it to the path ahead which would lead up beside me. I couldn't blow the path as I needed it to descend later.

Early after midnight the convoy came rolling down the hill, breaking as they went to keep from careening off the road. When the first truck, a heavy transport, reached the front of the trap, I blew the tree line for about twenty feet and twenty feet of trees stacked on the road. The lead truck crashed into the tree pile. The two waiting gunships opened fire, then I blew the rear trees and the road charges. Those who attempted running toward the lower front were killed, or surprised and turned back, when the charges were blown there. There would be no escape.

The gunships used a lot of 20mm rounds killing personnel attempting escape, and I fired with the sniper rifle non-stop. When the gunships switched primarily to 40mm and 105mm to hit all the trucks, I knew the end was near. When informed that there appeared to be no movement, yet personnel targets were still "hot", I began down the path to start Clean Up from the front of the line. There were many still alive and ready to fight, and a few rebels missed me by inches or less. About three trucks back I found the commander in the passenger side with a large shrapnel wound to his right shoulder. The damage had barely missed his neck, but tore his shoulder all to hell. He was alive and conscious, yet weak from loss of blood. I removed his weapons and strapped him in with his good left hand underneath and tied to the strap.

I proceeded checking the rest of the line, killing those who were left. On such a dry road at such an angle, blood ran downhill like many little creeks, and its smell permeated the air. The amount of blood released by the people in these convoys never ceased to amaze me. Then I returned to the commander. He looked at me and smiled, and said, "American". I nodded and said, "You're the commander." He nodded. He asked what hit them, and I felt he deserved that much, so I told him exactly what took place. I gave him water, and then I told him that he must know I couldn't leave him alive. He said he understood. He said he knew the Americans wouldn't allow anyone to know what they were doing, or how deeply involved they were. It was a relief to him to know that their convoys were being destroyed by American forces and not Salvadoran army, as that would have meant the army was an actual powerful force. He told me to go ahead, and I didn't want to hesitate further. I drew my .45, he closed his eyes, and I shot him in the head. I felt extremely sad and guilty, but continued to find his ID, and placing it upon his chest, I took his picture and returned to my roost. The chopper came and returned me to an airfield to climb aboard a C-130 home.

Bill asked me how I was. I told him I felt like shit. I told him about talking with the commander. He knew I would feel bad about this, and he patted me on the shoulder and we went into the debriefing. Lt Weasel was in rare form, not just picking at the whole plan and the kill, but he said I should have killed the commander immediately regardless of what else there was to take care of. I tried explaining that the commander was not a threat but that several threats still existed that required urgent attention, and I wouldn't have had time to deal with the commander until later anyway. He was restrained without weapons and badly injured, and that was enough at the time. He still went on ad nauseam about the proper way to do something of which he had no knowledge, experience, or intelligence. I decided that I

113

shouldn't tell the Lt about the conversation, and so I skipped to an immediate gunshot.

Shooting someone at close range is not as hard to deal with as using a knife, but it is much more troublesome in the mind than shooting from a distance. Seeing life leave a body, and the sudden complete stoppage of movement and life, is like glue that sticks in the gears of your mind. New ways of thinking, of channeling thought, become necessary. I wondered why such an intelligent man would be dedicated to his cause. I set out to learn more about these rebels and their cause.

Final Rest Camp

#9 – December 1980

Sometimes, for logistical reasons, or for reasons of distance, a weapons convoy may require camping overnight before continuing on. In this particular case, the convoy was congregating before leaving the next night. This took place in a box canyon with only a single road entrance with high walls on either side of the road. ~100 trucks were lined up nice and neat waiting to leave the next night. The entrance to the canyon was protected by 8 guards. Four guards were on the inside of the entrance, or close to it and wouldn't cause a problem. Four guards were on the outside of the entrance, and needed to be dealt with.

The gunships loitered above waiting for my signal. The guards would have to be killed one by one using a knife. The night was dry but sultry. The guards were spread out on either side of the road and the first pair were separated from the others and the entrance by ~50 yards. These four guards stayed off the road on either side. I was on the east side of this road and moved to kill the first guard, but just as I was about to drive in my knife he turned around. This was surprising, but I didn't hesitate and drove my knife up into his lung and heart, twisted, removed it and jammed it into his throat before any sound could emerge. I laid him down slowly and looked for the second guard.

He was ~10 yards further south on the west side of the road, so I crossed over behind him. I approached quickly but quietly, put my arm around his throat, and ran my knife into his kidney, turned it and pulled it out, then ran it into his liver, twisted, and he dropped. I decided to stay on the west side and creep up to the guard on that side closer to the entrance. I found him pacing north and south, consistently with about 10 seconds in each direction. When he turned north I quickly came up behind him and plunged my knife into his back and sliced his liver, twisted, and he dropped slowly with my help.

I decided to go back south a little to cross the road to the east. Once on that side I slowly made my way to the last external guard. Unfortunately, he was sitting on a boulder with his back against a larger boulder. The only sure way to get him was from behind. An overhead strike into his chest was out of the question, as these often fail because they get blocked. Once blocked I would either have to shoot or fight close quarters. Neither was acceptable. The shot would surely echo down the entrance (even with a suppressor) and I would be facing an entire army alone. Close combat is dangerous enough with a weapon. Once you are fighting you automatically reduce your chances of living 50%. If you lose your weapon your chances are seriously down. As I approached from the back he was smoking a cigarette. When immediately behind him he took the cigarette from his mouth and with my left hand I put my hand over his head and my fingers into his eye sockets and pulled back hard while simultaneously slicing his throat with my knife in my right hand, and the blood gushed, he became disoriented while choking on his own blood, and fell over squirming, then he just stopped while the blood continued.

I immediately retrieved my explosives and rifle. It was then that I first noticed being covered in blood. My hands were sticky with blood and left bloody prints on the explosives and my rifle. I set charges deep into the middle of the entrance without being seen, then retreated back to place charges at the base of the walls. Once I verified the charges I went ~25 yards down the road on the side and blew the road and side walls. The entrance was filled with rocks and debris 20 feet high. I could already hear the gunships firing and massive explosions taking place inside the canyon. As expected, several personnel attempted climbing the debris pile for escape, but I cut them down, and the gunships fired 20mm into the other side of the entrance. Soon, there were no more escapees and the gunships reported slow to no movement. I went over the pile and performed the Clean Up. There were several survivors ready to use their weapons, and they died in the attempt. Several wounded were killed in accordance with CIA orders. Any truck not burning soon was, and I left to go back over the debris pile.

I called for the chopper to pick me up. They landed in the road and when the gunner pulled me in he said, "Holy fuck! What happened to you?" This caused the pilot and co-pilot to turn around and look, and they asked if that was my blood. Assured that I was OK and the blood wasn't mine, they just looked with mouths agape and shook their heads. We returned to the airbase and I entered the C-130. The pilot saw me laying on the webbed seating and said, "What the fuck have you been doing? Don't get that blood on my seats." I suppose he thought that was clever and funny. I just flipped him off.

Noticing the amount of blood on my clothing and boots, arms and hands, and face, when we landed at Hurlburt I requested time to get cleaned up and change my clothes. Lt Weasel denied this request and ordered me into debriefing immediately. I gave my account, choosing not to tell the Lt anything regarding my thoughts, because he would just berate them. As he talked, and this is the first time I can remember consciously doing this, I *completely* tuned him out. I know from looking at the clock before and after that his mouth started moving and continued non-stop for 30 solid minutes. I had been looking at my clothes and the blood, noticing how it stained my hands and caked in my fingernails. Then my mind wandered, back to the mission, other missions… floating and wandering, maybe even hiking. When he finished and asked if I had heard him, I looked down again at the blood on my clothes. I noticed in places that the cakes were thick and hadn't fully dried, leaving them soft and fluid underneath. I had not heard a single word he had said, nor had I wanted to. I rose slowly and extended my hand for a handshake. He took my hand even though he was grossed out by the blood on my hands, and I shook, and I pulled him in tight and bear hugged him and said, "Thank you for all your advice." When I released him he had blood spots all over his uniform. He turned green and I thought he was going to puke, and he left the room, not to return. Bill looked at me and laughed, and asked, "You didn't hear a word he said, did you?" I shook my head no and took my leave to go clean up.

Kit

December 1980

Since meeting in August before school started, we began some phone conversations. This was not ideal as the only phone I could use, short of going to search for a phone booth, was in the barrack's common room. No conversation was private. Further, when I called her number, the majority of the time her sister would answer, and sometimes her dad or mom. Her sister was just a controlling nosey bitch, and I could tell she had provided much information to the parents, and that Kit had also told them some things. I couldn't fault them for being concerned about their daughter, so when they asked me questions about my work, I tried to be truthful, yet there was so much I couldn't share, and there was also much I wouldn't share with them.

Bill was very supportive of Kit. He thought the world of her and he too thought we were a "cute couple" sharing real love. Bill said she lightened my heart. I didn't think it right to withhold from Kit so much about what I did, so I asked Bill how he saw it, and what he would do. He told me I should be honest with her regarding the danger, and some details minus exact locations could be shared with her. I told him I wanted to marry her. He was floored, but very happy. He helped me find a deal on an engagement ring and told the clerk to box and wrap it when I became nervous and wasn't paying attention.

Kit arrived in Fort Walton in December, after classes let out for Christmas break. When we talked, when we walked, when we laughed, when we made love, I knew how much I loved her, her wit, her laugh, her commonality, her lust for life, and her love for me. She knew who I was and accepted me, and made me

119

feel so strong and loved. She was a strong person, a kind person, a loving person. My heart pounded for hers and hers for mine. I was extremely nervous, and not even the operant programming could clear the panic from inside me.

On the second day, I took her to dinner. We drank beer and slurped oysters. When I looked into her eyes, they smiled so brightly at me it made me weep a little. I brought out the ring, wrapped as a present. She thought it was just a gift, and it was, but not *just* a gift. When she finished removing the ribbon and paper and opened the box... she stared at it and looked at me with tears in her eyes. I said, "I love you, and I want to marry you." She took my hand, squeezed it hard, and said, "Yes." The waitress, who had been observing the whole time, began crying.

I told her, to be fair, I needed to tell her a bit about my work. We discussed the danger, and the death in an abstract way. I told her about the baby found by the road after the ambush. I told her until my term of service was up, I would have to continue doing this work. By this time she had moved to my side of the table and hugged me. She said she understood, and she still wanted to marry me. She said that once I completed my contract her dad could most probably help me find work in California.

The winter weather in Fort Walton Beach sucks, it's cold, rainy, and cold. The moisture from the Gulf permeates all of your clothing with cold and goes straight for your bones. That week the weather was miserable, but the love between us made us warm. She was beyond the moon, and I was the happiest I had ever felt up to that time.

Kit still had no plans for her college degree beyond general education. She wanted more than anything, she said, to be married and having children. She said she was looking forward to a life and growing old with me. We discussed her parents and I told her I knew this would be difficult for her to deal with them. She left and said she would talk to her Dad and Mom. I knew this would be tough for her. Her parents and her sister had certain ideas for her future, and I wasn't really among those plans for them. Kit would return in the Spring and we would finalize plans.

Box Bandit

#10 – January 1981

Russians supplied socialist rebels throughout Central America with arms, just as the US supplied capitalist and fascist dictators and rebels with arms. I'm sure the Russian interest in doing so was to create trouble for America on its borders, the way NATO and the CIA troubled Russia on its borders.

Nevertheless, the UN was susceptible to hear of the trouble Russians caused, but proof was needed, especially regarding the delivery of weapons. Intelligence was sure of Russian military cargo planes landing on remote strips and roads in El Salvador and Guatemala to offload weapons for rebels. There seemed to be no way to definitively prove it.

In a meeting held with AFSOC, State Dept, and CIA personnel, I informed them that the Russian cargo planes they were attempting to track were similar to the C-130s, low-level fliers that could land and take off on short unimproved run ways, could operate in stealth mode, and most likely held black box recorders for flight and communication data that may be obtained. Another meeting was held a few days later and the CIA brought specifications for the plane in which the location of the recorders was identified under the cockpit deck. It was further reported that the plane(s) in question were often stationed at a Nicaraguan air base on the western coast. I was asked if it would be possible to infiltrate the base and collect the recorders from one of the planes they were attempting to track. After two more days of reviewing the mapping and images of the area, another meeting was held at which I offered a plan.

122

There was no sense in bringing along a multitude of weapons. I carried my M11 with suppressor and my knife. I also carried a custom made back pack that I requested and was produced by the CIA. The bag was padded and contained copper mesh in the lining to prevent signals from the black boxes from signaling to the FAS/DAA. The area was completely flat and covered with brush and trees. It was too far and exposed for helicopter support, so I was dropped at low level from a C-130 Combat Talon, along with FRS gear for extraction. I went in the early nighttime, stashed the extraction gear, and made my way to the base. Surveying the area I spotted the plane and found an area by the chain link fence with crates piled ~forty feet long and four to six feet high with tarps thrown over them. By now it was daybreak and I had to find a spot to hide and rest until the shift change for swing shift occurred. I found shade and a blind in an overgrowth of shrubbery, and rested and waited until just before the shift change. Fifteen minutes before the change I made my way to the fence. There were alarm wires running through the fence at the top and bottom. I spliced a longer connection in the lower wire in order to cut it and peel back the bottom of the fence for entry. Once inside the fence I pulled the fence back down and tacked it with a piece of wire and hid behind the crates.

I could see the Russian plane about 25 yards from my position, parked in front of a hanger another 40 yards from the plane. The rear cargo door was down, and I watched as maintenance personnel began clearing for the end of their shift. The guards were also supposed to change shifts, and I saw them returning from various locations. Just as I was about to make a dash for the plane, another guard came walking around the other end of the hanger. He hadn't spotted me and looked as though he were inspecting the fence line. I hoped he wouldn't come on the other side of the crates.

123

But as he approached, still unaware of my presence, and not appearing particularly concerned or alert, he shifted and moved on my side of the crates. I carefully crouched between two crates with a tarp running over them. I could see his feet as he slowly walked by, like he was meandering. It was still light, and I had to get to the plane before the next shift came out. There was nothing for it, I carefully pulled my knife and quickly emerged... He was six inches shorter than me and with my left arm tightly around his throat and jamming his jaw and gullet my right arm drove my knife into his back with a twist. He made only a small grunt, his breath left, and he dropped like a rag doll. I moved his body deep under a tarp, and rearranged a few crates to cover blood spots on the cement, and I made a dash for the plane.

As I approached the plane I could see vehicles heading out again and some men walking in my general direction. This plane had parachute and equipment bins along both sides of the interior about 6.5 feet up. There were a few parachutes and equipment bags in the bin to my left toward the cockpit, so I climbed in, lay on my back, and stretched myself as tight as I could against the outer hull and pulled the parachutes and equipment bags in front of me. There was a small jutting bulkhead just in front of my head, so if maintenance personnel went in and out of the cockpit, they wouldn't be able to see me.

I lay in that bin holding pretty still for the entire swing shift. Two maintenance personnel came inside the plane at various times, going into the cockpit, coming out. When it became dark they hooked up a generator and turned on the lights. Staying still that long, in one position, always watching your breathing and sound is not easy, especially if you become distracted. For a couple of hours I was concerned they would find the dead guard and lock the base down. But when you're feeling sure you're not going to be found, you start to think of other calming things to pass the time without falling asleep.

Failing on the calm aspect, I thought of my fiance, her smile, her eyes, her hair, her body, her smell... of swimming, of sex. I thought about loving her and making love to her. Remembrances of touching skin and hot fluids in the hot sun. I pondered all of the sex I had been part of with her, and found it was good. No matter how dirty I was or had been, she was able to match and join in, never questioning sexual motivation and willing to take part and explore. She let me delve deep into her body and mind. Then I thought how fucking comical, that I was hiding for my very life in the cargo rack of a Russian plane on a hostile enemy base; I can hear maintenance workers, and I'm thinking about hot sex and find that I'm rubbing my hard cock. Undoing my fly I extracted my cock and let my load fly on the cargo bag beside me. It was dangerous and delicious fun, but I hadn't been rubbing at the end, and found myself still quite excited. I calmed my breathing and went back to thinking.

I pondered all of the sex I had been part of, found it was good, and examined more. I thought about couple's threesomes... being a third, and soliciting a third. I thought about how different an experience the threesomes made up of all single, unattached partners were, compared to threesomes involving a couple with a third. I thought how being a third is a fantastic experience, but sharing a third with someone you love is an even better experience. I thought about how the mindsets of the couple and the third are paramount, whereas the singles' threesome requires no such consideration other than sharing. I thought about being bisexual and only my bisexual fiance (and participating lovers) knew about it. I thought about seeing the eager horny excitement in the eyes of women lovers seeing two men pleasure each other. I thought how sweet the experiences and how unfair that I had to hide it...

The lights went out and the generator disconnected. Lights outside the hanger were dimmed. It was ~2300 and the end of the swing shift. The night shift consisted of few workers and even fewer works of maintenance. I was relieved that they had left the rear cargo ramp open to level. I could have used one of the side hatches, but those doors make some serious noise if you're concerned about who may be around. I climbed out of the bin as noiselessly as possible, which wasn't easy because my ass and my hips had gone to sleep. When on the floor, I had to wait for my stiffness to abate, then I suddenly had to pee, a lot. I stood by the rear cockpit bulkhead wall and peed for what seemed like several minutes. It ran down the wall and underneath the floor. The relief was wonderful and I suddenly felt full of energy!

Climbing the first short ladder I crouched to go under the cockpit deck where the avionics equipment was located. Using a small flashlight with red lens I located the boxes, removed the mounting hardware, and cut the wires on both ends. Then I quickly placed them inside the special bag. Looking quickly in the cockpit I discovered a bonus, a copy of a cargo manifest with a date a few days earlier and while I couldn't really read it, I could see weapons and locations listed. I stuffed it in the backpack and wasting no time made for the rear cargo door. Lying down to peek out and observe, and finding no one about, I hopped down and ran for the fence. After one more quick check I removed the wire tack and went through and then replaced the tack.

After running back to my drop point I ate a candy bar. I was so hungry from having not eaten beforehand to keep my bowels empty. I radioed the Talon for extraction and put on the FRS harness. The Blackbird came from the south and I could see it coming in so low over the trees I thought it was going to hit them. I sat and waited and he pulled up abruptly at the last

second and caught my tether and yanked me skyward with a jolt.
The cargo masters hooked the tether and the pilot lowered his
altitude again. They pulled me in and we stayed low until far
enough north and we headed back to Hurlburt, refueling in flight
on the way. They said they had been loitering at sea for a few
hours waiting for my call.

Back at Hurlburt, the man who trained me hugged me and
said, "You did it! Watch out, the Lt is pissing himself..." The
CIA officer gratefully accepted the black boxes and paper. He
told me he would let me know what they found. Lieutenant
Weasel, Program Flunky was not so happy. During debriefing he
harassed me about not checking in. I attempted explaining that I
was stuck in a storage bin in a Russian aircraft with people about,
and my radio was squelched to keep silence but still allow my
signal to be traced. He yelled about rules, following the rules, his
rules, about following orders, his orders, he harangued, he kept
getting in my face. Bill told him to "sit down... back off...
etc..." The Lt had me so angry I put my hand on my knife, but
Bill, who was behind me, placed his hand over mine and pressed
the handle against my side and continued demanding the Lt sit
down and behave or he may get hurt. I told Lt Weasel I
understood how to stay alive, and if he doubted it, he should
accompany me into the field to see how long he lasted. I needed
to breathe, so I told the Lt he had all the information he needed,
and if he didn't like what he read, he could make it up himself,
and I walked out. It's amazing how you do a thing, and all seems
right, then some asshole comes along to try and fuck you waving
his pencil dick in your face. How the fuck such an idiot is placed
in command of men is astonishing.

The CIA officer and State Dept rep returned and told me
the data collected from the boxes showed exactly where the
planes had been and landed in El Salvador and Guatemala, and
the manifest contained detailed delivery of weapons. They were

ecstatically happy and thanked me for obtaining the boxes and paper. I was awarded a medal from the CIA. Bill was very happy. The CIA officer was happy. The State Dept rep was happy. The Wing Commander was happy. The Group Commander was happy. Lt Weasel's boss (the Scout Program Commander) was happy. Lt Weasel was not.

Having been told that this mission saved lives, I'm of two minds. Great! But who catches the US delivering weapons to oligarchs, right wing dictators, and apartheid regimes such as Israel? Who catches the US committing or participating in genocide and murder for the capitalist or Neo-Christian or Zionist causes? I mean, I'm glad I could help stop the Russians from delivering at least some weapons, but **we** were delivering weapons all over Central and South America, as well as half the planet. You just *claim* that you are for Democracy, and lie through your teeth about about the Enemy, and suddenly it's OK to slaughter *en bloc*. When your treachery is pointed out, you transition your argument in support of Capitalism, Western Security & Society, and God.

Colombian Powder Burn 2

#11 – February 1981

Following Colombian Powder Burn (1) the gunships could no longer be utilized in Colombia, nor could the obvious presence of active US military personnel be allowed. The Colombian government and people were aware of the gunship use because there was little reason at the time to hide US involvement in counteracting the drug trade, but there was serious uproar over US weapons and personnel acting within their borders. In return for more help in acting upon the drug (cocaine) growth and trade, the US "promised" to act only with Colombian authority (the DEA with Colombian personnel).

But that's not how the CIA operates, so, it's business as usual. Why the CIA wished to eliminate cocaine processing labs in the jungle is not too hard to understand… The CIA was running cocaine and making deals with cartels and FARC guerrillas in order to illegally fund weapons for Contra rebels of Nicaragua. Sometimes, deals required eliminating opposing factions' supply.

Much of Colombia is national forest, and the entire southeast of the country is a vast jungle filled with cocaine labs. These labs produce tons of cocaine every year. They're all sizes, hidden, difficult to get to, and protected by cartel personnel who enjoy killing like you may enjoy eating a piece of pie. FARC guerrillas didn't even mess with cartel facilities, yet they patrolled much of the outlying area. FARC guerrillas passed from revolution for a cause to insane killing and torture almost immediately after their inception. They would gleefully kill, torture, ransom, anyone who wasn't one of them… except cartel personnel.

Being dropped in such an area requires serious thought. Being spotted by FARC coming in is the most serious concern. I was dropped at 2300 with weapons and explosives in a small valley ~4km north from the processing lab. This was close enough to avoid FARC on the way in. I made my way quickly to the processing facility, found a blind, and started reconnoitering the area utilizing night vision goggles; there were no lights and no work being performed at night. The area itself was about the size of a football field, with the main processing area taking up about 3/4 of that. There were water and gas tanks, and dozens of barrels of acetone, kerosene, and gasoline. There was a personnel building, close to an above ground gas tank, where the workers and personnel slept. They seemed to have left leaves soaking for the night in vats. Everything was underneath tin roofing with camouflage netting over the top. There were four cartel guards patrolling the grounds.

I crawled into the main processing area. Luckily, they had placed many of the chemical and gasoline barrels in line along the processing area, which would make setting charges, all incendiary, easy and effective. I crawled along the line placing charges between the barrels and on the vats. The guard stayed on the other side of the barrels, and when I had finished, I crawled to the outside, got more explosives, and along the exterior to a storage shed. The buildings were tin walled and roofed and raised from the ground with enough room to crawl beneath. I placed a charge under the floor of the storage, and under the floor of the personnel building where I could hear movement and talking inside. I crawled behind the gas tank and set a charge under each end. There was a large transport truck and I crawled underneath and placed a charge on the tank. A jeep next to it also got a charge on its gas tank.

I made my way back to the blind and collected my weapons, and readied the charges. This was going to be a huge fireball, and I needed some distance. I went north to a safe distance and set off the charges in three very short stages. The explosions and fire were immense and fire raged toward the sky and lit up the entire area. I could see all four of the guards running and screaming on fire. The personnel building was completely a raging inferno.

I turned and ran fast toward the extraction point. I knew FARC guerrillas would see this and come to investigate immediately. When I reached the small valley I stopped and hid, and called for extraction, had just gotten an ETA of 20 minutes, when I noticed movement across the valley heading in my direction. With the goggles I could see five FARC guerrillas heading toward me. They still had their weapons on their backs, so I knew they hadn't spotted me, but they were moving fast. I notified the chopper to loiter in the immediate area while I dealt with this situation.

At this point I needed to make a decision: 1) Hide and let them pass (they most certainly were headed toward the fire); or, 2) kill them all now. In my previous mission to Colombia I was caught by FARC guerrillas because of a twisted ankle, and the details of that ran through my mind quickly, and I felt such hatred and anger at them that it didn't take long to accept and enact option 2.

I set myself up at 15 degrees to the left of their approach, and fixed my suppressor. At twenty-five yards I sprayed down the line, then again. I approached them cautiously. The first four were dead with chest and abdominal wounds, the fifth had a wounded leg and a bullet graze on the arm. He turned and looked at me with a smile, but when I raised my rifle he quickly turned

131

that into a begging face. He was all of 17, and I didn't understand what he was saying, but all that was running through my fore-brain was a former mission with a very similar young man with my knife and an attitude toward my balls, and I shot him in the head. For extra measure I shot the first four in the head as well.

It was extremely necessary to leave quickly and I called in the chopper. The pilot saw the five bodies and asked what the hell happened? I told him, "Witnesses".

Neither then nor now have I felt compassion toward those men or guilt or shame over their killings. Both groups lived on the insane edge and had forfeited morality for drugs and money, and power and money. FARC guerrillas turned to attacking and abusing their own constituency for money (kidnappings, theft, murder). The personnel building could give me some guilt, but in such a remote location, with no town or village nearby, the workers would be long-term dedicated cartel personnel; at least, that's what I choose to tell myself. What I do have guilt over is helping the CIA in its own drug trade and personal wars. The CIA, while President Reagan was starting the all out *War On Drugs*, was subverting that policy, probably at Reagan's request, in order sell cocaine and other drugs in order to fund weapons (illegally!) for Contra rebels, which was specifically outlawed by Congress. "I don't recall [Mommy]", said Reagan.

Laughs, Fun, and Strangeness

During the time of these missions, everything wasn't all death. Of course, there was sex, some satisfying, some not so much (women who have high opinions of themselves – large egos – are as annoying and unsatisfactory as men with large egos). Most days fun could be had at the beach. Watercraft were available for rent, and the waves at FWB and Destin are fantastic at times for body surfing. Midnight movies in town were always available and fun, and fishing was always available.

I had made a bong out of PVC, galvanized pipe, and a thimble for a bowl. I painted it with the gunship gray polyurethane paint, painted the metal black with a red band at the top where the bowl sat, and glued a Spectre patch on the upper part, and called it Spectre Bongtoke. This bong became popular in the barracks. One day my best friend and I took the bong off base and got stoned. We probably should have waited longer before coming back to base, but, we didn't. As soon as we pulled up to the gate, we were stopped. There were two MPs, one of whom we smoked weed with regularly. The other took all the action. He ordered us from the car and led us into the guard shack. He searched my friend while the fellow smoker had to search me. He told me to place my hands on the wall. My hands were in my pockets feeling the small bag of weed I had, so I curled it up in my fingers and put my wadded hand up on the wall. So, at least we didn't get caught with the weed. However, the other guard searched the car and found the bong under the seat, and produced it for all to see. This was a more minor offense to actually having the weed, but we were busted for being in possession of paraphernalia. We were allowed to drive onto the base and report for punishment later. My friend lost a stripe

133

and partial pay for 6 months because it was his car (yeah, I don't know what that had to do with it either). Lt Weasel was extremely unhappy, I lost a stripe and pay for three months – I was lucky I was in a job that required the rank, and they needed me in that job. The Spectre Bongtoke ended up on the shelf of the Commander of the 16th Special Operations Squadron.

There were other drugs available. Some got hooked on cocaine. Most took speed at one time or another to keep awake. Combat soldiers have used stimulants since time immemorial to make it through battle and fight with more intensity. Some, like the two I discuss below lost all sense and got hooked on heroin. Their lives were going pretty good, but they sought more. It was quite sad to watch them going down the tubes, but you really can't convince an addict what they're doing is harmful until they have a crash. They started out with small amounts they would bring back to the barracks to cook. They invited me to watch them because I had field medical training and they wanted someone there in case anything went wrong. I agreed, just because I was curious, though I spent the first half hour trying to convince them not to do it, and they refused to listen.

They injected using their own needles. They had barely taken the needles from their arms when they started swooning and then passed out for about 20 minutes. I watched them, felt their heartbeats, and waited for them to regain consciousness. They finally came to and thought they had just been out a few seconds. Neither seemed attached to place or time anymore, but rather they just seemed to be floating with stupid smiles, unaware of how fucked up they really were. As another 45 minutes passed they started to gain energy, and suddenly, they wanted to go to the mess hall to eat. I told them go ahead, but I wasn't going with them. This event happened every third day, then every two days, then every day. I had stopped going and quit trying to dissuade them from this habit. They were both excellent mechanics, and one of them had a Chevy Vega hatchback (it was a small car). After getting sufficiently fucked up, they decided to replace the stock 4 cylinder engine with a V-8. Why? Who the hell knew! Because they could? They completed this in about a month and started running all over the area at top speed. There was a large bridge, with decorative stone railing, connecting Fort Walton Beach with Destin over a waterway. These two were speeding around the corner on the East end, lost control on the bridge, and went right through the stone railing into the waterway below. They really should have died, but stoned people sometimes get the greatest breaks in an accident. However, they were thoroughly damaged; nothing that wouldn't heal, but they would feel pain later on in life. The driver (his car) got the least physical damage, and he was drummed out of the AF. The other, with a leg and hip cast, arm cast, neck brace, badly bruised face, broken nose, and black eyes... he found religion and asked for help getting off heroin. They helped him heal, helped him with counseling, and he got clean, but they still discharged him after he healed.

The stupidity of service men and women can be quite astounding. One day the maintenance squadrons held a beer picnic at the little park by the end of the runways. Sometimes, small alligators who lived on the base would come up from the creek beside the park and look for food, especially with people there. Seeing drunk men and women, who signed up to guard the free world, panic and show fear toward what were basically Florida squirrels, was quite amusing. But when they started throwing full beer cans at the alligators' heads, that wasn't funny at all. When they got good and drunk, two Sergeants convinced all who would listen (too many) that they should all head butt... yes, like ramhorns. I asked what the hell they were talking about, and asked why they would do this. They explained that it made one tougher and it was a bonding ritual. I called bullshit and said all they would get out of it was a headache and perhaps a

135

concussion. They said, "No. Seriously… watch!", and they proceeded to demonstrate. They backed up like they were going to do a chest bump, but they rammed their foreheads together with drunken gusto. By the time they were done, their foreheads were swollen out about 2 inches (their hats wouldn't fit anymore), blood was dripping down their faces, their noses were swollen, and they turned to me with a look of superiority and said, "That was great". There are times in life that you see things that can't be fathomed, and this was one of those times. I refused an invitation to headbutt, but found myself more astounded when two of the women started butting heads, and a third started butting heads with the men. A distinct feeling of having entered the Twilight Zone came over me, and I left.

Drugs of the Sierra Madre

#12 – March 1981

The US Drug Enforcement Administration (DEA) has the authority to investigate and work with foreign countries to stop drug smuggling into the US, usually by working directly with foreign governments and police to stop drug runners and product from being sent. DEA agents carry weapons in foreign countries, but lack the military style force that you see with raids in the US. In foreign countries they must rely on foreign federal troops, and/or state/local police to enact warrants and raids. Sometimes, lip service is paid by the foreign country to the DEA in order to show service, yet keep drug lords happy at the same time. Such a place where this had occurred with growing frequency is Mexico. Without strict *Federale* swift action, the DEA is practically helpless, unless...

The CIA on the other hand, has authority in US law to stop threats it sees to the US. While this threat assessment system is relative to policy and leadership, and has no serious regulation, the CIA has powerful authority to order death, destruction, and US military forces into action for its' own classified purposes. When the DEA learns to beg hard enough, the CIA may help; which they did in the *Sierra Madre del Sur* in southern Mexico.

I was approached by AFSOC, DEA, and CIA personnel in February to come up with a plan for March. A drug processing facility was located in the lower mountains, manufacturing thousands of pills of speed and barbiturates daily, that were then sent to the US. A SEAL team and an Army Ranger team were coming up with plans as well and the CIA wanted to choose between them. Committing an action in a country such a Mexico, requires deliberate planning and delicacy. You can't just bring in a gunship and destroy things; you can't just bring in a large team of combatants more ready to fire weapons than think.

After reviewing the imagery and intelligence, I formulated a Scout plan and submitted. In a few days I was told to prepare what I needed and to pick a date within two weeks. A carrier was situated off the western coast, and I was flown to the carrier from Hurlburt Field, Florida. The CIA had provided a stealth Blackhawk helicopter. Blackhawks were relatively new in use at the time, only having been in production since the mid-70's. The stealth version was flat black with baffled engines, composite crafted rotor blades, and made to excel utilizing night vision in blackout conditions, and built for high speeds at low altitude.

All explosives and gear were loaded on the chopper, a short briefing was held, and we left as the sun went below the horizon. The area of the processing facility (a small factory) was controlled by a drug cartel. It was in a high desert location several kilometers from the nearest town or residence. There was the factory building which had only two doors – a personnel door and a loading door. These doors were made of heavy gauge steel and were kept locked from the outside during shifts. The building had a mansard roof with an industrial air conditioning unit, and a powered vent stack. Power was supplied by a large generator 50 meters south with an underground fuel tank. A natural gas tank was within 10 meters to power equipment and processes inside. A phone cable provided communications with cartel managers elsewhere. A well with powered pump provided water for personnel, processing, and a sprinkler system. To the north was a parking area for workers' cars. Straight east was a long winding road leading to cartel entrance boundaries and checkpoints that the workers had to pass through. Five guards were on the outside. One stood constantly in front of the locked personnel door and never moved. He was the one who let workers in, locked them in, and unlocked the door for them to leave at the end of their shift. Four guards walked in concentric circles around the property, each one in his own opposite solar ring. The rings were ~30ft apart. There were several trees with large branches and even larger twisted roots. A sixth guard was inside the facility where he was locked in with the workers for the entire shift.

To the entire SW & NW area was nothing but rock & ravine… Directly west was open to a box canyon 2km long, .5km high, and ended at a shear wall that was flat on the top. It was over this wall that the Blackhawk sped like a demon and dropped to the canyon floor and continued for .5km and stopped. I took my personal gear, M11 with suppressor, M16 with scope and suppressor, knife, and an odd assortment of killing tools. The explosives and other tools stayed in the chopper, to be called for later, and the chopper lifted and turned and was gone to sit waiting at the top of the canyon wall.

There was a some moonlight and I made my way quickly to the canyon entrance and waited for the outer guard, as his route would take him close by there in the trees. There was no chance of using my pistol or rifle, even with suppressors, until the last guard. I was ready with my knife, but when I saw the guard, I knew I had to reevaluate my method. He was ~6'5", with muscles on muscles, at least 265lbs, and he had a neck like a bull. I wasn't even sure if I could get my knife into him or if I could get it deep enough (yeah, he scared the hell out of me). I let him make another round and came up with a new plan. I ran a trip wire across his path under a heavy branch, and climbed the tree out on the branch with my garroting wire on d-rings and waited.

When he tripped and fell forward, I jumped into his back and lungs with my feet, then dropped into his lungs again with my knees, then sat on him while slipping the garroting wire around his neck. He was so stunned it was almost as if he raised his head

139

to make it easier. But I soon learned how badly people will fight to live. I pulled hard like riding a bull, and he fought hard like he was a bull. It's not like TV or a movie, people often die hard, and take a long time. This went on for what seemed like too many excruciating minutes, with him fighting the whole time. And then… he just stopped. I fell over exhausted, then noticed I had pulled the wire all the way back to his vertebrae, and blood was everywhere. I became so angry… probably the most angry I've ever felt, at myself for a myriad of reasons, and maybe at him for just not dying neatly. I kicked his head and it separated from his body.

After a few minutes I calmed myself and continued. In succession I placed my knife in the backs of the three remaining circling guards. Looking at my watch, I noticed I was ahead of schedule, so I took some more time to calm down. I needed to make a single shot connect and I needed to slow my breathing. I picked a spot with a clear shot from the west at about 50 yards, and just sat and breathed. When my heart slowed sufficiently, I took aim at his head and fired, and he was down. I called the chopper to drop the other supplies and he raced down canyon, dropped them, and raced back.

I unpacked the explosives and tools. Medium charges were placed deep in holes beside the building, not to destroy the walls, but to shake the building hard to displace chemicals and dust into the air. I dragged the bodies of the guards and placed them over some of the filled holes, and took the required pictures of the bodies for the CIA. I placed a large charge down the fill neck of the generator fuel tank (the generator was located directly above and would go as well). I left the LNG tank running to the inside alone. I cut the phone wiring, then climbed on the roof and cut the air conditioning power and cut the power to the filtered exhaust system. I lowered a huge incendiary charge down the exhaust stack with extended antennae. When on the ground again

I cut the power to the water supply pump, and placed incendiary explosives on the tanks of some of the vehicles. By this time I could hear pounding from the inside on the metal entrance door.

The chopper was notified that all was ready, and when they saw the building go, they should come extract me. The vehicles and fuel tank & generator were the first to go, with the explosions rocking the ground. Then the ground was detonated around the building which shook it violently without destroying it. Then I detonated the incendiary charge in the exhaust stack. There was an initial explosion followed in milliseconds by an even larger explosion with parts of the roof blown away, and a giant fireball engulfing the interior like a huge fire pit. The 30 workers and guard inside had no chance whatsoever. By the time I was getting in the chopper the rest of the roof and the walls were caving inward on a white hot raging fire, and vehicles could be seen speeding up the long winding road.

The pilot lifted, turned, and sped through the canyon at top speed. I saw the wall coming at us and blurted out, "Oh fuck!", but he pulled up and slid over it like it was nothing, then turned and looked at me and laughed.

When we got back to the ship, I was still over-hyped. I *needed* some time off. My fiance lived near Los Angeles, and I desperately wanted to go see her and talk. I requested time off via the radio with my Lieutenant to go there before returning to Florida… Request Denied! Lieutenant Weasel insisted I return to base immediately and report for debriefing. OMG how I hated him!

I used to have dreams about strangling him, knifing him, shooting him… Now I don't think a lot about him except when talking about him. What I think about now are my confused feelings over this mission. I, like many others, have taken hits of

141

speed to get through critical missions, projects, etc... Soldiers in every army take speed to fight longer and harder. I've never been a fan of barbiturates, but to start a war over such things when education and legalization is a better answer, seems to be, to egregiously understate it, overkill. Ideology, *faux* moralism, the DEA, and the American Drug War created these cartels, not users.

I've tried to understand my anger over cutting off the guard's head, and I still don't really understand it. I suppose I wish I could have made it quicker and easier for him, even though I know he would have done the same or worse to me had he caught me. The guards were ruthless cartel personnel, and my pity stops a little short, but *seeing the results of your own handiwork can be quite jarring* unless you're a psychopath, sociopath, or sadist. But the workers inside the building were just people from the local area who needed jobs. My original plan called for using the door guard's key to enter and kill the inside guard, which could have been achieved easily enough wearing a mask and forcing the workers to run, but that was rejected completely.

We returned to Hurlburt late in the evening, and I was supposed to report immediately to Lt Weasel for debriefing, but I was *so* tired and angry. I went back to my room and bolted the door on the inside. I wanted and needed to see Kit, to talk to her. I put ear plugs in and slept almost non-stop for 24 hours. A few times I heard pounding on the door, but I ignored it; with the bolts not even the First Sergeant was getting in there. Late in the afternoon the next day I got Bill and reported to the Lt. He berated me and chastised me for 2 hours straight. He berated the whole plan and execution. I was never closer to killing him than right then, and Bill knew it and stood close beside me. When he finished blathering I got snotty and demanded to know what was so fucking important that he couldn't approve me a little time to recover. He began belittling again and said I didn't deserve it,

142

because "you don't work hard enough"! I got up and walked out, even as he was ordering me back.

Kit

March 1981

We had known each other a year now. She returned in March and we celebrated, made love, and celebrated some more. We saw the Rocky Horror Picture Show and Led Zeppelin's The Song Remains the Same at the midnight movies. We made love.

When we stopped to breathe, we started talking about marriage plans, and her family. We had previously discussed some detail – we would have to get married in California, but not until my term was up. Lt Weasel would not allow me time to get married, so I insisted we put it off for a year and a half until my time was up, I would come to California, get work, and we would be married. She liked this idea, more for the time it would give her to work on her family.

While her Mom was all for her getting married, her Dad was not, and the Mom came around to that way of thinking. Kit's sister would get them to join her in ganging up on Kit. Basically the argument was "he's not an officer", "his work is too dangerous", "you'll be a widow or stuck as a military wife on some god-forsaken base." She tried to assure them that I was getting out before too long, that we had decided to put off the wedding until then, and she would never be living on a military base. As for the danger, she wanted to know why they were always praising veterans and the military, yet when she wanted to marry just what they praise, they were extremely negative. It all fell on deaf ears.

Kit was still extremely happy, but I could tell they were wearing on her. The officer & NCO remarks hurt. I knew what I

144

did, and I knew what pilots did, and I knew what Major Fleming and Lt Weasel did. She insisted we were going ahead, and I could only accept that. I wanted to talk with her about some of the things I had done, but it just didn't feel safe to do so. The killings and how they made me feel seemed too intense to discuss, and I was afraid I would scare her off.

We spent time swimming, body surfing, naked swimming, and fucking on the beach at the tide pool. At night we would get a gallon of beer from the drive through and take it to the beach and watch the sunset as we held each other.

She said she would return in June. I hugged her and told her I loved her, and she hugged me back and told me she loved me, and I felt it to my very core.

Sandinista Arms

#13 – May 1981

Nicaragua has infuriated the United States ever since they had the gall to elect a socialist president, it was unforgivable and the CIA and US President could not stand for this. Supplying arms to the right-wing Contra rebels was forbidden, but we subsequently know how that went; yet the CIA and President had other ideas to support the Contras. They certainly needed the support because, although they were ruthless, they were also few in numbers and seriously weak compared with the Sandinista army. Contras, without help, serious help, were limited to border raids along the north and slipping back into Honduras for safety and marauding among the locals.

A plan was presented to me to logisticize and enact. The Sandinistas had a major ammo and weapons dump NW of Wiwii and totally inaccessible to the Contras either by skills or numbers; yet the CIA wanted the ammo dump blown with indications left behind to give the Contras credit. In other words, the US would blow the dump and shower credit upon the Contras for infiltrating the Sandinista forces, to make the Contras appear stronger and more intelligent than they were.

Reconnaissance images showed clear areas of storage for weapons, ammunition, and explosives. This would have to be taken care of with all incendiary explosives, in order to keep crates burning white hot to disfigure the weapons. Intelligence showed that the main dump was surrounded by a chain-link fence with only 2 guards within the perimeter. There were at least 40-50 guards patrolling the wide exterior (50 yards out or more), but only to the S, SW, W, NW. The E/SE approach was toward the

146

town and seemed to be considered no danger to them. The NE approach was quite rocky and seemed unassailable to them, so they didn't bother patrolling that area. In this NE approach was a flat table top rock outcropping .5km from the dump, and this was the way in with the help of a Blackhawk stealth helicopter provided by the CIA.

We came in at the drop of the sun. The Blackhawk followed the river toward the town then sharply turned west staying barely above the ground. The pilot, utilizing night vision, spotted the table top and landed quickly with great skill. We unloaded my gear and the explosives and I stepped out of the way while the chopper lifted and spun around and was gone within seconds. I went light my own gear, M11, M16 with scope & suppressor, knife, and minimal ammo – there would be no sense in starting a firefight in this place – and wire cutters. The explosives were many and heavy, comprising three large stuffed ruck sacks.

I made my way slowly, and quietly, in a straight line from demarcation to the fence line. Not seeing either of the guards yet, I cut the fence to peel an opening and brought in the explosives and hid them behind some crates. It was imperative to kill the two guards inside the perimeter before proceeding, also because they were going to be used to sell the idea of Contras. I searched for the guards and found them talking in the center, then they split up in opposite directions. This needed to be done as quickly as possible or I would lose time searching for the second guard again. Seeing the direction of the guard heading in my direction I rounded some crates ahead of him and jammed my knife upward through his neck into his brain and twisted. He dropped and I left him there for now and immediately headed for the second guard. I found him quickly. He was slowly walking away from me and I approached behind a row of crates, cut over directly behind him, and simultaneously put one arm around his throat and my knife in

147

his back with a twist. He dropped and I dragged his body over to the other guard. We were hidden from outside patrol view, and I brought over the hidden bags.

A few other items I brought were Contra colors and hats, and a long string of M-80s closely bound. After placing the incendiary explosives all on RC detonators of the same frequency. I dressed the bodies in the Contra gear, then placed the bodies close to an explosion point where they would be burned somewhat. I placed the string of M-80s close to where they were and stretched out a long fuse and exited through the cut wire. About twenty yards outside the wire I lit the fuse and headed further toward the table top. When the M-80s started exploding the surrounding troops started rushing toward that area firing when they got close. I detonated the dump. Initial fiery explosions led to a cascade of fiery explosions which killed some of the attacking Sandinista troops. I called the Blackhawk and it was already waiting by the time I climbed on the rock. We took only a few seconds to view the entire dump in flames, then we lifted, spun around, and we were gone within seconds.

Subsequent intelligence reported that Sandinista officials bought the ruse – that two of their troops had helped Contras stage this insurgent action, and that there must have been at least 100 Contras who had crossed the border to make this happen with the help of traitors within. US government officials, led by their favorite President yammered on about how the brave Contra rebels, not unlike our Founding Fathers, fought for Freedom. Pundits questioned if the Contras were stronger and smarter than we thought they were. The CIA agent hugged me like he was in love with me and I thought he wanted to kiss me.

Having reflected on this for many years, and seen the US perform these kinds of shenanigans again and again all over the globe, I see how wrong I, we, are when allowing our government under the secret guise of the CIA to destabilize legitimately elected governments. Daniel Ortega never did himself any huge favors as a statesman, but he was elected legitimately and democratically, and that's the business of his own people. We, through our unregulated and uncontrolled Presidents and CIA, make socialist leaders and governments what they become. The *faux* student groups and business organizations, the repeated lying and covering up of right wing atrocities and death squads (you can see it now in psychopaths' unabashed orgasms of delight for Israeli apartheid and genocide), the relentless destabilization programs and attacks and coups and assassinations. America has become obsessed with communism and Zionism to its' own detriment. Every socialist is not a communist, but some people never learn, and in the end embrace fascist ideals and solutions, inevitably becoming what they hate the most.

Heads Full Of Holes

#14 – May 1981

Rebels (indigenous people) in the El Salvador civil war controlled much of the mountain areas, even close to major population centers. They constantly moved their camps, equipment, and supplies at night to avoid detection. The CIA ruthlessly and tirelessly sought information on these movements.

This convoy was relatively small, 30 trucks and ~300 personnel (mostly men and some women). I was told the trucks contained mostly weapons and ammunition, and a few supplies. They would be traveling through a high plateau area that was mostly very dense forest. Approximately halfway through their route they would pass through a large open plain that would allow all the vehicles to be seen... and trapped.

I was dropped in this area in the early evening of the previous night with RC detonators and explosives, 8 RC switch controlled Browning .40cal machine guns that would fire in bursts after activation, and enough ammunition to kill everyone three times over. The open area was a circle ~300 yards across. I spent all night setting up the machine guns at the perimeter, leaving myself a wide space from which to operate, without the risk of crossfire; and placing RC explosives in the road, at the front and back choke points, and at various places surrounding where the trucks would be stopped – It was imperative to keep personnel close to the trucks and from attempting escape into the wooded areas. I placed RC detonator explosives at each gun emplacement for destruction before extraction, and notified operations that the trap was set.

During the next day I attempted as much sleep as possible in the shade of the trees away from the road. The sun and the heat were oppressive. It was a dirt road, not very busy (3 or 4 cars and 2 buses during the day), but, combined with the heat, enough to keep one awake and vigilant when they're not supposed to be there.

~0220 I was contacted by gunships Wicked Wanda and Big Ben loitering in the area at 30,000 feet. I gave them a fix on the center of the trap and they made equipment adjustments. They notified me at ~0245 that the convoy was coming down the road and they dropped to attack altitude of ~20,000 feet. I told them to wait for the explosions in the road and that would be their signal to open fire from opposite vectors, keeping equidistant in speed and track as they circled. When the lead truck came to the front of the trap, I exploded the front and back road choke points. The gunships opened fire with constant bursts of 20mm rounds, and with the trucks stopped still I set off the rest of the road explosives. All of the road explosives were incendiary in order to set the trucks on fire in the open space. If one was attempting to leave the line, it was blasted by a 40mm shell from above, and the occasional 105mm shell. As the 20mm fire continued, and some of the personnel attempted to leave the line, I started the Brownings which continued firing in bursts, and set off the explosives surrounding the trap line which encouraged the runners to turn back to attempt shelter again, to no avail, with the trucks.

All firing was over in 25 minutes. I was informed by the gunships that there appeared to be wounded movement, and to be careful during "cleanup". Cleanup, invented by the CIA for CIA controlled operations meant that everyone must be dead, appear to be unconscious and about to die, or they must be "dispatched" (meaning they must die). No witness to US personnel, equipment, or involvement may be left behind. Weapons are destroyed, ammunition is destroyed, humans are destroyed.

That job fell to me. You must carefully slink and sneak your way through the burning wreckage and bloody gore to attempt to locate survivors and runners (who've run, crawled, or dragged themselves into the woods), and even if they beg you for help, which they do, you must put a bullet in their head. A few managed to elude damage or death and reach the tree line – these had to be tracked and killed. For some, ripped and torn to shreds, yet still living, it's a mercy. For others, it's just sad CIA murder. But since it's an undeclared conflict, who's going to bring notice. On this particular occasion, I used 55 .45cal rounds… yes, you read that right. I "dispatched" (shot in the head) 55 wounded or hiding rebels (indigenous people), men and women, for no other reason than offending the CIA by still being alive and/or seeing my face or were aware of the death fire from above.

Upon inspecting the trucks and cargo I discovered that there were no weapons at all being transported, save the personal weapons held by the rebels. Every truck had only food. I documented the cargo, destroyed the weapons I brought and the ammo cache and extracted. Upon reporting to the CIA officer in charge, he asked me why I didn't destroy the food. I answered with another question, "Why the fuck did you tell me there were weapons when there weren't, and have me help kill 300 people for a food shipment?", to which he replied, "They're the enemy dip-shit because I say so, and you kill them and destroy ANYTHING they have, because I say so!" If he had been on that plain with me and said that, I would have reported him as a casualty and burned his body.

When looking back at this there is an attempt to calm myself with having followed orders, but the Nuremberg Judge stated it best that following orders is not an excuse. When a young man, you pride yourself with doing the President's work, doing it all for the American People, for Freedom and Democracy; but, when old or out of the brain wash, you realize all of that is crap, that you did it for oligarchs and corporate interests tied to the US and a skewed and insane US policy that still prevails regarding social ideas, and US policy which supports right-wing fascist regimes and dictators exclusively around the world.

The faces have haunted my dreams for 40 years, and force a reckoning upon me. There are those who would say this is no more tragic than anything else… maybe not for them, because apparently they've never looked into pleading eyes with tears and pulled a trigger to blow someone's brains out. There are those who would dismiss this as the nature of war, yet the US wasn't at war even though the CIA was doing its' best to conduct one for another country – this was 1981AD, not 1981BC, yet the governments and secret operators maneuvered like ancient court sycophants, battle lords, or even the pre-WW1 instigating French (Yes, the same French who instigated Vietnam and so many other imperial colonial wars). Yet this was being instigated by the US (Land of the Free, Home of the Brave) who had been instigated by the English and French to come to the colonial feeding table many times with weapons and force in hand (coconuts from the Philippines anyone?).

My shame, guilt, and sadness will never end, nor should they. Governments, politicians, and the majority of the US population will never feel anything over this, yet they all should. They will continue to send young men without developed frontal lobes into asinine situations to kill and destroy for ideological, not moral, reasons. Those young men will continue to pay the mental price of their actions for their entire lives, unless they succeed in ending their own life sooner. It would be sweet justice indeed if the disgraced President or Senator slit his own throat for pushing,

153

ordering, and enabling these boneheaded plans instead of leaving the suffering to those who acted for them in good faith. But it's not in the nature of a President or Senator to act that bravely, only talk bravely.

"On Great Lone Hills"

The Mormon Tabernacle Choir burned this into my heart when a boy. Now it burned my heart considering all the death I had dealt, and helped to deal from above. It's a patriotic song, and shows a longing for Peace, but Peace gained at the expense of Truth will never last. In two world wars, German soldiers stormed into war wearing belt buckles emblazoned with the words, "*Gott Mit Uns*" – God With Us. Since the supposed end of WW2 the US has made the world sick with its own colonial version of God With US, even when slaughtering in the mountains of Central America and elsewhere. I stood on those hills and slaughtered for every American and their God.

View Central America today and you will see what the American God has wrought, Corruption. The American God truly "walks abroad in garments of might", but there is no "path of splendor" or crowning of light – only death, power, and corruption. Granted, these words were written in defiance of the Nazis, but they are words that every American, including land thieves and slavers, have known and felt incessantly from the founding of the republic.

On great, lone hills, where tempests brood and
gather,
Primeval Earth, against primeval sky,
We, faring forth, possessed by fervent longing,
Have found a throne, eternal and high,
Have knelt at last in wordless adoration,
Till fire and whirlwind have both gone by.
With ardent song we greet the golden morning.
By faith upborne, remember not the night.

155

The whole wide world, triumphant hails the
dawning.
God walks abroad in garments of might,
The hills, behold, are now a path of splendor,
Transfigured all, and all crowned with light.

Hymn from *Finlandia* – Jean Sibelius
Words by Veikko Antero Koskenniemi
Performed by the <u>Mormon Tabernacle Choir</u>

Guatemalan Swamp Convoy

#15 – June 1981

Guatemala had seen non-stop US meddling and regime change, right wing death squads, and a very determined rebel backlash.

"Damn'd spies and informers, damn'd friends and damn'd liars"
- Swift

It amazed me how much correct detailed information the CIA could obtain about rebel activities – meaning someone sold out their countrymen. This was a large convoy, ~100 vehicles with some pulling artillery pieces. Heavy trucks were transporting personnel (~1000), small arms (M-16, AK-47, M11, 9mm Beretta) and ammunition, WWII era Browning 40cal machine guns with ammunition, 7.62mm miniguns with ammunition, and shoulder fired rockets.

The convoy was traveling through a very large lowland area on a bad dirt road that arced around a lone hill of 150 meters in height, with semi-steep sides. This was the chosen point for ambush. The convoy would pass this hill at approximately 0200. Early in the evening I was dropped by helicopter on the hill with my gear and explosives. The lowland area was dense swamp jungle, and the area east of the road, and around the sides and back of the hill was swamp.

I went down the hill and mined the road to the south of the hill, and placed RC charges at the base of a very large tree to force a fall across the road when detonated; and buried RC charges in the road along the length. I went back up the hill and

157

waited. At 0145 three Spectre gunships arrived and loitered after marking my position. I notified them of the charges and when those detonated, that was their cue to open fire. At 0210 the convoy began going around the hill. They reached the point of the mines and the first truck exploded. I detonated the tree and it came crashing down across the road, then detonated the road charges. The gunships opened fire, one starting with the front of the convoy, the second tearing up the middle, and the third, first destroying the rear escape route, then proceeding to tear up the convoy from the rear.

I used a sniper rifle from my position, especially to keep anyone from ascending the hill. At one point Wicked Wanda (one of the gunships) notified me that five rebels had ascended the face of the hill and were approaching my position, but they were too close to me to fire on. I switched to my M-16 and moved in their direction and laid low. I noticed them at about 25 yards in a close group and began firing in bursts, and they all appeared to drop. Upon coming closer, one of them lifted his rifle but I shot first and hit him in the chest. The others were dead and I reported to the gunship and returned to my perch. From this height and surround view I could shoot and kill unendingly. I went back and forth on that hill, firing and killing, until I ran out of sniper rounds, then I started using my M-16 again.

In 1981 an AC-130-H Spectre gunship in full stealth attack mode carried twin 20mm electric Gatling guns, a 40mm Bofors gun which fired multi-round clips in rapid succession, and a 105mm Howitzer cannon. Each 20mm round explodes with the force of a grenade with corresponding shrapnel. The twin mount was designed to place a round in every square foot of a football field size area. Depending upon needs, every 10th or 20th round is a tracer round with red phosphorus which burns when exposed to oxygen. The idea is to give a pilot a visual perspective of where his rounds are heading at night, or low visibility conditions –

tracer rounds are also utilized in small arms such as the M-16. Those rounds also cause extensive burns and painful death when hit by the round or shrapnel. A 105mm round can vaporize a human being when it explodes next to them, or it may vaporize half their body within 25 yards. Concussion and shrapnel will kill for several yards after that; and, if white phosphorus is utilized, which is supposed to be against international law, yet gets used anyway, a person will suffer an excruciating death from chemical burning which will not relent until the chemical reaction is spent.

The gunships fired 20mm and 40mm rounds into the jungle across the road to kill those trying to escape. In 45 minutes the entire road below was aflame, and the gunships reported no one moving, and heat signatures in the jungle area had cooled. I began my sweep of the convoy and road from the front. The few that were still alive were dispatched. Extra explosives were used to destroy undamaged weapons and equipment. This convoy had carried ~1000 people, who were now all dead, in pieces, and in parts. Again, the amount of blood was phenomenal, soaking into clothing and boots, and permeating the nostrils, throat, and mouth. I ascended the hill again, called for my extraction, and a Combat Talon plucked me out. The government forces later came and took control to show how they had destroyed the rebel invasion.

I've been asked how my own kill responsibility on such a mission could be counted. Spectre gunships had a rack pod of cameras (video and still, infrared and normal) in the front door hatch (these were unpressurised aircraft). One of the cameras would be locked on me and record my activity, and would be monitored by a technician inside the electronics operations booth inside the center of the gunship, who would notify me of enemy approach and generally keep an eye out for me. This booth was sound deadened and was extra protected by Kevlar plates surrounding the entire booth. Tapes of the missions were always recorded and sent to the CIA and AFSOC. My firing rate and hit ratio was known, and figures represent that as well as my own reports.

This scene took place before a turn in my thinking regarding the Central American conflicts and US involvement. You get used to the variety of explosions rained down by these gunships, especially when you're not receiving the death from above. But when a dry road has been turned into mud by the blood of humans; when you see bodies with burn holes that may have started as small shrapnel wounds, yet burned out to holes the size of grapefruits to basketballs from exploding tracer rounds (red phosphorus) or exploding 105mm rounds that contained white phosphorus (yes, it's illegal); when you see bodies half to almost fully vaporized by 105mm rounds; when you see bodies missing their top, or their bottom, or their leg, or their arm, or their head… Sooner or later your brain, heart, and soul must pay the price for participating in this. That time came for me a few months later, and I no longer wanted to live.

To this day I feel the guilt and responsibility of these actions. It astounds me that I went so long with such a *laissez-faire* attitude about killing. When people say "Thank you for your service" it makes me cringe. While other people rise and sing the National Anthem, I feel disgust and pain. When at meetings where people rise to "Pledge Allegiance", I can't make myself say it, and I want to stop my kids from saying it. At points you use excuses to defend yourself, against yourself. "They would have killed YOU". "They knew what they were getting into when they joined". All the excuses are true, yet the overriding fact remains, that this was a civil war and we (the US) had no business being there, which means I had no business being there. This wasn't civil war over moral issues of freedom and justice (except for the indigenous people who comprised the bulk of the rebels), this was civil war to further business interests and power and strengthen

160

colonial power – just like everything Britain, France, the US, etc… sticks their noses into.

Nuns

#16 – June 1981

Blood red stains on habits black,
Fell before my roving eye,
Hands uplifted to their god,
Now in blood mud dirt they lie.

> *Nuns of El Salvador*
> – Rubicon

    El Salvador. Oligarch families formed the power in El Salvador under the auspices of the US, and military leaders trained by US forces and the SOA exacted rule. In the '70s, liberation theology took hold with a vengeance for the people to attempt to hold on to their land, homes, and villages which oligarchs and US interests wanted to control or own. There was, of course, an opposition based on socialist ideas. Roman Catholic Arch-Bishop Oscar Romero was the most outspoken critic of the regime and US support of that regime. US President Jimmy Carter, spewing the usual anti-communist rhetoric vowed in Oval Office conversations to squash any and all socialist sentiments in Central America. He complained about Romero to Zbignew Brzezinski, who in a recorded call to the Vatican demanded that they silence Romero, "or we will". Low and behold, in March 1980, in a country practically guided by the CIA, Arch-Bishop Romero was murdered while officiating in front of his congregation. Nuns of all orders were helping the people and rebels with humanitarian support, because the oppression was *that* strong, and evil reigned in a civil war of the Haves seeking to have more.

Another convoy was to be destroyed, consisting of ~30 heavy trucks filled with weapons, ammunition, explosives, and personnel, and ~15 support vehicles, mostly all terrain vehicles with machine guns bolted in the bed or rear area, a few maintenance vehicles for the larger trucks, and a small fuel tanker. The rebels controlled the mountain areas, and moved these things around to avoid detection. The CIA received information of the move and I was ordered along with Wicked Wanda and Big Ben to destroy this convoy. After reviewing imagery and times, I conferred with the pilots and picked the best location for an ambush trap, along a high mountain road which left no room to maneuver or escape.

A troop helicopter dropped me with gear and supplies (explosives) on top of a hill opposite the road the convoy would be on. In the middle, between the hill and road, was a fairly deep ravine, with serious drops on the road side. I positioned myself on this hill across the main ravine ~100 yards away from, and with equidistant view of, the road.

At the location of the ambush the road wound slowly back and forth around ravine drops with an extreme slope above and an extreme drop-off below. This section wound like this for ~2km, enough room for all vehicles to fit in the trap. Wicked Wanda and Big Ben marked my location via radio signal to avoid firing there, because from 20,000 feet away, everything on infrared camera looks like target blips. A shallow bridge-like connection led from my side to an area in the front of the road trap. Previous to the convoy's arrival I used charges to fell trees across the road at the front of the trap, well before the connection spot. I then laid RC mines at various distances down the road.

At ~0030 the convoy had fully entered the trap and had to stop for the fallen trees, I exploded the road charges, then painted the lead truck with a laser which Wicked Wanda hit with its 40mm gun and proceeded onto the second truck. Simultaneously, Big Ben used its 105mm Howitzer to destroy the road to the rear, then began hitting the trucks from that end. On this occasion, in addition to my M-16 with scope, I took a sniper rifle. As trucks, cargo, and personnel were destroyed by alternating 105mm and 40mm cannon fire, and repeated bursts of twin 20mm Gatling guns, rebel personnel were attempting to flee. Some attempted climbing up to no avail, with 20mm rounds or my sniper rifle picking them off. Some attempted going down, only to meet the same fate or simply fell to their death. Some saw my flash and fired in my direction, and I heard rounds wizz by, but was alright by changing locations. Many were attempting to traverse the road, explosions, and burning wreckage to get out the ends, only to meet their death by 20mm rounds or sniper fire.

After 15-20 minutes the constant firing ceased, and after ~40 minutes all firing ceased, and Wicked Wanda and Big Ben left the target area. They still detected live human targets, not moving, but they had to go. I had additional orders from the CIA – *no survivors* to tell about the gunship attack, and I was to check the road and trucks to ensure that all weapons, ammunition, and people had been destroyed – euphemistically named by the CIA, Clean Up. *I really **despised** this part of the mission.* It's easy enough to locate intact weapons and ammunition boxes, toss a grenade and destroy it; but its quite another to search for survivors and kill them. There were a few who were only slightly wounded and still wanted to fight. Who wouldn't? But there were some who were conscious and expected mercy, a hospital, medical attention. But while in a declared conflict the US still doesn't follow rules of humane treatment, in undeclared conflicts, especially run by the CIA, no such rules apply. The CIA officer in charge of this mission, who I had worked with many times, declared that you could kill whoever you wanted and as many as you wanted, so long as it fulfilled the orders, the US wasn't implicated, and it didn't interfere with the Agenda.

I started at the front of the road and approached the first truck. It had a gaping hole blown through its engine compartment and the cargo area was a burning splintered wreck. Bodies lay everywhere, torn to shreds by shrapnel, exploding 20mm or 40mm rounds, just blown apart, burned by explosion or tracer rounds, or half vaporized by 105mm shells. I found a few trucks with cargo areas still intact, and tossed in grenades. I found rebels alive and mangled so badly that shooting them in the head was their best blessing at that point; and there were, as always, a few who feigned being wounded or dead and tried to escape, to no avail.

When you carefully wend your way through such a mess, being careful and watchful for enemies who may fire on you, you naturally crawl or get on your hands and knees. The day had been dry. The road had been relatively dry. However, common to these convoys in an ambush trap, that many bodies bleeding out in such a confined area had turned much of the ground into mud made with blood. You would find yourself standing in puddles of blood up to your ankles, crawling through blood, kneeling in blood... and you could smell it – an overwhelming metallic smell that reeked of iron.

I also found what I had feared; what I thought I saw through my scope... nuns. Nuns in headdress and work clothes. Out of ~400 rebels, I counted 30 nuns and/or novices. They were all unarmed. They were grouped together, many with hands clasped in prayer, holes torn through their bodies and heads, some

165

with a single sniper wound. From a distance, I could think, "Was that a nun?" But immediately it would seem impossible that there would be nuns. I couldn't really tell, so I kept firing.

Nuns had been supplying humanitarian aid to villages throughout the country under threat and terrorism of the government – food, medical attention, etc... Often they traveled with rebel convoys to new locations to assist the people and provide succor. This raised so many doubts and questions in my mind about what we were doing there, about the morality of what we were doing. I wasn't being religious, but I wondered why women who wanted peace in the world would be so convicted to help in an obvious civil war. I started to ask myself what the rebels were fighting for, instead of accepting the word of my commanders, especially the CIA.

Having finished what can only be described as macabre clean up, I returned to my hill location. I called for the Combat Talon, and they dropped a Fulton Recovery Unit. I donned the harness and let up the balloon, and they yanked me off that hill and pulled me in, and I thought how badly those rebels would have liked this for an escape.

Back at the staging base, I rounded up the pilots and Electronic Warfare Officers and told them that nuns were in the convoy. To a man they replied, "Really? That's interesting." but didn't really care. When I told the debriefing officer, Lt Weasel, he said, "Who cares? The CIA doesn't care and neither do we. The nuns have no business sticking their noses in this." I became enraged and yelled, "You motherfucker! That's so fucked up!". The observing sergeant pulled me from the room.

I spent sleepless nights after this trying to understand what I was involved in; why people were so willing to invest their lives in fighting; why we were always supporting right-wing regimes with ties to US business vs supporting human rights and calling out mendacity. Learning more about the conflict, I learned that right-wing Salvadoran military and para-military death squads had targeted nuns for rape, torture, and murder because they opposed the regime and preached liberation theology. I started to feel like a Nazi.

Reflecting on the fact that the CIA always knew how many would be in the convoys – and they knew ~400 would be on this one – it has struck me that they knew nuns were aboard this convoy, but they chose not to make this known or debate the issue. With the intelligence they had gathered, and with what they did share, it's not possible they didn't know. Somewhere in Washington or Langley pictures of dead nuns torn to shreds by US fire sit in archives. The CIA, in many respects, is a lot like the SS, with detailed documentation and images of the death and destruction they have orchestrated. The United States Central Intelligence Agency knew those nuns would be killed, and they wanted them killed because they upset the Agenda.

To this day the sadness over having participated in this atrocity pervades my being. It's one thing to attack and kill those who don soldiering outfit and gear – they know what they're getting in to; but to slaughter those whose sole purpose is to support, protect, and provide aid to the afflicted and innocent...

Kit

June 1981

Upon returning from the massacre of nuns in El Salvador, I was *eager* to see Kit and be with her, to be human again in a positive way. She was to arrive the next day, so I slept more than usual to regain energy, and try and not let the massacre affect our time together. When I woke up about mid-day, there was no phone message on my door. I called the hotel, but she hadn't checked in yet.

After eating at the mess hall, I walked to the Post Office to check my box. There was a letter from Kit. This gave me a sick feeling, so I went back to the barracks before opening the letter. It was taped, so I used my knife to slice off the end. I tipped it up, and the ring I had given her fell out, and my heart dropped into my shoes. I pulled out the letter and read it. Her sister had never let up, and constantly harassed her Dad so that he demanded she end the relationship with me. She refused and he said he would stop paying for her college and kick her out of the house. I respected her love for her Dad and her Mom. I wondered if I had given her too much information about my work. But the fact is I had lost to money and college, that pure love had been thrown away for other addictions. My heart was now fully lacerated – I had never felt such love before, nor such pain. When I thought of her my heart was absolutely broken and ached with pain. I cried, but my levels of sadness and anger overflowed, and I had to get off base quickly before I caused damage.

I didn't want to be around anyone, so I drove to the Tide Pool beach and sat and cried some more. God how my heart ached, and my body felt like it was filled with lead, but my head was filled with fire! I just couldn't believe she wouldn't even call me, or come in person… nothing but that damn letter. Staring at the ring, I hated it. I threw it out into the middle of the tide pool, swearing like every love idiot before me that I would never fall in love again.

Woman is fickle,
like a feather in the wind.
She changes her words
and her thoughts!

Always a lovely,
pretty face,
in tears or in laughter,
it is untrue.

Always miserable
is he who trusts her,
he who confides in her
his unwary heart!

Yet one never feels
fully happy
who from that bosom
does not drink love!

Verdi – *Rigoletto*

White Phosphorus

One of the most obscene deaths in existence

"Weaponized chemicals are the equivalent of burning humans alive."

(email to the Chief ICC Prosecutor)

It's extremely important to understand weaponized phosphorus. Without doubt it is one of the most obscene, cruel, and painful deaths. I'm ashamed I've been involved in its use. Human Rights Watch has been documenting its use in the relative present, and has documented its use historically. We'll focus upon US and Israeli use, but you must understand its weaponized origins, and its extremely cruel effect upon the human body.

"White phosphorus is one of three allotropes of the element phosphorus. The other two are red, an amorphous polymer, and black, a graphite-like polymer. The substance known as yellow phosphorus is actually white phosphorus that contains impurities (e.g., red phosphorus) or that has darkened from exposure to light. Red phosphorus turns violet or purple when it is heated to >550 °C... [White phosphorus] has an unpleasant, garlic like odor and is extremely toxic. It is unstable in air—first forming white fumes before bursting into flames. White phosphorus has been called the "devil's element" because it glows green in the dark and is pyrophoric... Because of its instability, white phosphorus is typically stored under water, in which it is barely soluble. The allotrope is soluble in hydrocarbons, carbon disulfide, sulfur chloride (S_2Cl_2), and other nonpolar solvents." (American Chemical Society)

Elemental phosphorus doesn't exist in nature, but its compounds do and are used to extract elemental phosphorus which gets placed into artillery shells, bombs, missiles, and rockets. Red phosphorus is allowed in narrow amounts for tracer rounds (bullets and smaller shells – ie 20mm, 30mm, and 40mm – that are fired rapidly via automatic weapons). As the round spins out the barrel its like striking a match and it's still burning upon impact; yet when these small shells and bullets fragment on impact or explosion, burning red phosphorus can be embedded in bodies. White phosphorus wedges can be embedded in bodies often flashing into fire later.

White phosphorus is extremely unstable in air, and has to be stored under water, where it takes the form of a glowing wax-like substance. While its use is allowed for signaling and other non-weaponized applications, use against humans is strictly forbidden, yet it gets used anyway. The use of weaponized white phosphorus goes back more than a hundred years. It was used by all sides in WW1 and WW2. The US specifically has continued its use extensively in Korea, Vietnam, Central America, Colombia, Iraq, Afghanistan, Bosnia, Libya, and more, and has pushed for its use in Ukraine which may expand exponentially with the delivery of Abrams tanks and ordinance; and the US has taught other governments to use it, and blesses the use. Generally, post WW2, it has been used exclusively against communists, socialists, and those opposed to capitalism and colonialism (meaning rebels seeking justice and indigenous civilian populations).

Proscription against its use as weapons against humans was placed in the Geneva Conventions (which Israel signed and ratified in 1951) which was adopted by the United Nations as Protocol III. Some in media claim Israel has not agreed to Protocol III, but they in fact signed and ratified Protocol III in 2007, and the United States not until 2012. The US is *extremely guilty* of violating these conventions. Israel has been documented using white phosphorus against humans since the time they invaded Palestine. They were in violation of the Geneva Conventions, yet the US applied pressure to allow them to escape punishment. The United Nations is well aware of Israel's use of white phosphorus, yet the US vetoes any Security Council action against the Zionists. Even the Zionist newspaper, New York Times, has admitted that Human Rights Watch is correct and has stated that Israel is using weaponized white phosphorus. The videos of Zionists' use have all the tell-tale signs; including the use on children. 70% of the casualties of Palestinians are women, children, and infants; this is done purposefully to destroy the ability of Palestinian civilization to recover through reproduction (cf: the expendability of men vs women in The Privileged Sex by Martin van Creveld).

Now I want you to understand what happens to humans when exposed to weaponized white phosphorus. I have first-hand knowledge of the US use in Guatemala, El Salvador, and Columbia. I was on the ground fighting and directing "traffic" while gunships attacked rebels; and afterward I performed what the CIA euphemistically called "Clean Up". AC-130-H gunships were fitted with a side mounted 105mm Howitzer. It's my estimate from direct observation that 20% of 105 shells fired by these gunships on these missions were white phosphorus and some of them a mix, which I'll explain shortly. When a 105 shell hits the ground and explodes, its casing fragments into hundreds of pieces; simultaneously the white phosphorus is thrown out in a cloud 25-50 yards in every direction. The phosphorus takes the form of sticky pulverized wax-like particles, waxy wedges, and gas. Many of the casing fragments are coated in the chemical. These shrapnel fragments (and wedges) can embed in the body, but will burst into flame, especially if the fragment is in the lung. If these fragments (or wedges) enter the abdomen or another location (including brains) a vast burning hole is going to take place and keep expanding based on the amount of chemical present until the chemical reaction is spent.

If the splattered particles are breathed in, it is certain painful death. This splatter can get anywhere and it sticks to skin and clothing, including eyes, nose, and mouth, but now it's starting to react to the air, and the splatter ignites. When this happens, small particles flash and burn, larger splatter burns and burns and burns. Hair will burn and skin will melt, even down to

173

the bone; ears will melt away; hands may take on the look of skeleton; 10% of skin surface burned with white phosphorus is an extremely cruel and painful death sentence, without immediate medical treatment (which we know Israel and the US blocks and withholds).

Now, I'm sure you would think nothing could get any more obscene. But the chemical engineers of the militaries went further, and developed mixes. Some of the phosphorus ordinance also contains elemental sodium. Sodium (elemental) is completely unstable in the presence of water; not so much the water in the air, unless its rain. The sodium will hit the human, and if they're sweating, or bleeding, or it gets in an eye, a violent chemical reaction takes place where the sodium steals oxygen from water based fluids, releasing the hydrogen, and burns violently until the chemical reaction is spent. I've seen this take pain and cruelty to a whole other level. Humans often urinate or defecate during the process of violent death. I've seen bodies where elemental sodium has stuck to the crotch on clothing, and urine will make it ignite and burn through to skin. We all know how sensitive the area of the genitals can be, so imagine, if you can, a raging, sticking chemical fire in your crotch.

All of these scenarios lead to death, but CIA Operations want absolute death and proof (pictures). As I've said, in many ways they are exactly like the SS. Some hadn't died yet. Some were completely unconscious and would never wake up. Some were still conscious, and some begged for help. You could see and hear their excruciating pain and gasps for air. When you see bodies sparking and flashing fire, you know the world has lost all moral bearing.

Chemical deaths are the most painful and heinous deaths in warfare. It makes me sad that my country is leading the way in use of chemical weapons; yet they are not alone. Countries claiming moral militaries, yet consistently use chemical weapons including weaponized white phosphorus, include Britain, France, Germany, Israel (claims "the most moral"), Japan, Australia, Russia, Saudi Arabia, and more. All of these have been threatened by the ICC; but as the British have proven with Queen Elizabeth, and the US failing to ratify the ICC charter (even after it helped to establish the court), the ICC bows to political pressure and threats of removing funding and they stick to only prosecuting third world or non-capitalistic entities. As the Chief ICC prosecutor told me via email, they just claim "no jurisdiction", which provides no hope for justice.

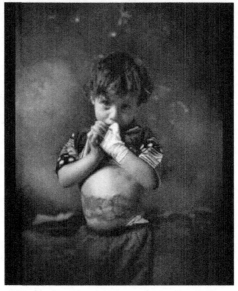

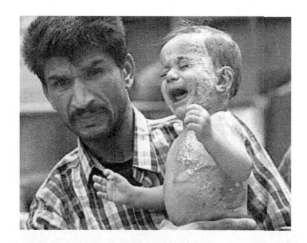

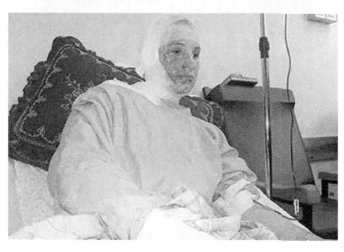

"If the TRUTH makes you uncomfortable, don't blame the truth... blame the lie, that made you comfortable"

Same malfeasin', same ol' crimes, we haven't changed, since ancient times.

Iron Hand - Dire Straits

Trackers

#17 – August 1981

I heard a slight groan, and I knew it
was the groan of mortal terror. It was
not a groan of pain or of grief – oh,
no! – it was the low stifled sound
that arises from the bottom of the
soul when overcharged with awe. I
knew the sound well. Many a night,
just at midnight, when all the world
slept, it has welled up from my own
bosom, deepening, with its dreadful
echo, the terrors that distracted me.

The Tell-Tale Heart – Edgar Allen Poe

I received notice that I would be traveling to El Salvador
again. Command and CIA provided satellite images of the area,
without specific location of the target because they couldn't detect
it exactly. Rebels had stolen a UH-1 helicopter and converted it
into a gunship. They had a large weapons and ammunition cache,
and there were purportedly several rebel personnel at the location.

Without detailed information, and given the high
mountainous terrain, it was decided that a Spectre gunship would
be ineffective at the location. I was given orders to destroy the
helicopter gunship, weapons and ammunition cache, all personnel
buildings, kill any rebel personnel I came into contact with, and,
as always, given special instructions that no US involvement be
suspected.

179

After reviewing the imagery I chose my path of entry and exit, loaded my gear, and was off on a C-130 Combat Talon to a base in San Salvador. My usual gear included a survival knife with a 10 inch blackened blade. Weapons and explosives, normally signed out before heading out, included M16 with scope and removable suppressor, M11 .45 caliber semi-automatic pistol and suppressor, and several packs of C-4 plastic explosive with remote control detonators.

As the sun was setting a US UH-1 attack helicopter transported me to a clearing 12.67 kilometers from the target area. I traveled on goat paths to the location and found the rebel encampment. The whole area was under camouflage netting, including the stolen helicopter which had been fitted with door and front mounted 7.62mm miniguns, and rigged rocket launchers. I scouted around the encampment and determined there were approximately 20 rebel personnel, two tin buildings (for eating and sleeping), a tin hut for small arms, a larger tin hut for larger weapons, and two buried ammunition lockers. The rebel personnel appeared unconcerned with being found. An access road to the site came from opposite my entry point.

Returning to entry point I found a blind among fallen trees, observed and waited. At 2215, having noticed 18 personnel had gone into the personnel buildings leaving 2 guards, I approached from my blind. The guards really weren't paying attention and looked like they were falling asleep. I decided to place explosives around the base of the personnel buildings first. Then I placed charges around the base of the weapons caches, and crawled to the buried ammunition lockers and placed charges in each with extended antennae sticking out. Last I crawled inside the back of the helicopter, removed an access panel, and placed a charge underneath the engines. When I got out, I placed another charge underneath the rear, then crept back to my blind.

All charges were armed and registered, and I detonated them all at once. The personnel buildings were disintegrated with all personnel inside, while the 2 guards were killed by flying shrapnel and my own fire. The helicopter blew off the ground and in two, with the front half landing in the personnel rubble, and the back half landing in the weapons and ammunition inferno. The explosion was so violent the mountain shook.

I documented the destruction of the targets and turned to leave in the same direction from which I came, when additional rebels arrived in pickup trucks. I kicked myself mentally for not having put charges on the trees to block the access road. They immediately broke off in pairs and began to search in different directions. I noticed two heading in my general direction and I immediately left the area.

After 1km I knew they had picked up my tracks and were following me. My speed was greater, so I thought I could easily outpace them. After 5km, I knew that anyone who could track that well in the dark would follow me to my extraction point (the same clearing). This was unacceptable. I knew they would torture and/or kill me. I knew they would put the extraction and the extraction crew in danger. I knew that once they saw me, they would know Americans were involved, and this was counter to my orders. I made the decision to eliminate them.

Gunfire was out of the question as it would soon have rebels overrunning me. I knew they were separated by several meters, and they whistled to each other from time to time in order to confer. The path had heavy growth on both sides, but on the high side was a particularly large tree with shaggy bark. I used my knife to cut the bark and pry out a partial circle to peer through to the path. Then I placed a trip wire low across the path about a meter from the tree and covered it lightly so it couldn't be seen. The first rebel came along the path and tripped, and I came around the tree and drove my knife deep into the heart of a woman. With shock in my heart and my knife still in her chest she clearly whispered, "Baby!", and then the life left her eyes and face. The shock turned to deep sadness. When I pulled my knife from her chest she dropped.

I propped her body up against the tree like she were resting and removed the trip wire. I gave three short whistles and hid behind a large bush on the lower side of the path. Her partner approached. He squatted down and was talking to her and checking her. I could hear the desperation in his voice. I didn't want to do it, but I emerged and drove my knife into his back with a twist. He died quickly without speaking.

Both had US M16 rifles, but at this point an odd coincidence caught my eye. They both had matching gold wedding rings. Upon closer inspection the rings had engraved designs that seemed to match. Searching them I found identification papers with matching last names. I realized what I had done and started to cry. I was sure they had left a baby behind.

Concerned that the bodies would be discovered, I took infrared photos of the bodies, documents, and weapons, then I dug a single grave off of the path in a flat area and buried them with their weapons. Feeling extremely bad about what I had done, I placed their hands in a clasp. I walked half in a daze ~7.5km to my extraction point. Radio communication with extraction personnel indicated an ETA of 30 minutes.

The sun was about to rise, and I could see details in and around the clearing that I couldn't see the previous night. There was a fast running stream close to the clearing in the woods. It wasn't until then that I noticed the dried and caked blood – on my hands, arms, clothes, and boots. Blood has such a distinctive smell... heavy... metallic... and it settles in the nose and mouth. I went to the stream and stripped off my weapons and gear, and lay down in a deep spot. I scrubbed my hands and arms, rubbed my pants and shirt. I put my head back and let the cool water rush over my face and body. For 10-15 minutes I let that water run over me, so thankful for it, but feeling extremely guilty for enjoying it.

Putting on my gear and weapons I heard the chopper coming and I signaled. The gunner pulled me in and I collapsed on the rear seat and stared aimlessly. It was going to be a hot day, but I felt cold... too cold.

The chopper brought me to the C-130, and I slept on webbing seats all the way back to the US. I was supposed to go to debriefing immediately upon return, but I was so exhausted I just went to my room and slept for 2 days. Knocks on the door demanded my attention, but I didn't answer. On the third day I reported to the Lieutenant for debriefing. He reported directly to the Scout Program Commander. He was an evil little bastard. Never having been in the field but knowing all the rules and how EVERYTHING was supposed to be done. I gave my account and expressed remorse. He looked at me with contempt and disgust. He told me I was weak, a crybaby, and a pansy. He told me there was no room for remorse in this business. I lost it and told him he'd feel remorse if I shoved my knife in HIS heart, and continued calling him every fucking dirty word I could think of. A sergeant attending the debriefing told the Lt to back away and he got me out of the room. For years, every August and in between, I tortured myself over having destroyed a new family, destroyed a love, ended a beginning...

One thing I didn't report was my failure to block the access road. If I had blown the trees and blocked the road for

~100 yards, they never would have gotten there that fast or been able to track so close. I knew from the moment of my arrival that a larger cohort of rebels must be nearby to support this encampment. Why didn't I block the fucking road?!? I was trying to hurry instead of being thorough. I would normally have blocked the road just for the sake of preventing escape. Why, this one time, did I blow it off?

My dreams of having destroyed a family haunted me constantly. Yes, I knew if they had caught me they would have perhaps tortured me, and killed me for sure, and exposed my body for the media to prove US involvement. Nevertheless, I began to realize I should not even have been there. For years this event has tortured my heart. In 2007, I found a way to send information about the killings and location to the Salvadoran Consulate in Washington, DC. No fingerprints, no printer marks – anonymous Cypherpunk chain re-mailers. I was never sure of receipt until 2021.

I'll let the words of the ODNI written to me a short time ago suffice:

"There is a conclusion to this. In August 2007 an untraceable email with PDF image attached was sent to the consulate of the foreign country involved. This communication contained details of the incident without revealing responsible parties. The PDF image was a map showing where the bodies were buried. The State Department was called in and attended the exhumation and autopsies. The bodies were that of two rebels, man and wife, 28 and 26 at time of death. The woman died of a single stab wound to the heart, and the man died of a single rotary (commando) knife wound which tore the liver. The woman was approximately 45 days pregnant, and the CIA liaison reported that the bodies had been buried with extreme care, side by side, with adjacent hands placed in a clasp. Though the CIA was sure who must have sent the email, the US Ambassador was overcome and a standing order was issued by the State Department that no action be considered or taken. The bodies were returned to their families."

    This woman is a regular in my dreams and nightmares – almost every night. Since telling my wife, the woman and her mates are trying to kill my wife, and I start stabbing all the soldiers within reach. I can still feel the blade ripping past her ribs, see the light and life fading from her eyes, and the dark whisper, "Baby!". As her head gave way and dropped back, I held her up, then laid her down. The sadness of having ended an entire generation of human and familial growth will always be with me... the sick feeling he must have had knowing that she was dead before he died... and the look on her face as her last concern was for her baby...

Puppets

#18 – August 1981

Oh, now I feel it coming back again,
Like a rolling thunder chasing the wind,
Forces pulling from the center of the
Earth again,
I can *feel* it!

Lightning Crashes – Live

A buried weapons cache was reported in a mountain location in El Salvador. This country was controlled by 13 right wing oligarchies with strong ties to American businesses. I was ordered to infiltrate the location, identify the weapons cache, and destroy it. Spectre gunships were not possible because the exact location was unknown (foliage and too much loitering time above the rebel area would give away direct US involvement); additionally, it was a hidden and buried cache and there would be no guards. I learned a lot about this nation's conflict after the last two missions. The right wing oligarchies supported a strict right wing government which carried their interests (and US interests), and supported the use of right wing para- and military death squads committing murder, rape, and torture to assert control, all with the assistance and instigation of the CIA. Bishops, priests, nuns, villagers, and anyone opposed to strict capitalism were all fair game for murder and rape, terror legitimated by US presidential decree and Congressional leeway given to the CIA in law.

I felt completely unsettled with this mission, but I was 20 years old and second guessed myself. I also felt relieved that I probably wasn't going to have to kill anyone. Inspecting the usual provided satellite and reconnaissance imagery, I chose my point of entry, ingress and egress paths, and loaded my gear on a C-130 to a local base. While I always kept my own knives, a CIA weapons locker was provided from which I drew an M-16 with scope & suppressor, and a .45cal semi-automatic pistol with suppressor. I had requisitioned an explosives package with RC detonators, and that was provided and checked before climbing in a Huey gunship and leaving for the drop zone. It was night with slight moonlight.

The drop zone was approximately 15km from the target, and the little bit of moonlight was enough to follow an animal path along the ridge of a long range of hills. The target zone was a forest of thick and tangled trees of mid-level canopy. A clearing had been hollowed at the lower level leaving the higher canopy untouched which hid the location from above view. There were no guards, and with night vision goggles I was able to locate where digging had taken place. A buried large rectangular concrete block box was located with a locked metal hatch. I cut the lock to look inside and found an attached ladder going down approximately 12 feet. The container appeared to be about 12 feet deep by 12x24, and contained M-16s, AK-47s, various caliber pistols (mostly M11s), a few shoulder fired rockets, and various explosives. Checking the surrounding area I found three more smaller metal containers about the size of large commercial dumpsters. These last three were unlocked and held ammunition for the weapons inside the larger container.

After taking various pictures of the caches, I placed a very large charge in the bottom of the large container with an extra incendiary charge. Several boxes were place over this and I extended the detonator antennae to reach out the top of the container. Then I placed mixed charges in each of the smaller containers and latched the lids. I backed off about 100 yards and checked the signals then let it rip. The ground shook violently and magnificent balls of fire erupted from the ground. I took a few more pictures and immediately left the scene.

Close to the extraction point was a little village about 125 yards downhill from the western ridge I was on, and blocked from immediate sun on the east from another ridge. When I reached this point it was daybreak, the sun was not over the eastern ridge, yet there was light. There was a rock under a tree on the path, and I sat to rest and look at the village. I was enjoying myself because the early morning seemed pleasant and beautiful, and I was very happy that I hadn't had to kill anyone.

There was a central square with a small fountain. The streets branched from the center in four directions, and the fourth direction was toward my position and the road dead ended. The square and streets were surrounded by living and business quarters. On the street branch closest to me a native girl, all of 15 years old, her skin the color of rich brown-red molasses, danced in circles in a multi-colored skirt and white blouse with colored embroidery, proudly twirling her skirt. She looked so happy, and I felt happy watching her be happy. It was a beautiful scene and I thought it must be her birthday. She was so happy.

Then a jeep (US provisioned) came barreling into the square, around the fountain, and came to a stop 10 yards from the girl. She froze, and still didn't move when the two men, Salvadoran military, ordered her to stay. The jeep was provided to them by the US. The M-16s they carried were provided to them by the US. The .45cal pistols they carried were provided to them by the US. No one emerged from the buildings inside to stand by the girl. These military men, supported by the US, by

US taxpayers, and hell, by me, were known for cruelty, rape, and death. I observed through my scope.

One stood directly in front of her, the other a few yards back to the north, their right sides facing me. They appeared to ask a question, but didn't like the answer, so the front one smacked the girl hard across the face. The girl cried and tried to walk away, but he grabbed her arm and made her stand still. The rear trooper appeared to giggle and twitter like a hyena, then circled her and pulled her shirt down over her shoulder, popping buttons. I fixed my suppressor and continued to observe through my scope. The front trooper walked around her slowly, pawing at her as he went, then stopped in his original position. He used his rifle to lift her skirt above her waist, rubbed the muzzle in her crotch, then handed it to his partner, who smiled and giggled more while he continued to point his rifle at the girl. The girl cried harder and was stiff with fright. The front trooper lifted her chin with one hand, and used his other to push her blouse down past her shoulders, exposing her breasts. I could see where this was going, and it was going there fast.

I chose the rear trooper as the first target, because that would allow me time to focus on the other before he realized what was happening. The rear trooper was still and his head provided a stable and viable target. A suppressor doesn't eliminate noise, but it does a fair job reducing it and reducing flash. An M-16 round traveling in a downward trajectory with wind at its back… can't miss. An M-16 round is meant to tumble upon impact and break into multiple fragments to cause the greatest amount of damage possible, and this one didn't disappoint. The trooper's head fairly exploded in the direction of fire. The girl started. The front trooper hadn't heard the shot, he was so intent on his own kill. He looked at her shaking, then turned around and saw his partner crumpled on the ground. His turning provided a larger target and the next round went into his chest, but he was still up, so I put another round through his head and the back of his skull blew out, and he dropped immediately.

The girl panicked for a few seconds then ran off in fright. No one emerged from inside the buildings, which angered me. I packed up and continued on my path for extraction. On the ride out I fully realized that I was fighting someone else's war... and I was helping the wrong side. What the fuck was I doing this for? We were supporting, and being, fascists (corporatists), and I felt sick knowing I had become what I hated most.

I never felt guilty killing those two, they were psychopaths and deserved it with all the pain that they may have felt; unfortunately, I don't think they had a chance to feel anything or enough. The fact that no men or women in the village emerged to help the girl angered me to rage. Surely they heard what was happening. Surely they heard the girl crying – I heard from over 100 yards! Surely someone was peeking out of their shutters. Why would no one help?

These killings were never reported nor documented. If Bill had been around, I'm sure I would have told him in private. I possibly could have told the CIA Operations officer, as his attitude as previously expressed was that "it doesn't matter who dies so long as the mission is completed successfully without any knowledge of US involvement". However, I kept it to myself. It was a decision that I don't regret making, yet it also feels like a Catch-22 inside a bizarro world. I never even told details to the former 1st SOW chaplain to whom they sent me when I told them I wanted out. I told NO ONE these things for forty years, yet they lived in my head constantly, and still do.

This event has taken on new life for me in the last year. Just as I had withheld my military trauma from my wife, she had withheld her own trauma. When she was 18, a psychopathic

190

football player named Curtis The Rapist, from M_____ Center, took her in a storage/workout room at a school dance. He tried forcing sex which wasn't working, so he became even more violent and tied her up on the floor to a bench with cord, and he raped her with extra violence and malevolence. When he was done, he left her there to free herself, after threatening her life if she ever told anyone. Like most rape victims, woman or man, she blamed herself and was sure no one would believe, and she was deathly afraid that her father would find out and kill the boy and be sent to prison. Curtis The Rapist made sure to express forcefully that she deserved it and if she ever opened her mouth to anyone, he would track her down and get her. So she kept it to herself. The painful irony for me is I could be there to save a native girl in a foreign country, but I couldn't be there to save my future wife.

I so want to believe that the girl lived a long and happy life, but I'll never know, just as she'll never know who killed her attackers. My wife, a bit of a Buddhist spiritualist, communes with her, which makes me cry when I think about it; I'm an atheist, yet I hope with all my heart they hear each other.

Alexander Pope

An Excerpt from
Epilogue To The Satires – Dialogue II

  F: Hold Sir! For God's sake where's th' Affront to
you?
Against your worship when had Selkirk writ?
Or Page pour'd forth the Torrent of of his Wit?
Or grant the Bard whose distich all commend
[*In Pow'r a Servant, out of Pow'r a friend*]
To Walpole guilty of some venial sin;
What's that to you who ne'er was out nor in?
      The Priest whose Flattery be-dropt the Crown,
How hurt he you? He only stain'd the Gown.
And how did, pray, the florid Youth offend,
Whose speech you took, and gave it to a Friend?
  P: Faith, it imports not much from whom it came,
Whoever borrow'd, could not be to blame,
Since the whole House did afterward the same.
Let Courtly Wits to Wits afford supply,
As Hog to Hog in huts of Westphaly;
If one, thro' Nature's Bounty or his Lord's,
Has what the frugal, dirty soil affords,
From him the next receives it, thick or thin,
As pure a mess almost as it came in;
The blessed benefit, not there confin'd,
Drops to the third, who nuzzles close behind;
From tail to mouth, they feed and they carouse;
The last full fairly gives it to the *House*.
  F: This filthy simile, this beastly line
Quite turns my stomach –
        P: *So does Flatt'ry mine;*

192

And all your courtly Civet-cats can vent,
Perfume to you, to me is Excrement.
But hear me further – Japhet, 'tis agreed,
Writ not, and Chartres scarce could write or read,
In all the Courts of Pindus guiltless quite;
But pens can forge, my Friend, that cannot write;
And must no egg in Japhet's face be thrown,
Because the Deed he forg'd was not my own?
Must never Patriot then declaim at Gin,
Unless, good man! He has been fairly in?
No Zealous Pastor blame a failing Spouse,
Without a staring Reason on his brows?
And each Blasphemer quite escape the rod,
Because the insult's not on Man, but God?
  Ask you what Provocation I have had?
The strong Antipathy of Good to Bad.
When Truth or Virtue an Affront endures,
Th'Affront is mine, my friend, and should be yours.
Mine, as a Foe profess'd to false Pretence,
Who think a Coxcomb's Honor like his sense;
Mine, as a Friend to every worthy mind;
And mine as Man, who feel for all mankind.
  F: You're strangely proud.
        P: *So proud, I am no Slave;*
So impudent, I own myself no Knave;
So odd, my Country's Ruin makes me grave.
… Ye tinsel Insects! Whom a Court maintains,
That counts your Beauties only by your Stains,
Spin all your Cobwebs o'er the Eye of Day!
… All his Grace preaches, all his Lordship sings,
All that makes Saints of Queens, and Gods of Kings,
All, all but Truth drops dead-born from the Press,
Like the last Gazette, or the last Address.
  When black Ambition stains a public Cause,
A Monarch's sword when mad Vain-glory draws...

Posthumous Letter To Bill

12 January 2022

It's been 43 years since I first met you. Talking about you with my wife, she suggested I write you this letter, and I'm already crying.

It was immediately after initial commando training that I transferred to Hurlburt and you took me under your wing. We trained in the forest around Hurlburt, in the swamps, on the beach, in the water, in the rivers... intensely and non-stop. Soon we were going with the gunships on their record breaking air refueling flight to Guam, and then to the Philippines for more training.

In the Philippines you ran me ragged evading captures, teaching infiltration, and reaction, and "subduction of life". You drilled into my head not to panic, even when fear of the act attempted to overwhelm me, even when the odds seemed impossible to overcome. You made me repeat and live, "If you panic, you die". You taught me how to survive and turn odds in my favor under circumstances of capture. You looked into my eyes trying to convey that you understood what I was getting into, while I still wasn't aware of what I was getting into. You showed care, concern, and support, but remained aloof because I believe you thought I would probably die with the way this program was to operate.

When, still in the Philippines, I became too edgy, you took me to Marines you trusted and told them to take me to a "good" whorehouse. Then we trained even harder. You knew my first mission before I even had a clue. We trained for Eagle Claw in the desert at White Sands. We practiced low level skid drops and FRS pickups. You taught me to read terrain maps with different eyes. You trained me to look at every possible angle of what may happen. Though you didn't talk a lot, you used to attempt drilling what you did say into my head with your eyes. You trained me to react quickly, to not let hesitation or fear prevent necessary action… to accept the moment and act, otherwise, I would die. Though you always said the mission was important, and human life was important, *you* stressed that *my* life was important.

Immediately before my first mission, you opened up a little about your own experience in Vietnam, but you remained personally closed. You told me how you had been demoted for punching an officer (it's always those asshole lieutenants). It seemed you were still dealing with your own demons. When we finally went to Egypt and Saudi Arabia for Eagle Claw's final preparations, you assured me I was ready and capable, and still continued giving me advice. When I returned from placing the lights and setting initial charges and sabotage markers, you actually smiled and seemed happy to see me.

When the insertion was made for Eagle Claw, you warned me not to trust the skills of Delta Force, that Army Rangers couldn't think outside their training and that SEALS tended to fall apart when on their own. Things which I found to be true under fire and which I related back to you. When we returned from Desert 1 you actually embraced me.

You rarely let yourself loose. The only exception I remember distinctly was a doosy. When we returned from Egypt the gunship we traveled on, Wicked Wanda (appropriate for this scenario), stopped in England at a base north of London. You, me, and the whole crew went to town to a pub. It was a beautiful pub with rubbed oak woodwork, and private snugs off the main room. We all sat in the main room drinking and you were getting

195

pretty loose. In walked a beautiful, 30ish, blond woman with milky breasts the size of howitzer shells. She was very friendly and sat, talked, and drank with us. I think she saw you staring at her breasts, then she announced that if we wanted, we could all fuck those breasts, one after the other in rank. Each load of cum was to remain where it was. The gunship crew voted that you and I would have to go last because we weren't actually "their" crew… Which made us thirteen and fourteen. You surprised the hell out of me by saying, "That's fine. Let's go." We went into one of the side rooms, pulled the curtain, and she pulled her top down, saying, "Nothing but the dick between the breasts… no touching anything else." The captain came, and went, as did the co-pilot, EWO, and the flight engineer, gunners, and spotters as she fingered herself. Then you fucked her tits with all the lube of the cum, and you blew a wad up into her face. I was last and with all the hot cum I didn't last long at all but it was intense. She said to one of the gunners, "Hand me some of those towels love" and she cleaned up, gave each of us a kiss and walked out smiling. She was happy and I'd never seen *you* so happy.

Upon departure for my first Central American mission you grabbed my face and intently stared into me with your dark burning eyes insisting that I remember that the nighttime was shorter than I would think, and you embraced me tightly. "Don't overthink and don't waste time" you would say. "Get in, act, get out", and "don't get involved in anything not associated with the mission". I often wonder what you would say concerning my last mission. Just like telling you all the details of the other missions, I would have told you if you hadn't died. I would have told you there was no way for me to ignore it… that it would have taken a heart of stone and a moral lobotomy like CIA agents and politicians have.

You attended all my debriefings except the last three. You always supported me and defended my right to my anger with Lt

196

Weasel. You kept me from threatening his life more than once. When he kept haranguing me over not reporting in (when I tried to keep radio silence), and he got in my face, you saw me put my hand on my knife and you held it down against my side without saying a word. You calmly told him once that he had no right to second guess my actions when he had no training or field experience in these matters. You told him once when he was getting out of his chair again (to yell at me), "With respect Sir, if you don't sit down and stay there I'm going to knock you into the chair!" More than once you told him to back away or he'd get hurt. *You always trusted what I did and trusted I would make the right decisions, something I had never experienced before.* The sergeant you arranged to fill in for you when you took leave did exactly as you did. You must have filled him in very well. Thank you.

You took a long overdue vacation leave in June. I didn't learn you were dead until October. No announcement was made, and I was only informed after several inquiries. You died hauling a trailer full of firewood with your Jeep, and it flipped over on the highway and you broke your neck. All the things you went through, all the times you survived, only to die taking care of a simple chore! No one knew anything about you. No one knew when or where of a funeral or service. Lt Weasel wouldn't give me the time of day concerning you. It was simply... you were gone! I cried non-stop for 2-3 days, and then on and off for another week or more; and I still feel your loss 40 years later. You were somewhat of a father figure, but you were a strong, supportive, caring figure who actually cared whether I lived or died on those missions. You taught me so many important things and gave me such strength of purpose. The skills and behavior you taught me kept me alive through hell, saved me when I was caught, and even helped me at other times to keep my head. Thank you.

197

I'm sorry I didn't know you better or more. I'm sorry I didn't push harder for more of your information, life story, history... I do remember that you were drafted for Vietnam. I do recall that you said you had divorced shortly after Vietnam ended because she had aborted your baby without telling you and had been going out with another man while you were gone; and instead of getting out, as you had planned, you stayed in to deal with the pain. I'm sorry you had to deal with that pain. You were a good man and didn't deserve that.

You were very supportive of Kit and I, but after I returned from the mission killing the nuns, I found a letter from her in my box telling me it was over, and it contained the ring you helped me find. I threw that ring in the tide pool across the highway from Hurlburt. I know, a waste of money, but, you feel like taking it out on something and the ring was all there was. Her parents (especially her father) and her sister (who you remember disliked me) convinced her that since I wasn't an officer, and because I was in such dangerous work, that a relationship with me was a "dead" end, in more ways than one. They were probably right. What chance has a volunteer killer have to obtain love outside of a war? How much longer could my luck hold out, regardless of skills and training?

You were there when they awarded those medals to me, and you genuinely seemed proud of me, and you took my pictures when the Wing photographer seemed to snub my presence. I often wonder now what you did with those pictures. Before each presentation you would remind me that they really only like giving awards to officers in the AF, based upon the primary air combat role; but you would assure me that I deserved those awards and not to let the presence of all the officers affect my bearing as one who "out performed them every step of the way".

When I last saw you at the beginning of June, you knew I was starting to have trouble justifying the killings of non-combatants, killings to stop food shipments to starving villages (not just rebels). You knew I was starting to question the policies. You didn't know about the last three missions. The objectives were obfuscated to allow misconduct and force political killings... killing of nuns, pregnant woman and husband, rapist Salvadoran army guards. These things hit me slowly, then with the force of a hurricane. My god how I wanted you at those debriefings and just to talk with about the details! My god how I needed you when I told them I couldn't do it anymore, killing for a corporatist political agenda (fascist)! I felt like I had become what I hated most in all the world, a Nazi fucking stooge! They made me meet with every fucking commander on the base. I met with the squadron commanders. I met with the Group commander. I met with the Wing commander. I met with the former Wing chaplain whose advice was "Don't let the bastards screw ya"! EVERYONE in the CSG had an opinion on what a low-life commie simp I was! Scared! Unpatriotic! Treasonous! Yellow! Pussy! etc... Lo and behold, Major Fleming showed up himself to berate me, and tell me how worthless I was except for killing; with his little Lt Toto barking by his side. Yet after all that, even at the last minute, after having stripped me of my medals, awards, etc... they told me they "could make all this go away if you'd simply go back in the field"... but I couldn't. It seemed like in a manner of two months, my entire world shattered in my hands... my entire belief system of who I thought I was or wanted to be blew up in my face, leaving me permanently wounded and scarred.

Last year I learned that the Major (who retired as a Colonel) had written a book taking credit for going into Iran. He said he took in a collapsible motorcycle to run around in that canyon. He seemed to have forgotten the village to the north and the Iranian army unit stationed in that village, or the radio tower,

199

or the communication lines, etc... After I stopped laughing (he forgot a pack shovel to bury the lights), I was enraged, and I've been that way ever since when I think about him and his useless foppishness. Lt Weasel still makes me burn with rage.

But that's a tangent. You were very important to me... for me. If not for you, I never would have survived, never married, never had children. *I regret yelling at you in the Philippines that you were a sadistic fuck.* You knew what I was heading into, and you tried telling me, but I didn't listen well enough. But nevertheless, you did prepare me, and I remembered the things you taught me, because you were an excellent teacher. Talking about you with my wife yesterday, I could once again see your eyes burning into me, willing me to learn, stay alive, and stay human. I could see your face clearly again for the first time in years.

I've missed you since 1981. I wish I could talk to you now. I loved you then. I love you now.

Rubicon

Up Against A Wall

I'm woven in a fantasy,
I can't believe the things I see
The path that I have chosen now has led me to a wall
And with each passing day,
I feel a little more like something dear was lost.

It rises now before me,
A dark and silent barrier between,
All I am, and all that I would ever want to be,
It's just a travesty...

The Wall - Kansas

Following the last mission, I could no longer justify what I was doing. The Salvadoran and Guatemalan regimes were clearly corrupt and evil. They couldn't have survived without US backing and active CIA and military support. Looking around the world, and throughout US colonial history, the US made a habit of supporting right-wing governments and dictators. If locals got out of hand or demanded fair play, we sent in troops to slaughter the "socialists" and "communists". Even at that time, the US all-out supported apartheid South Africa, just as they support apartheid Israel to this day, regardless of the slaughter taking place.

...The moment is a masterpiece,
The weight of indecision's in the air,
Standing there,
The symbol and the sum of all that's me,

201

It's just a travesty,
Towering, blocking out the light and blinding me,
I want to see.

You can't just quit in the field, you'd probably end up with a gunship round vaporizing your existence. No new orders had yet been issued, but I knew they were coming. At the time, I thought Bill was just on vacation. He had been gone longer than expected, but god how I needed him! I went to Lt Weasel and informed him I would no longer go on these missions. He was incensed and ordered me to continue. I told him there was no way I would ever go out again. He called me every derogatory name he could think of, and threatened to have me arrested, I told him to go ahead – his order was invalid. You can't order someone to violate the law and the conventions of international law.

Then the shit hit the fan, in my direction. Lt Weasel called the Major. The Major flew down and involved all the base Commanders. The Major lectured me for 3 solid hours on integrity, following orders, communism, socialism, Russians, those "trying to destroy our way of life", etc... He scolded me how our leaders knew best and we should do as we're told for the greater good. The CIA knew who our enemies were, and we should take their word for it, even if it were wrong now and again.

The Major sent me to talk with the 8th and 16th Squadron Commanders, the Group Commander, and the Wing Commander. I told all of them the same, that I could no longer support right-wing fascists; that I could no longer kill on the word of another that it was the right thing to do, when all indications explicitly screamed it was the wrong thing to do. The CIA's operational orders were wrong, a violation of international law. We (Americans) were slaughtering and killing the wounded for the sake of political ideology, secrecy (about out involvement), and to hand off successes to the inadequate and power hungry death squad militaries of foreign fascist governments. They were all very nice and semi-supportive, but all of them were of the pilot, kill from a great distance without guilt, guild.

And so it went,
The children lost their minds,
Crawling over bodies
of those who gave their lives.

And the fists begin to throw,
And the fire starts to blaze,
Don't you think they know
They're the fucking human race?

They said the world does not belong to you,
You are not the king, I am not the fool,
They said the world does not belong to you.
It don't belong to you.
It belongs to me!

And So It Went – The Pretty Reckless

I was sent to see a psychiatrist at Eglin AFB. He spent and hour with me, listening as I spewed out my problem with indiscriminate killing. Since he was a psychiatrist, I told him the details of the missions, the killing of wounded, the blood, the killing of unarmed civilians, and the nuns. The tears running down my face could have filled a lake. When I finished he told me that he felt I had a problem with authority, perhaps having to do with my father. I asked him if he got his diploma from a Cracker Jack box. I asked him if he had been listening at all, or was this some sort of boilerplate diagnoses specifically made for military use. He said thanks for talking to him and he would write his report.

When the report arrived, the Major and his yippy dog went to town with it, accusing me of failing to be a team member, of not following orders, of having problems with authority related to my father. I asked for a copy of the report and they gave it to me. No where in the report was mention made that the subject (myself) no longer wanted to kill for ideology and profits. Though the DSM 3 published in 1980 had included PTSD as a diagnoses, and this information was certainly available to the psychiatrist (he had it on his shelf), no mention was made of trauma, killing, or death and the fact I didn't want to do it anymore. That a trained psychiatrist with an advanced degree couldn't see this or report on it spelled out the lengths the military will go to establish that nothing is their fault, that soldiers are faulted by there inability to "suck it up buttercup" and continue obeying assholes.

The Wing Commander asked if there were anyone else they could have me talk with. I told him that if there were someone outside the military, I would talk with them. Considering what was involved in the missions, it made sense that they sent me to the former Wing Chaplain, a retired priest. We spoke for a couple of hours, and while I couldn't divulge all the information on the missions, I made it clear that I was being ordered to kill without cause and even slaughter the wounded, and that I just couldn't do it anymore. I told him about the psychiatrist and his false report. He understood and pointed to a plaque above his mantle. It had a Latin phrase and he asked me if I knew what it meant. I told him I didn't, and he told me, *"Don't let the bastards screw you...* I can't tell you what to do, but you have to live with yourself and your conscience... Don't let them tell you what you *have* to do."

When I returned to the Wing Commander, he seemed sad at my sticking to my refusal. He contacted the Major, and escalation of pressure mounted. I was given every dirty job to perform publicly, and the information concerning me was leaked to practically everyone on base. Soon, men that I'd known as good friends turned on me like rabid wolves. From these, and from the Major and his barking dog, I was called coward, commie, yellow, pussy, wussy, slacker, traitor, scared, chickenshit, and so much more. I was threatened with prison, and some said they should hang me or put me in front of a firing squad.

I felt so extremely alone. I wondered where Bill was. Lt Weasel wouldn't discuss him with me. I asked around incessantly and was finally told that Bill had been killed in an auto accident. He was transporting firewood using a jeep and trailer, and flipped it on the highway and broke his neck. I thought of all he had been through in Vietnam and his life, and to die, that quick while moving firewood. I was never able to tell him about Kit. This hit me very hard, and I cried for days… now I really felt even more alone.

Unbeknownst to me at the time, the former 1st SOW Chaplain was pushing hard to try and help me. Meetings were taking place in the background, and then I was called in by the Major to discuss my separation. Apparently there had been arguments about how far to take the punishment, and then whether to allow an honorable discharge. Also apparent was that the Major (my Commander) and his dog Toto were for maximum punishment and dishonorable discharge. Others argued against this, the Chaplain the most forcefully. What the Major offered was cruel and petty. He brought up the AFEES Major's objection attached to my entrance waiver. He told me what a disgrace I was; that I shouldn't have even been allowed to join. He stripped me of my medals and awards, save my Marksman ribbon, "to remind him of who he really is". He said my DD-214 (discharge document) would be redacted *in toto*. If I didn't agree to this, I would be given a dishonorable discharge. At that time, a

205

dishonorable discharge carried heavier weight than now in the world of employment. Such a damning record was a blackball when seeking employment. I couldn't take that chance, and I was alone in my deliberations, so I agreed.

While the paperwork was readied, I continued with public humiliation work, and received continued public repudiation. When I went to the mess hall to eat, I was left to sit alone feeling angry eyes upon me. During this time, Lt Weasel would constantly alternate between verbal abuse and being my best friend. When he was my best friend, he would relay to me how much the Major and he cared about me. He, and the Major, right up to the last day when I signed the documents, would offer that "all this could just go away… everything will be restored, including your rank and medals… this whole incident will just be erased… all you have to do is go back in the field." This, after telling me how worthless I was and how I shouldn't even have been allowed in – and yet, they still wanted and needed me to go and destroy willy nilly.

On the last day, I went in to sign the paperwork. When they showed it to me, my heart took a dive. The DD-214 had been stripped, completely. I had seen an updated copy previously, and now, it was empty. After all I had been through, to have my life reduced to nothing… No deployments, no awards, no citations; rank was gone; time-in-service reduced. *I had been redacted from service.* True to his word, the Major had left my Marksman ribbon, to remind me. And then, to top the shock, the reason for separation was listed as "APATHY – DEFECTIVE ATTITUDE". This hurt more than anything. First, because it wasn't true. Second, with this printed on the record, even with an honorable discharge, this document was useless to me for employment. They had taken away the accrued paid leave I was owed (from all the times Lt Weasel refused my requests for leave). I was royally screwed!

At this point I had no alternative but to sign. I missed Kit. I missed Bill. I received my copies and drove off the base, alone… so very, very, very alone.

Coming Down

At twenty-five, and still alive,
Much longer than expected for a man...
At twenty-five, all hope has died,
And the glass of my intentions turns to sand...
And shatters in my hand.

<u>25</u> – The Pretty Reckless

Driving out the gate alone was daunting, and I had yet to realize how far I would fall in coming down. I felt free, but there is much insecurity in freedom. For a moment I thought I would drive to California and attempt to get Kit back, but then I told myself, "No! Fuck that bitch!" She had been there for me early on when I felt alone, and made me feel life and love. I truly loved her, but when I needed her most she wasn't there, and I felt nothing now but intense pain. She sold herself for a college education she didn't even plan on using.

The guilt and shame over what I had done began growing. Soon, my sleep became disturbed with dream reenactments, and I would wake up exhausted. I took a job selling coupon books over the phone. When payday came I was issued a check, so I went to the business' bank to cash it, only to be told that account didn't have enough funds. I nearly lost it in the bank. I drove over to the phone center and told the man his check bounced. He said, "No problem, I'll write you another." The anger raged in me and I threw him against the wall with my hand on his throat and told him, "I want cash!.. NOW!" He fumbled in his pocket and paid me. I hated that job anyway.

I tried a series of nothing jobs, but when I couldn't pay
rent any longer, and I couldn't make my car payments, I decided
to try something else. I bought a listing of companies with jobs in
the Gulf oil industry. I stole a plate from another car and lifted
the sticker and put it on my plate. I drove to Louisiana and
applied at several companies. One told me to stay at a certain
motel and they would cover the cost (to be repaid) until they sent
me out. This was one of the worst motels you've ever seen. In a
beautiful scenic area of Podunk, Louisiana, above a bar and the
rooms were filthy and had windows onto an old hallway strewn
with trash, the kind that gives you thoughts about being robbed or
worse.

After a few weeks of eating nothing but snack foods, they
finally sent me out on an oil rig about 75 miles out. The work
schedule was a week on and a week off. Finally with some
money for rent, I found that my cousin (by adoption) was
working in Fort Walton Beach at a stereo store. She had a two
bedroom apartment and agreed to rent me a room. During the
week off I searched for work closer to FWB without much luck; it
was the off season for tourism and few jobs were to be had.
While on the oil rig, I became steadily more tired. My sleep had
become riddled with dreams about killing, and waking up in cold
sweats from fighting. As I slowly descended into major
depression, I began laying awake for hours in my bunk on the rig,
and my mattress in my room. My thoughts would spin and race
for hours until I was only getting an hour of sleep each night.
After a few months my thoughts became dissociated, and
somewhat psychotic. I could see the faces of many that I had
killed. Begging faces, defiant faces, scared faces... The woman
and her husband entered my dreams angry that I had stolen their
lives and ruined their family. The detached head of the cartel
guard growled at me. Every day the guilt, shame, and sadness
grew to the point where I found it hard to function normally.

209

I wanted peace and quiet. It seemed reasonable to me that I could use one of the life rings (a rectangle with a net bottom deep enough to stand in), and I would use this to float away to a desert island and live my life in peace – I would escape. Yeah, I know, but when you're *that* tired and out of it… I put my plan into action and was floating away from the rig in the middle of the night, and I really thought I would end up on the beautiful desert isle. During the next day it rained and the waves crashed over me. After several hours of this, I began to vomit constantly. The rain subsided and a long lonely night turned into a hot sunshiny day – then I *really* got sick. I puked to the point of dry heaves. One more long and lonely night in relatively calm water, but I was so very cold now. About mid morning I was so out of it, and suddenly I found that a Coast Guard helicopter was hovering above me. They were telling me something through their PA, but I couldn't make it out, and I found I couldn't make sensible words either.

They lowered down a basket and strapped me in, and we headed for New Orleans. While in the ER a rep from the company owning the rig came in and asked me to sign a waiver; I was very compliant and did just as he asked. They put me in the psych ward, but since I wasn't insured, they transferred me to the State hospital north of Lake Pontchartrain. Here I was poked and prodded and asked non-stop questions. I tried to deny that I had done it on purpose, but apparently while I was out of it, I had confessed almost everything. What I didn't tell them was about my military service, because I had a fear that they may get the military involved and/or they would lock me up in there and throw away the key. The doctor who ended up with my case had a huge heart. He held my hand as I cried and told me I had major depression. I took the tricyclic he prescribed, but when it started giving me headaches and to make my heart pound, I started spitting them out.

210

I called my parents, told them where I was and that I needed help getting out. My dad was pissed beyond measure and wanted to leave me, but my mom insisted otherwise. They hadn't heard from me in months. They rode down with one of my sisters. The doctor told them, insisted, that when we arrived home, they should get me treatment immediately. That didn't happen for reasons belonging to all. We retrieved my car from the company parking area and headed north.

There were late snows when we arrived. My parents, who lived on a lake, were at work, and I sat festering all day. I couldn't let go of the shame and guilt... it only grew stronger. I had come to the point of wanting to die constantly. I couldn't tell anyone what I'd done because I was so ashamed. I looked out the windows and felt trapped by myself. There was a bottle of Jack Daniels and four full bottles of heart medication on the counter. I washed down all four bottles with the Jack and waited for the nothingness. Then, my stomach was being pumped at a small clinic in a small town. I woke up while this was happening and tried to stop it, but they strapped my arms down, and I was out again. When next I awoke, they were putting me on a life-flight, and the kindest nurse looked at me with pity and told me everything would be alright. I turned my head because I had to vomit, and it got on the chopper floor, and I told her how sorry I was. She just wiped my face clean and told me not to worry about it, it was nothing and she'd have it cleaned up in no time, and she smiled sweetly at me.

Then I was out again. When I awoke this time, I was in a hospital in another city in another state. I had been in a coma for three days. I felt and saw the straps holding my arms and legs and I thought, oh shit, I've done it now. When you really want to die, but then you wake up realizing you've failed, it's not a hallelujah moment. The doctor wasn't sure if I would live, and I hadn't wanted to, but I did nonetheless. If this had been a hospital in my home area, I would have been committed. But seeing that this hospital was in the next state, I was returned to my parents under the promise of getting help.

My mother would ask me, "What happened to you?" But then she would just as easily turn off her emotions and not listen. There was no one to listen and no one to help. PTSD wouldn't be considered a useful diagnoses for military veterans until the '90s. I was still "only a man" in need of sucking it up, buttercup! This was usually proclaimed by "virgins talking about sex".

All I could think about was wanting to die. When the weather turned hot, and sticky, a new manifestation occurred. I would look at my hands and they would be covered in blood, and I could smell it. When this first occurred, I would hide my hands in my pockets and be totally freaked out. When removing my clothes I saw there was no blood, and I started to accept that I was seeing things. I soon realized that I knew that there was no actual blood on my hands or caked into my fingernails, but when I looked, I saw it. Even today, this still happens in hot sticky weather, but I've learned to ignore what I see, because I know its not there. The smell of diesel as it passed forced my mind to wander back to the bases and flightlines and burning jet fuel (an extremely dirty poorly refined fuel that looks like dirty pond water).

I first sought help from the VA. In order to get psychiatric help at the VA, you have to be interviewed by a military psychiatrist or psychologist. I was sent into a room with a psychiatrist and I explained what problems I was having, and why. He listened and then said, "There's nothing here that indicates your problems are related to military service." He showed me my redacted record, looked at me in disgust, treated me with disdain, and sent me out without allowing me to explain.

I realized that they had no access to records of my activities, but his attitude showed me he wouldn't have cared anyway and would have found an excuse to drive me away. I drove the 45 minutes home feeling pain and deep sorrow. God how I wanted to die!

For two years I was like this. Majorly depressed, in and out of psych ward treatment (for which I was billed). One "doctor", dressed in cowboy hat and boots, told me to "suck it up" and told me he was going to medicate me. I told him no one was going to medicate me without my permission. He threatened to force medicate me, so I threatened to kick his ass. He said he would review my case, but I no longer felt safe there, so I ripped the bar from the shower wall and went to break out. Six sheriff's deputies were there in no time, and four of them wrestled me to the ground and hand-cuffed me. I was taken to the state hospital and placed on suicide watch. Never would I tell any of them about my military service – I just didn't trust them. I had tried telling my Mom once, but she had always been emotionally scared, scared to discuss painful or sad things, so I gave up.

Needing some relief, and some change, I began running again and working temp jobs. I attempted utilizing my DD-214 once for employment, but the looks and sounds of disapproval and disgust I received made me put it away never to be used again. Running helped clear my head and allowed me to think. Contemplating my situation, I realized I could tell no one about the killing or my sexuality, ever. I decided that I would have to live with chains on forever, both with the military service and my sexuality. It was extremely lonely and suffocating, but I embraced this path. In 1980 the DSM 3 was published with PTSD as a diagnoses of the anxiety disorders. Yet no one, absolutely no one, asked me about my military service, and no one bandied about the PTSD diagnoses, and I didn't even know it existed at that time (and apparently neither did psych

213

professionals – and the VA proved itself that they would do anything rather than treat what the military had wrought).

As always, the virgins talked about sex. Chicken hawks are so free to give their opinions on who should die and who is righteous, without any knowledge or experience about what they're talking about. Praising veterans who don't seek praise, praising the military and "decisive" politicians who don't deserve praise. Reagan pontificated on his righteousness while continuing to destroy Guatemala. The CIA continued running their rabid dog operations, killing anyone and everyone who opposed their agenda; and Americans reveled in their power while choosing ignorance over Truth. The CIA was documented moving drugs via Cessnas and MAC transports to fund Reagan's Contra "freedom fighters" and fund Israeli apartheid, eminent domain, and slaughter in the Middle East. America fully supported apartheid South Africa. You know, *apartheid*, an international crime.

The nightmares and flashbacks persisted, but I improved enough that I was able to sign up for classes at the community college. I took the standard general classes, but focused on music and singing. I wanted to be as far away from killing as possible. I wouldn't be there long before my life was spun around again, and I would cross another vast Rubicon.

Learning To Fly Again

Well, the good ol' days may not return,
And the rocks might melt and the sea may burn...

Well, some say life, will beat you down,
Break your heart, steal your crown.
So I've started out for God-knows-where,
I guess I'll know when I get there.

I'm learning to fly, around the clouds,
But what goes up, must come down.
I'm learning to fly, but I ain't got wings,
Coming down, is the hardest thing.

Learning To Fly – Tom Petty & The Heartbreakers

The community college was a nice change, studying for a purpose that made human sense. I attended my classes and got good grades. I avoided much human contact because I felt so guilty, and I was sure others could see it, like I had a bloody mark of Cain on my forehead. I was singing in the choir and enjoying music theory. I had picked up bad hay fever while in Florida and southern lands, and many a day I attended class with tissue stuffed in my nose because it wouldn't stop running. Even cold capsules weren't all that effective, or turned my nose into cement. But looking like that, I was sure no one would be interested in such a wreck.

Performing in the choir led to an invitation to join the show choir. A full scholarship was offered and I jumped at the chance. The show choir had an elaborate stage show in a very

215

large auditorium built a few years before. We sang show tunes with little dances, funny skits, and sickening patriotic songs.

One day while practicing, a beautiful woman stood in front of me with long black hair (infused with natural coppery gold) and the body of Athena. She was long and tall at 5'9", with legs and hips that could knock out a man (or woman) at 100 yards. Now, there are not too many women who can dance with feeling and abandon so that they are so beautiful and mesmerizing lost in the sweep and momentum of their bodies, music, and feeling. This woman is one of those. I watched her dance and focused on the fluidity and suppleness with which she moved. When she swayed, I so wanted to touch her hips and hold on to them. She finally turned around and looked at me, and she was so stunningly beautiful I hesitated and I felt babbling brain syndrome coming on. Trying to think of something to say, I stuck with a compliment that I truly felt, even though I stole the line from Johnny Mercer: "Jeepers creepers! Where'd you get those peepers?" Her eyes being large orbs with sky blue iris and yellow/green perch bursting like the sun around her pupils. The shape of her lids turned them into a beautiful perfect almond shape; and when she smiled, a big beautiful inviting smile, it raised her cheeks and pinned her dimples and made her eyes so bright you could die happy right then if this were the last thing you ever saw. Her name? Julie, and she hit me like a bolt of lightning!

While I am a ravenous animal, I am not a psychopathic aggressive animal about sex. Making a woman uncomfortable wasn't in my makeup, or at least I didn't want it to be. Trying to stay calm, I talked to her more and more, and fantasized about her more and more. She found out that I ran everyday, and she asked if she could join me. We only ran a few miles on the indoor or outdoor tracks, and ran up and down stairs. When she wore shorts, she displayed the most beautiful legs you've ever seen.

216

The strong muscles moved back and forth under her skin like a ballet. Her calves she inherited from her dad, and they're rich and powerful. Her thigh muscles, powerhouses of sublime dance training. I loved looking at her legs, the exquisiteness heightened all interests.

As we ran we talked, about practically everything. When I found out she was currently involved with two other guys, I felt it best to stay back from throwing my hat in the ring. I would have to wait and see what happened, and show her respect. I wasn't planning to compete for love, I had a different idea of choice. So we became even closer platonic friends. She shared with me, and I shared with her. When I started dating a woman she knew, the heir to a local ice cream & dairy business, Julie seemed disappointed, but continued talking and asking about those dates.

Those dates weren't the best of events. This woman was a bit entitled. She had a very nice body, but she had a not so nice personality. I took her to a Sherrill Milnes concert, and during the break, as we talked by the hall windows, she told me I was "mumbling again". I said, "Excuse me?" She said, "You mumble all the time, and it's annoying". Strike 1 and 2. She was insistent that I come to her house, which I did. She made hot jello. I had never known anyone to drink hot jello, but it was also sugar jello. I was not big on sugar, and when she asked if I wanted some I politely said no (why not tea or coffee?). That didn't stop her, she insisted that I drink some and shoved a mug in my hands. We went into the living room and sat on the couch. She drank her jello and seemed annoyed (quite often) that I wouldn't drink mine. She then wanted to make out, and said I could stay the night. She had a very nice body, but she had on so much makeup covering her skin, it reminded me of my older sister. It was a real pre-Seinfeld moment. You could see makeup cracks going in every direction, and her attitude had fully turned my interest off. I just couldn't do this anymore with her. I excused myself telling

217

her I had to get up early for work, and got the hell out of there, feeling like I had just dodged a bullet.

Julie had no end of fun with this. She didn't hide her amusement or relief very well. It was then that I fully realized how much she was interested in me, but I just didn't want to interfere in relationships she had going, or get caught in a triangle or square of sorts. The show choir was picked to perform in Washington, DC for a banquet. Our sappy patriotic repertoire would blow them away. We stayed in double rooms, and during one night a man showed up at my door looking for Julie, he told me his name, and he was dressed to the hilt and carried a bouquet of flowers. This was one of the guys Julie spoke of being involved with. I took an immediate dislike to him, and probably treated him rudely. My roommate laughed at me and told me I was in love with Julie. He asked me why I hadn't asked her out, and I reiterated all the excuses. After the concert we all went to Georgetown to go to the bars. I was feeling out of sorts so I drank beer, after beer, after beer. Julie had me cut off, and I thought what fucking nerve! But I could tell she cared about me.

On the long bus ride home, Julie sat in the seat next to me. She put her legs up across mine, and I got the stiffest boner. I hoped she wouldn't notice, but she tended to grind at it with her calf. Even after going to the bathroom and returning, the boner wouldn't go away. It was a several hour bus ride and I had that stiffy the entire trip. I still wasn't sure how to handle this as the other men seemed to still be in the picture.

Things went on like this for some time, until the final concert of the season at the college music hall. There was an after party at a student's house. Midway through the night Julie approached me with glee and purpose in her eyes. She grabbed my hand and told me to follow her, she wanted to show me something. She took me into the bathroom and locked the door.

218

She took my hand and guided it between her legs, which I found to be extremely wet. We kissed and she undid my belt and pants and pulled them down, stroking my cock while trying to remove her own pants and underwear. She sat on the sink deck and her shirt was open exposing her breasts. They looked so beautiful and perky framed by her shirt. There were knocks on the door to use the bathroom, and we said just a minute, and then ignored them. It felt so good to be inside her, warm, inviting, and exciting. I asked about protection, she said not to worry, she was on the pill. Looking at her beautiful body and the zeal in her eyes made me thrust harder, and I came so hard I thought my organs were being sucked dry. We kissed and kissed and finally became cognizant of where we were and the knocks continuing at the door. When we came out of the bathroom people just stared with knowing and shocked looks.

After this, there was no holding back. I tried to be with her constantly. We fucked everywhere. We fucked in the fields, the park, the cars (wherever we could park them safely). We fucked on the music hall mezzanine entrance landing at the college. We were fucking in the car at the park after it was closed and a policeman stopped and checked what was going on. The windows were completely fogged and we scrambled to get our clothes on. We fucked in the cornfield entrances. We fucked in the field beside her house and I got poison ivy. We. Fucked. Everywhere!

I had fallen hard for her, her beauty, her camel toe, and her little quirks and characteristics endeared her to me. She would run and suddenly jump trot like a filly, especially when we crossed streets. When she talked, the end of her nose would bob up and down like a bunny rabbit. She would tell me how my touch was electric to her, and I held her hand whenever possible. She took a Shakespeare class performing A Midsummer Night's Dream, and fed me dewberries and love.

219

At some point I bought a new ten speed bike and road the 12 miles to her house to get her before school. She's not a morning person and she would stumble through the dark hall at her house with tattered pajamas, unlock the door, and let me hold her on the couch. We rode bikes to school and I sang to her. I was definitely in love. I wrote her bad poetry – praising her "melons of meat". I wrote love letters, expressing that the need to make love to her was like needing food, water, and air to breathe. We had the same thoughts. We finished each others sentences. We were best friends.

I wanted to propose to her, but couldn't without telling her something about my background. I sweated out many a night arguing with myself about whether or what I should tell her. *This was a living torment to me.* Right or wrong, I just couldn't talk about my sexuality; this was only 1984 and bisexuality was not considered "normal". I refused to take the chance, and I thought what would it matter anyway, I'd be married, permanently. This mistake would come back to haunt me. Also, right or wrong (wrong again), I couldn't bring myself to discuss my military service. I made up lies about what I did in the AF. The depression couldn't be hidden. She had already noticed how intense and depressed I could be. I told her about the oil rig and the hospitals, and then I told her Dad. I thought at one point I could talk with him about the military, as he had been a WW2 infantryman, but I chickened out and couldn't, so I stuck with the tale of depression. I just felt that if I told everything, it would be overwhelming and she would bolt, or her parents and sister would cause such a negative stir that we would be broken up. I didn't want to lose her… I couldn't lose her… and I stuck with the wrong decision. Wrong in the sense that she had a right to know all information, and wrong to let my fear get in the way of her deliberations.

For Julie's birthday, I bought an engagement ring with all the money I had, which wasn't much.

"Ain't got no money, but I sure got a whole lotta love…"

Ain't Got No Money – Bob Seger

I taped the ring in the bottom of a large shoe box and covered it with crumpled paper and wrapped it up. When she opened it, she finally saw the ring and looked surprised. With her Mother watching in horror, I got down on my knee and asked her to marry me. While I could practically hear her Mother behind me whispering No… No… No… Julie said yes, she would marry me, and she hugged me and told me she loved me. I felt relief and a happiness I hadn't known in quite some time.

In the months that followed before the wedding, we worked out differences of continuing school. I had been accepted to the Eastman School of Music in Rochester, NY. Julie had been accepted to Michigan State. This was a difficult thing for us to work out. MSU held nothing for me, but Julie insisted she needed the program there. She suggested that we could just continue a long-distance relationship. I was having none of that, as my previous experience with such told me it was a mistake of major proportions. I couldn't lose her and survive. I refused to lose her to a college degree. I told her I would go with her to MSU and we set the wedding for August.

We graduated from the community college with honors. We both signed up for MSU with transfer credits giving us two years completed. In late-summer I filled out an application for married student housing in Spartan Village, and we would move in when school started. The wedding planning was causing no end of problems with Julie's parents and her sister. Her parents

221

were against her marrying me, her father even offered to buy her a car if she refused to marry me. Her sister was/is a controlling, evil, manipulative bitch from the 7th circle of Hell. She whispered in the parents' ears constantly, stirring up animosity and trouble. A few weeks before the wedding I came over to get Julie, and I was in a really good mood. I entered the side door and called out hi. Her mother entered the kitchen area and shouted at me, "This is all *your* fault!" Then the sister entered the kitchen from the living room and told me I should get out, which I wasn't about to do. Taking force into her own hands, she attacked me and scratched my face with her claws. I threw her down across the room into the kitchen table and she landed on the floor. I told her if she got up I'd knock her on her ass again. Julie came from the living room crying uncontrollably. I wasn't sure what they had been doing to her, but it was obviously a gang attack. I took Julie out and got her in my car. Her Dad followed her out ordering her to stay and tried reaching in the window to grab her. I took her to her brother's house and she stayed there. Details of the wedding were finally worked out, even if feelings were not worked out. We married in the front yard of her parents house with stone cold faces surrounding us. My cousin played his trumpet and we had a pig roast. That night we left to start our life.

Married Life, Children, Problems, and Renewal

Julie and I have been married for almost 38 years, and we've *known* each other for almost 39. Through that time the effects of PTSD, especially anger, have wreaked havoc upon us. I have been severally triggered by bosses, ignorance, failures, and more. There have been repeated attempts to die, hospitalizations, every antidepressant known, antipsychotics to deal with dissociations, violence, failure to perform sexually due to the medications, and failure to have sex due to other factors of Julie's that will be revealed ahead.

Julie has stuck by my side through all these things. I've attempted very hard at times to drive her away, because the urge to die would become overwhelming. In the late '90s I became so sunken in depression, like I was drowning, or I was in a deep muddy pit with no way to climb out. The nightmares of killing had become once again an intense nightly affair.

The dreams *qua* nightmares started slightly before military separation. There is always the blood, gallons and gallons. Begging and pleading faces. Sudden stoppage of life force. There are extreme looks of surprise as my knife enters a back, throat, or brain. There is the savage bull ride of the cartel guard. There is always the woman with a knife in her heart whispering "Baby!" as she fades into oblivion. There is the husband checking her with a sinking despair in his voice before my knife enters his liver, and he too succumbs to death. There are the thousands of bodies blown to shreds, or with gaping, burning holes passing all the way through them, some of them still

223

breathing in pain beyond your comprehension. There are the dashed hopes of those who thought they had escaped only to be tracked down and shot. There is a baby no longer with a mother to love and care for it. There is a choking smell of blood suffocating me as I sleep. There is running and running so that I wake up exhausted like I'm still in the field.

Years ago, Julie would begin to wonder why I didn't come to bed. I would make pots of coffee deep into the morning; I would do anything to stay awake until I passed out because I didn't want to face the dreams, the feelings, the craziness. Julie had been the recipient of kicking, punching, knifing, and running in my sleep. She once again took me to the VA after bouncing around psychiatrists that I refused to talk with, because I just couldn't trust them. The result, meeting with their psychiatrist was the exact same as before, with the same rudeness and disdain. He refused to listen at all.

The failure of the psych appointments, medications, my guilt and shame took a toll on me. It also took a toll on me what I was doing to Julie. I felt that I had destroyed her life. I had also had a deleterious effect on our son. He absorbed guilt for my problems. Once, when he was 13 and having some growing problems, I sat with him at the kitchen table to discuss solutions. The nature of the problems seemed related to the type of mindset that got me off track with the military. I tried telling him there were things I did in the military that I wasn't proud of, and which left a lifetime of regret within me. I was going to lay it out for him, and Julie was standing there listening, and I thought now's the time. But as I looked at his innocent little face, I realized one important thing about him – he was the type to try and outdo me in whatever I had done. Words started choking in my throat. In the end, there was no way I could tell him this information, and I left him with the lame, "I've done a lot of things I'm not proud of." I knew this decision couldn't stand. It felt like a mistake immediately, and proved to be so.

It amazes me how a trained killer can be so bad at killing himself. As children are born you feel more guilt over the act. Sometimes you start to think about it even as you're trying to change and stay alive. When we were living in Salt Lake I had a job as the swing shift clerk at a gas station. The owner was an ex-cop and he kept a chrome plated 9mm semi-automatic pistol under the counter. He asked me if I knew how to use it, and I answered I did. He said not to be afraid to use it if necessary. That evening when it was slow, I pulled out the pistol and popped the clip and removed the slide to look. I took it apart, examined it, and put it back together in seconds and loaded a round into the chamber. I realized how smooth and easy it felt to me, and how easy it would be to blow my brains out then. I thought of Julie and our son and cried, and I popped the clip again, emptied the chamber, and put the gun back under the counter. This weapon was too tempting for me. I left a note at the end of my shift explaining that I couldn't work there anymore, because I knew if I did, I would be dead or I may kill someone else – and that scared me more than dying myself.

Mentioning our son reminded me of when he was born in 1989. He was conceived in our Chicago apartment in love in the cold of late fall. Julie had been to a conference in another state, and returned via a ride from my sister. I so looked forward to seeing her. When they arrived, my sister went to sit in the living room, and when Julie came in she pinned me against the wall in the entrance hall. She lifted our shirts and she kissed me with desire and rubbed her chest against mine. I said, "I think you missed me", and she said, "I guess so." We went to bed that night eager to recharge our love, and we did. Sometimes we came so hard that our backbones would shudder and slide. This was one

225

of those times, when you think there's a baby in that cum racing for the egg.

It wasn't planned but it was welcome and exciting. Julie had previously had a miscarriage and took awhile to recover from that emotionally. Julie could no longer eat our favorite food, pizza, but she ate the Chicagoland area out of watermelons. It was an extremely hot and humid Chicago summer. I saw the blood on my hands regularly. Julie looked like she was going to explode, and she would come over frequently to see me at work. It was very difficult to maintain a conversation while thinking about blood on my hands. Somehow this transformed in my brain to I felt myself to be a monster. Then I thought, what if my son has my genes, and what if he's a monster like me. I talked to Julie about this, but of course she had no clue what I was talking about, and it probably scared her. One day one of the contractors found me behind the building where I worked crying. He asked me what was wrong, and I said I couldn't help the feeling that my son would be like me, and be a monster. He had no clue what I was talking about, but he tried to make me feel better. I cried incessantly over this, but remained sane for Julie and our boy. When he was born I was there, and falling in love with him immediately put my fears to rest. Julie had gone through hell with this birth. The boy was 22 inches and 11.5lbs. The placenta was huge and weighed as much as he did. The "doctor" hurried her through labor because he wanted to go play golf, and he gave her an episiotomy, cutting through her sphincter muscle leaving her with problems to be corrected by a real doctor years later. She and I have complained about the "doctor", but never about the love producing a 6'3" strong carpenter and hockey player.

After the VA fiasco, I became depressed to an extreme degree. The pain in my heart and my head I found too hard to deal with anymore. I was still sure I could tell no one. When Julie went to the school with our son, I started drinking for pain relief, because I was going to cut my wrist. I sat on the closed-in porch and sliced length wise, because I had read this was the way to do it. The blood seemed slow, so I cut across as well. Still the blood seemed slow, so I used some wire snips and stared cutting through every vain I could see. The blood flowed much better now, and I had lost a lot on the floor rug and was getting light headed. I wasn't paying too good attention, and the event was taking too long, and Julie pulled in with our son. They found me on the porch and called 911. A community paramedic arrived first, and while he talked with Julie I ran out the front down the street. I was so dizzy then and out of breath and he caught me ¾ of the way down the street. His partner brought the ambulance down and he put me in the back and tried to apply pressure on the wound, so I started pumping my hand to force out more blood. He yelled at me to stop, but I continued even as he tried forcing me to stop. I kept pumping my hand and then my other one for solidarity, then he yelled at me, "If you don't stop that it'll be the last thing you ever do!" I thought this so ironically funny, and then I passed out. They sewed everything back up, but I can still look at the scars to remind me.

Our second son was born in 2001. Years before I had had a dream about his birth. Julie was in an all stainless steel operating room, and there were electric blue, green, and red lights shining off the stainless steel, a beautiful scene with the colors and the feeling was joyful and loving. This son was conceived while Julie was playing hockey on a women's team. She had lost weight and tightened into looking like Audrey Hepburn. There was a tournament on the far side of the state, and we stayed in a hotel room. She looked so beautiful and she was aggressively horny. There was a mirror beside the bed, and we both watched as she rode on top of me, grinding, and we came together; again with the kind of power that let's you know something has happened. He was somewhat planned. We had had trouble with fertility for some time, and we both remember this night with delight. Looking at this boy, now a strong 6'5" man, we are thankful for the love that produced him.

There were other events and other psychiatrists. At one point I became very uncommunicative, and had the affect of a drooling vegetable. I didn't want to eat anymore, it made me feel guilty. In a lucid moment with the psychiatrist I asked about ECT. It scared the hell out of me, but I wanted to get better for Julie. We set up an appointment with a very caring doctor at a hospital, and he talked us through it, and we said, yes, let's go. He applied 17 sessions of ECT, and my brain did begin to reset. When I told Julie after a session that I was hungry, she cried.

But yet another time I was feeling the guilt and shame again, and feeling very alone in my secrets. My little brother who had died of SIDS, was buried in a cemetery close to where we lived. I felt at the time that I should have died and he should have lived. I really felt that I shouldn't be alive. The ideas you come up with in the mist of depression can be nonsensical, yet they may seem perfectly sensible to you. I had lithium and antidepressants at the time, and drove to his grave and swallowed them all with booze – I was sure I would be gone.

When I awoke in the hospital I was strapped to my bed and the intubation tube was still down my throat. They had told Julie they did all they could do, and they were just waiting to see if I would wake up. Julie came to see me and I wouldn't look at her, partly because I felt so ashamed, and partly because I blamed her for saving me. I know it sounds stupid, but that's how fucked up your thinking can get. Throughout treatment I played whatever game I had to in order to get out. Lucky(?) for me insurance has strict limits on who's going to stay and for how long. When we arrived home again my anger grew toward Julie for just not letting me die. We ended up fighting and I threw her on the bed and told her I was going to kill her, and I choked her hard. Our son yelled and told me to stop, but I wasn't listening. I saw Julie right then only as a threat. But then I truly saw her and relented. She has forgiven me, but I will never forgive myself. The knowledge that I could kill someone, outside the theater of battle, is as bad as any event which had caused PTSD in the first place. I can still see her face pleading with me. This is absolutely the lowest and most painful point of my life. It is the event which gives me the most pain – and there have been so many of them. At this time she still had no idea what had happened to me.

I decided to try and attack my PTSD in a different way. Immediately after military separation I had tried to deny my own guilt. Even though I knew better, I tried convincing myself I wasn't at fault. Later I tried convincing myself that none of it ever happened; yet at the same time, I was working oppositely by writing letter after letter to AFSOC and others on open channels attempting to retrieve my records, because I started to question myself and what I knew to be true, and I wanted to piece together a period in my life that seemed like a whirlwind of activity and confusion. I changed my diet dramatically and began walking more, which was at least as effective as the medications which I quit taking.

We were trying to have another baby. We were again seeing a fertility doctor and we fucked like rabbits, constantly. We both felt desperate, we both felt like we were broken physically. We poured our emotions and love into our sex and in the summer of 2004 our first daughter was conceived. She was born in 2005 and I had never seen anything so beautiful associated with me to that point. I couldn't fathom that I could help produce something so wonderful and beautiful. She was the easiest birth for Julie, and for months after she had cute little pointed elf ears. She's proud to point out now that she is above average for height as she had spent so long listed as average in height. Her intellect has always been above average, and she tears through schoolwork like a hot knife through butter. She is intensely ready to take on the world.

As the anniversary of killing of the couple approached in 2007, I devised a plan to try and get the couple returned to their families so they would finally know what happened to them. I obtained the email address of the Salvadoran embassy in Washington. Utilizing Cypherpunk chain remailers, I sent an email of explanation along with a pdf map of where the bodies were buried. It tore me up every August that no one knew where they were or what had happened to them. I heard nothing about this email until 2021.

Although the dreams never stopped, they occurred every night, my brain seemed to gain better control over them. I started working out intensely almost every day, and then started lifting weights. I felt better emotionally and I felt stronger, but I admit I tended to get obsessive about the workouts. But I really was feeling well and strong, regardless of the dreams and guilt. A big turning point came for me when I decided to stop denying what I had done, and accepted it and the guilt for my part – this was 32 years after the fact.

In 2009, my body was feeling well, and my mind was driven to seek physical love with Julie. Julie had kept her figure through all the years. She's always worked hard and plans to live to 100. We had thought that our baby making days were over, so we made love with abandon several times per week. I ate her, she ate me. A favorite was finger fucking her from the side while fucking her mouth, and when she came, I came in her mouth. We fucked and screwed in every position imaginable... and then we got a surprise. At 44 Julie was pregnant. Our last child, our daughter of joy was born. She is a joyful child, even as she starts teen years. Her wit is only exceeded by her beauty, and a lucky man, woman, or X is going to have their hands full someday.

Without the love of Julie, and without the added love of our children, I wouldn't be alive today. We lifted weights together and Julie pulled a 315lb deadlift. At 55 I bested at a 555lb double for a deadlift, and a 455lb double on full squats. Then psoriatic arthritis hit me hard, and Julie's rheumatoid arthritis was hitting her. We walked more. My problems, which Julie knew nothing about, had caused problems for our marriage, and Julie had problems to which I wasn't yet privy. We started attending Marriage Matters classes to help us work through things. The biggest thing to come from those classes was sharing thoughts and emotions. As we walked many items of dissension started to come out, as well as items that caused dissension.

About 58-1/2 the dreams started increasing in intensity again. I felt an intense need to evaluate what my life had become, and how it had become what it was. I needed to understand better the 2-1/2 years of my early life that seemed to take 40 years away from me. I began writing letters again through open channels (from which I had never obtained an answer), but this time I took a chance and started openly talking about classified missions and names. I received a reply from a Colonel in AFSOC basically telling me to shut-up, and that he was forwarding my letter to the Office of the Director of National Intelligence. I waited to hear from them.

In the mean-time, Julie and I continued walking and talking, and I decided I no longer could, or wanted to, keep from her what I should have told her years ago. I told her about my past sexual experiences, a little at a time, but with each new revelation Julie shuddered. I told her about Kit, and this probably made her the most angry, because she had specifically asked if I had ever wanted to marry anyone else, and I lied. I started telling her about the military work, the killings, etc...

I spent a good two years in total meltdown over Kit and the military killings. I thought I would never meet another who was suited to me... until I met Julie. And from this past occurs three of the biggest blunders I have ever made with Julie:

1) Because of the previous failed relationship and my inability to process it properly I was reluctant to tell Julie enough times how much I loved her, how at times I felt I would burst with the love I felt for her, how at times I cried alone with relief that she was there in my life... Idiot that I was/am, I didn't want to jinx it!?!

2) I lied to Julie then about having any relationships, what they involved, how many, etc... I didn't open up to her about these until last year. The reasoning doesn't matter, even if I convinced myself at the time it made sense; and, as time passed, the criticality of the mistake grew and overwhelmed the reasoning as bullshit. I shouldn't have kept this from her. I should have let her make her own decision with all information. Now it's more shame and guilt while attempting to calm and gain back her trust about telling her things of which she already was suspect.

3) I also lied to Julie about my military service. While she would be kind enough even now to say I may not have felt I had a choice, the same applies from above – she had the right to all information and the right to make her choice based on all information. Over the last six months I've come to regret not telling her about the service in a very profound and deep way. Again, there simply is no excuse, other than self-servicing, that

232

explains my not telling her. I've caused severe pain in her life from this, and she had no way to comprehend. I've stolen her choices and years from her life out of selfishness. Worst of all, I let her, just like our son, believe that she was the cause of my suffering and problems... and I never wanted that.

We continued talking, and I told her about writing the letters asking for and demanding information. She asked why this was important now, and I told her that even after 40+ years, the problems associated with the events still troubled me greatly. I don't feel shame or guilt over any sexual activity I've participated in (quite the contrary), but I feel extremely shameful and guilty for not talking to Julie honestly about it when she asked – and she did ask directly. The killings, no matter what anyone tells me, or tries to help excuse for me, I am responsible for directly and, in part, generally. There was always a choice, and I made the wrong ones. The sadness, regret, shame, and guilt will always be there. That I lied to Julie about this oh-so-many years ago, and allowed her and our oldest to grow any amount of years thinking they had caused my pain... gives me such pain and guilt!

Last year the letter from the ODNI was received (redacted for compliance). After receiving this letter the puzzle pieces started flying automatically into place at warp speed...

Office of the Director of National Intelligence

From: ████████ dni.gov

05 May 2021 0947

Mr. ████████ (████):

My name is ████ ████ ████████ ████ for ████████ ████████ All of your request(s) have been forwarded to me for disposition. Since 2005 you have submitted 10 requests for records. Too many requests for classified records brought up red flags, and we felt it best, after reviewing your requests, to handle all of this through a single office.

As you know, your work involved classified operations for at least three different intelligence agencies. These agencies have requested that all material involving those operations remain classified, which includes your work. All classified material is maintained classified originally for 50 years. The operations you were involved in would normally not be unclassified until 2030-2035. However, at the urging of then Vice President Biden, former President Barack Obama doubled the classification time of Central American operations and Operation Eagle Claw until 2085, at which time the then current executive and staff will review the material and determine whether declassification of the material is warranted.

While we sympathize with your difficulties in obtaining VA assistance, these materials and information are unavailable to them normally as release waivers are required through properly authorized channels that the VA itself must initialize. Simply tell them classified records are involved. Upon review redacted and relevant material may be provided directly to them.

The issue of your DD-214 is a closed matter. Again, while we sympathize with your inability to make use of that edited document, you will see below that it was the result of a compromise to provide you with an honorable discharge yet satisfy the the Command's need to "punish" you for what they deemed "betrayal of force structure". No amount of pressure will get the military to correct the document.

However, after reviewing your records, the debriefing records, and the associated CIA and DoDIA operational records, a team in this office (including a psychologist) have determined that you were punished far too severely and may have PTSD related to your assignments. While changing records is beyond the scope of this office (you may always appeal directly to the Office of the President), we have been authorized to provide you with some information concerning your unedited records, to answer a few of your pressing questions, and hopefully provide you with some closure in an operation that seems to bother you.

Records indicate you were awarded the Air Force Cross, 2 Silver Stars, 4 Bronze Stars, Defense Superior Service Medal, AF Good Conduct Medal, the CIA Distinguished Service Medal, as well as various other ribbons and awards. You were credited with eliminating over 300 enemy combatants (117 confirmed). These stunning achievements are born out of 18 combat assignments involving 14 operations, all of which were completed successfully, excepting Eagle Claw which failed due to human error of other personnel. All of these awards (excepting the CIA medal) were revoked upon your military separation. This was part of the compromise which allowed you to have an honorable discharge. More drastic measures were contemplated, yet the former 1st SOW chaplain intervened forcefully on your behalf as he was convinced you were having a sincere crisis of conscious. You were left with your Marksman ribbon "to remind him of who he really is" (Major ███████████). While you had friendly support from the Wing and SOS commanders, Major ██████ was your program commander and he pushed for maximum punishment.

Your account and observations about Operation Eagle Claw are all correct. Limited information was declassified and released publicly. Major ██████████ was never on the ground in Iran, but he was well connected politically and was able to make claims and assertions without repercussions. Others soon followed and the multitude of stories and "first-hand" accounts by persons not there has flourished. There have been too many spreaders of disinformation, false names and narratives, but this actually serves the US interest in protecting still classified information, including your own, which serves the safety of yourself and others.

The following account (without location or names) is provided to you from debriefing records, operation records, and other sources. We hope this will give you some closure to an obviously distressing event in your life. In August 1981 you returned from a foreign mission and were debriefed in detail.

You were ordered to infiltrate an enemy mountain camp location and destroy their weapons cache and a stolen UH-1 helicopter which rebels had converted into a gunship, and destroy obvious personnel quarters. You were dropped 12.67km from the camp and traveled by foot on goat paths to a secure blind outside the camp. At 2215 you approached the camp and attached RC detonation explosives to the helicopter, weapons caches, and a personnel building. You returned to the blind and detonated the explosives, ensuring that the targets had been destroyed.

As you were leaving to return along the same path, you noticed the arrival of additional rebel personnel. They spread out in pairs for search in different directions and two were headed in your direction. You immediately left the area but the two rebels picked up your tracks and continued to follow you for approximately 5km.

At this time you realized that anyone who could track that well at night would follow you to your extraction point (the same drop zone) which may expose yourself and extraction personnel to a firefight. You also evaluated your orders that no evidence of US involvement could be left behind, and you felt your only option was to eliminate the following rebels. At the side of the path was a large tree. You split the side bark with your knife and pried it out enough to peer through and placed a trip wire across the path. When the first rebel tripped you sprang out and put your knife into the chest of a woman. It was clean shot to her heart and she died almost instantly, though you said she whispered "baby" clearly.

You removed the trip wire and propped her body against the tree as though she were resting. Having observed that they whistled for each other from time to time for conference, you gave three short whistles and hid behind a bush on the opposite side of the path. The second rebel approached and squatted down talking to the dead partner (checking her) and you emerged and drove your knife into his back with a twist. He died quickly without speaking. Concerned that the bodies may be discovered, you took infrared photos of the bodies and documents in their possession. You then dug a single grave off the path and buried them with their weapons.

235

After this you hurried to extraction and returned to your US base. In debrief you indicated the woman's last word, that the names on identification indicated the two were married, and she either had a baby left behind or she was pregnant. There was a heated argument with the Lt conducting the debriefing which ended in expletives.

There is a conclusion to this. In August 2007 an untraceable email with pdf image attached was sent to the consulate of the foreign country involved. This communication contained details of the incident without revealing responsible parties. The pdf image was a map showing where the bodies were buried. The State Department was called in and attended the exhumation and autopsies. The bodies were that of two rebels, man and wife, 28 and 26 at time of death. The woman died of a single stab wound to the heart, and the man died of a single rotary (commando) knife wound which tore the liver. The woman was approximately 45 days pregnant, and the CIA liason reported that the bodies had been buried with extreme care, side by side, with adjacent hands placed in a clasp. Though the CIA was sure who must have sent the email, the US Ambassador was overcome and a standing order was issued by the State Department that no action be considered or taken. The bodies were returned to their families for burial.

All reviews (AFSOC, CIA, SEAL Commander, DoS) declared you had no other options under your strict operational orders. The SEAL Commander stated that it would have been virtually impossible to take two prisoners alone and get back for extraction safely. Simply, you had no other choice.

You stated a feeling that all your assignments seemed like a whirlwind of intense activity, and indeed they were. Our psychologist feels you were not given adequate time or assistance to deal with these issues. We encourage you to seek assistance from a licensed psychologist utilizing your ███████████ plan to further work through these issues.

As I said, no amount of pressure will get the military to change records such as this, but we felt compelled to at least place a request to have original awards placed on the DD-214 and remove the negative monikers "Apathy" and "Defective Attitude" which we feel were unfairly applied. Honestly however, they are just going to ignore it and deny any punishment outside the authority of the UCMJ. Further, the military and political offices are filled with idealogues who still hold fast to old beliefs concerning Communism and its threats, and they are unlikely to look favorably upon your record after the point of conscientious objection.

Your record was exemplary, filled with intelligent decisions and planning, and only terminated by your objecting to unbalanced support of right wing governments. However, the point of reiterating these events and citations to you is to reassure you that you did indeed participate significantly and made the best possible outcomes from difficult situations. Some of your work contributed to a reduction in lives lost. In January 1981 you planned and successfully completed a mission to retrieve avionics equipment from a foreign military aircraft located on a foreign base. Data from that equipment helped the State Department in halting weapons and ammunition deliveries to rebels. The successful tactics which you developed have been used in training intelligence operatives in many agencies.

Your observations about the longevity of the Scout Program were correct. Scouts were to be a special operations replacement of Forward Air Controller and Forward Observer roles that dated from WW2 through Vietnam. AFSOC wanted to expand the role with the idea that individuals would act where SEAL or Ranger teams could not effectively operate. You were 1 of 6 in the program commanded by Major ███████. The 3 senior NCOs were mainly involved in training foreign troops. TSgt ███████ who initially trained you, died in late 1981 in an automobile accident. SSgt ███████

████ was called into your role when you left, and he was killed during his first mission in the new area. With this death the program was re-evaluated and was found to be outside the scope of AF ground personnel. New advancements in optics and technology, followed by the advancement of drone technology allowed much of the same capabilities while keeping personnel out of harm's way. The remaining senior program members were reassigned and the program shut down.

This is all this office is able to assist you with given the classified nature of material information. We will not be able to answer further inquiries, but as noted you may make direct appeal to the Office of the President at any time.

Your answer to whether you may write a book account of your activities is yes, with the exceptions that:

1) You may not use your own name or the actual name(s) of any personnel - military, governmental, or civilian;

2) You may not use actual Operation names;

3) You may not use actual operational locations;

4) The account should appear to be fictional.

This Office thanks you for your service and wishes you success.

Sincerely,

/// ████ ████ ███ ///

, ODNI
ODNI ████

Uncaged And Making Amends

But I'm gonna break
I'm gonna break my
I'm gonna break my rusty cage and run

Rusty Cage – Soundgarden

Having finally told Julie about my bisexuality, I felt like I had been released from an old rusty cage. It did cause problems between us for awhile, mostly because I had lied and hadn't told her sooner, but also because people who find out their SO is bisexual immediately go through a period where they think they aren't enough for their partner, and suddenly they feel like they are competing with another half of the human race. It takes time to think through, talk, and understand this, but with reassurance, it can calm down and make a richer marriage.

Having unloaded all of these things to Julie, I sensed a stirring related to other problems in her own past and behavior. She finally told me that when she was four, her mother had sexually assaulted her; and, on top of that trauma she had been raped at 18 by a psychopathic football player named Curtis The Rapist from M_____ Center, and he had been extra vicious in his attack, tying her up and forcing objects into her; telling her how much she deserved it and how much he knew she wanted it. Curtis The Rapist made sure to express forcefully that she deserved it and if she ever opened her mouth to anyone, he would track her down and get her. He left her tied up in an equipment

238

room at the school and she had to free herself and find a way home (miles away). She never told anyone or reported it because she felt shame, like it was her fault; and, she thought her dad would kill the boy and end up in prison.

I behaved very badly at first. I just didn't want this to have happened to her. I hate her mother but I just didn't want to think her capable of this. The more I thought about Curtis, the more I wanted to kill him, in the most violent and vicious manner possible. I said as much and this scared Julie half to death. I needed to get off that horse before I committed myself and Julie to consequences. Julie had kept this secret for as long as I had kept mine. Over the years she has worked relentlessly on pulling herself out of the hate and madness produced by these traumas. She dealt with her own traumas at the same time as trying to help me with she knew not what, until now. But Curtis must now know that his secret is exposed; that the psychopathic perverted cunt he is is known by many. Poor stupid Curtis; "revenge is a dish best served cold" (a timeless Pashtun proverb).

Having the ODNI letter in hand, I decided to come clean with my kids (except for the youngest – not yet). To Julie and the oldest, I felt compelled to explain that the years of depression, anger, and suicide attempts had nothing to do with them – that they did not cause my problems or pain. I know they grew thinking they were at fault somehow for my own problems. I needed to apologize in the most sincere way, to both of them. I made copies of the letter and sat down with Julie and the three oldest. I asked them to read the letter first, then I explained the whole ordeal from beginning to the present. Discussing these things openly is very painful – I still can't talk about those events without tears, but I needed them to understand the quality and quantity of the events. I apologized to all, but I stressed apologies to Julie and the oldest. I told them I was so sorry for having allowed them to feel that any of it was their fault. I told them I hadn't told anyone these details since leaving the military. Some people you just can't trust, and some people you feel too much fear over releasing the information to them. Some people live in ignorance no matter what you tell them. Some people listen to what you say, feel the pain, yet revel in the killing (virgins talking about sex). The letter spelled out my direct kills, but it failed to mention that I had planned and help execute gunship missions where over 5000 people were slaughtered. I told my family I would have guilt, shame, and sadness over these lives for the rest of my own life – it is something I had accepted as true. The oldest thanked me and hugged me. He said things made sense now. Our relationship has improved. Julie and I started seeing a counselor to work through all the revelations and feelings they produced; it hasn't been easy, but we continue to work at it – and we continue to love each other emotionally and physically.

The other part of making amends is putting this in writing. It took over 40 years of pain and suffering, the guilt of decades, and the powers of aging, to decay and release the locks which held this in. I'm not like my wife, I can't forgive those who aren't sorry for what they have done, caused, or the havoc they have wreaked. I can't forgive the lying Presidents, every lying and ignorant politician, zealots of any religion or ideology. I can't forgive ignorant or unfeeling military commanders, the CIA, the DoDIA. I especially can't forgive people like Truman, Eisenhower, Kennedy, Johnson, Nixon, Carter, Reagan, Bush Sr, Clinton, Bush Jr, Obama, Trump, or *especially* Joe Biden. The others had their short moments in history, but Biden has worked relentlessly behind the scenes since the early '70s manipulating imperial foreign policy. How many young men and women have died dancing to the tune of a piper who has never participated in or experienced war as a soldier?

Lies And Damned Lies

While it is true that "I don't know what I don't know",
it is also true that once I do know, if I turn a blind eye
or fail to act I am guilty of committing the sin of
ignorance upon myself and my fellow men.

– Juan Idalgo

Not long ago I saw an Air Force recruiting commercial. A black general sits on a chair inside a hanger pontificating in an excited, deep growling voice that when pilots put on their helmets and visors, it doesn't matter whether they're black, white, red, yellow, brown, etc…, they are all just "kicking ass" in a multicultural love fest. Wouldn't all you young people with nothing better to do with your lives like to kick ass in respect and love, just like in a video game?

Three things about this made me cringe. 1) Pilots (men and women) may not care if the pilot next to them is another color, but they sure as hell don't care that many of their victims are brown or black or yellow – towel heads, inferior races, enemies of freedom and democracy, etc… 2) The days of gun blazing aerial dog fights are long gone. In the age of faster jets and turbofans, the biggest threat to a pilot is radar guided or heat seeking missiles. They fly high and fast and are able to destroy a target from miles away, even from outside the battle zone. They are removed from close combat and feel no guilt over killing, and they revel in "kicking ass" from miles away. A drone pilot on the other hand may actually view the faces of those they kill from high definition cameras, and for them guilt does happen. This

241

may also happen with close air support pilots (A-10 and attack helicopters), but to a lesser degree. But for the most part, guilt for meting out unjust death is not in the pilot's vocabulary. 3) They are specifically reaching out to a generation of young people who have grown up playing video games, and those kids ignorantly think that is what combat is like, and the asshole general knows this and plays upon it.

Lt Col Dave Grossman, an Army psychologist, the same who posited killing being akin to sex, has blamed violent video games for creating young people who are immune to feeling guilt about killing. But once again he misunderstands the problem and dynamics. He also blames commercial interests for the production of these violent video games, and here he misses the whole truth. Young people play those games for the entertainment value – they have **no** idea what real killing involves; what causes the problem is that they don't cogitate that real combat involves real pain, real suffering, and real death – there is no computer generated rebirth – and they are truly ignorant of the real consequences of battlefield actions until it's too late. The US military has no incentive to disabuse them of their ignorance before signing them on. Further, *the production of these types of video games is not solely commercial*. The US military invests money in these types of games, and they even produce free versions that can be downloaded and/or played from their websites – realistic battle without realistic death and destruction. The Army, Navy, and Air Force are as much a player in the video game, entertainment, movie, and TV industries as any commercial entity.

Women as well suck up the false narratives. If you follow TV and movie trends, you'll see the completely false narrative that women have been involved in combat and special operations since 9/11, wielding knives, automatic weapons, and *krav maga* all over the Middle East for decades. The media, from news to entertainment, enable and perpetuate these falsehoods. The truth of the matter is that no established force utilizes women in the field for close or front line combat (including the Israelis) – and this has nothing to do with chauvinism, and a lot to do with the fact that women just don't want to involve themselves in war until they've been programmed to want it – and yet, they still suck at it. Women in rebel forces often participate in front line combat, but that's more due to a desperate need than a want or skill – they still suck at it. Women have been allowed to become Navy SEALS since 2016, yet no woman participates in that front line combat. In Afghanistan, the US Army attempted an all woman unit (trained to a lower standard than men because they couldn't carry the weight nor meet the physical requirements) searching for weapons and conducting house to house searches. The experiment had to be terminated early because they were firing at each other and shooting friendlies, because they were operating in panic mode. The fact is the overwhelming majority of women *choose* not to participate in direct proportion to the amount of combat going on at the time (Judith Stiehm, <u>Arms and the Enlisted Woman</u>, Philadelphia, Temple University Press, 1989, p100; *Newsweek*, 5.8.991; and Laura Miller, "Feminism and the Exclusion of Army Women from Combat", Harvard University, John M Olin Institute for Strategic Studies, 1997-8, p19; all in <u>The Privileged Sex</u> by Martin van Creveld). Why is this relevant? Because it has been said that "war is a man's thing" (I had a woman therapist say this to me), and war represents "toxic masculinity". Because women are susceptible to the same lies fed to men regarding glory in war, of which there is none. In an insidious twist, many of the lies specifically fed to women don't come from the military, or from men, but from other women – feminists, Karens (who may threaten to throat punch you), and heartless revenge seekers. The US feminist group, National Organization for Women (NOW), wants women to be drafted, yet not a single woman of NOW has ever faced combat, close or far away, nor will they ever. They are a privileged class of women, like virgins talking about sex, trying to steal more privilege and power at the expense of lower class women who will pay for it supremely. Women's groups pushed to continue war in Afghanistan, for the purpose of "saving" Afghan women. Though never having to face combat or put their own lives on the line, they've decided that they are willing to sacrifice the lives of any amount of men and civilians to achieve their political and/or social power goals – *and not by asking, but by lobbying the halls of power to force the involvement of men.* "The road to women's privilege is paved with the corpses of men... In regard to the way they are raised, the work they do, the economic support they receive, and their position *vis-a-vis* the law, women have always enjoyed and still enjoy considerable privileges. Likewise, when it comes to fulfilling their obligation to society, women have enjoyed and still enjoy considerable privileges. The greatest single privilege is that they are hardly ever expected to shed blood for their people." (*In the Maw of Mars: The Principle of the Thing*, The Privileged Sex by Martin van Creveld, 2013, DVLC Enterprises).

Then there are the revenge seekers like Madeline Albright, ready and willing to sacrifice any amount of men and civilians ("500,000"+) in order to "free" Bosnia and fuck the Russian menace. There was Margaret Thatcher, ready and willing to sacrifice any amount of men and civilians to force a country to give back its own island. There was Golda Meir, ready and willing to sacrifice any amount of Palestinian men, women, and children via genocide and expulsion to the greater glory of the return of the Israeli kingdom (stolen from the inhabitants now and centuries ago). Recently, there are Marjorie Taylor Greene, Ginnie Thomas (yes, the Supreme Court justice's wife), Lauren Boebert, Marine La Pen, and Trumpettes – psychobitches from Donald Trump's harem of loony women, ready and willing to start Civil War. War and its causes truly know no boundaries of sex. Ignorance, greed, and the lust for power abounds in men and women. So no, war is not a "man's thing".

But the worst perpetrators of injustice have been US Presidents and business and international colonial powers. The Monroe Doctrine unilaterally made the US the policemen of the western hemisphere. The doctrine of Eminent Domain allowed Americans to fool themselves into thinking they had supernatural rights to other peoples' lives and land. The US fought Mexico for control of Texas under the same pretext that Putin is using now to attempt control of Ukraine. McKinley started war with Spain over Cuba, creating a false flag with the Maine explosion to force conflict when *Spain had already acceded to all US demands.* A US fleet battled the Spanish fleet in the Philippines and defeated them. While the US ceded Cuba its freedom, we decided to "keep" the Philippines for colonial purposes, including coconut plantations. US Marines and volunteers, trained at the Presidio, slaughtered thousands of Filipinos for the glory of capitalism, egged on by the British and French wanting, *needing,* the US to take its place on the world colonial stage.

A thorough reading of history (read The Long Fuse by Lawrence LaFore) will show the French instigated WW1, attempting to play both sides and to appear as Russia's friend, while attempting to control Alsace-Lorraine. The US became involved when the Germans, who Roosevelt and Wilson ironically disliked because of the Prussian military bearing, invaded after the French forced a mobilization of Russian and German forces and the French and English whined and complained. The war had caused the outbreak of civil war in Russia and the birth of false communism and then Stalinism. When the war was over, the French instigated and demanded the harsh terms upon the Germans which practically gave birth to Hitler.

After the bitter fighting of WW2, the world saw Stalinism as communism. They weren't even close in meaning or effect, but the cold war was on. Soon communism would be used as an excuse for interventions everywhere. Korea was a fairly easy sell to Americans unable to read subtext and thinking we were stamping out evil – a continuation of WW2. Vietnam was a harder sell after the losses in Korea. The Dulles brothers (John Foster and Allen) perpetuated the hegemony of US power around the globe. John Foster Dulles *strongly* felt perpetual war would be an acceptable price to pay for capitalism (his religion). They were privileged in the worst sense – spoiled, and tied deep in corporate interests. If the President represented the gods above ground, John Foster and Allen Dulles represented the underworld. John Foster was the political demon who saw capitalism as a religion, and Allen was the much darker CIA demon. But Vietnam presented a problem after Korea. There was no real communist threat in Southeast Asia, ideas maybe, fighting for rights and stolen land, definitely, but no threat – but there was plenty of unrest due to the colonial plantations of French Indochina and the British imperial interests still going. Natives wanted their land and freedom back, but **you can never tell a colonial power that they don't own what they've stolen**. The French whined and complained to the US that socialists (who wanted their own land and freedom back) were causing non-stop problems. The Dulles brothers, not caring about a communist threat, but caring for the colonial corporate interest, devised the insidious containment idea after WW2 to captivate ignorant Congressmen and Americans – The Domino Theory – Communism was running rampant and if one country fell to the evil, they would all fall like dominoes. They got Truman to speak this in a speech. This same argument created sufficient false fear to allow Kennedy to send "advisors" (thousands) into Vietnam, Laos, Cambodia, and elsewhere to assist in alleviating the "communist" threat. Lyndon Johnson created a Maine incident in the Gulf of Tonkin to expand the war. Nixon would have stayed, but he realized Americans were tired of this new splendid war, and he realized we would lose for a myriad of reasons, and he ended it after the needless loss of many lives.

But just as many Presidents do, Nixon just turned his sights elsewhere. Central and South America, victims of US corporate controlling aggression since the United Fruit Company, became a new focus of socialism and communism. In 1970 Salvadore Allende became the democratically elected President of Chile. A physician and head of the Socialist party in Chile, he had reforms in mind that were meant to help his people. A few of those reforms meant that US corporate interests (mainly in copper and wood) would have to take some losses in order for the country and its people to do better financially. US corporate interests couldn't stand for this, and they complained to Nixon repeatedly and Nixon soon berated the communist interests and he named Allende as their leader. He ranted and raved (the phone calls are recorded), and the US via the CIA elevated General Augusto Pinochet, a right-wing zealot, to chief opponent and he led a coup using US weapons, intelligence, and financial support. Whether Allende was killed with an American bullet or not doesn't matter. The CIA has admitted orchestrating this coup and his death, and the years of right-wing dictatorship and disappearances (kidnappings and death), is the result of American regime change. This regime change brought on years of corruption, murder, torture, and the "disappeared".

The US has committed or attempted regime change around the world, but never more frequently than in Latin America. Almost every country in Central and South America has suffered via US regime change. Even recently the CIA has been extra busy attempting to turn over Venezuela into US hands. Cuba has endured imperialism over the years, only finally to end up staying socialist via revolution against corruption from US corporate interests. The US assassinates, or attempts to assassinate, leaders that don't kiss US corporate ass. It has nothing to do with socialism, *per se*, but everything to do with US corporate money interests. Guatemala and El Salvador have suffered greatly from US intervention. Guatemala was forced into the US fold in the '50s, as well as El Salvador. Both countries quickly were taken over by oligarchical families stealing land and killing those who opposed them. The US has supported these death squads for decades, and even trained government leaders in death in the US. In the late '70s and into the '80s, civil wars broke out in both countries, due to the cruelty of the oligarchies supported by the US. Jimmy Carter initiated the assassination of Arch-Bishop Oscar Romero who spoke forcefully against the injustice – with the CIA paying assassins to gun him down in front of his congregation. Reagan expressed extra vehemence for Guatemala, and vowed to help destroy any socialist rebel forces and anyone who supported such – because the government forces were going to lose. To watch, as VP Kamala Harris recently traveled to Guatemala, and lectured them on corruption, and that the concern of the US may lead to more involvement is beyond the pale – her boss, Joe Biden, helped create that corruption and destabilization. Joe Biden is not the "new FDR", he's the old Harry Truman, and that's a serious problem.

Reagan and Bush Sr helped create the Taliban in Afghanistan, because the CIA couldn't help itself and funded terrorists to terrorize the Soviets on their southern border. When the Soviets had enough, after they had been promised repeatedly by the Afghans that they would put an end to the cross border incursions, they invaded and installed a leader favorable to Russia. This brought out all the stops for the CIA to fund terrorists because of the obsession with communism. They couldn't let them fail or change on their own, the CIA had to force it. Clinton continued this policy, and started Albright's war in

Bosnia, all while continuing the policies of cruelty in Latin America.

George Bush Jr continued these same policies, lied to start war and commit torture kissing the ass of the Israeli apartheid regime by starting war in the Middle East. Because fighting Iran seemed too iffy, George Sr used the CIA and politicians and bureaucrats to mislead the Iraqi dictator, whom they formerly loved, into taking Kuwait, so that war could be initiated. Saddam Hussein was left in power initially by George Sr because he felt his absence would create instability. But the CIA and George Jr and his neocons wanted control in Iraq, that would eventually lead to Iran. George Jr and his team, including the officer who helped cover up the Mai Lai massacre, lied to the farthest extent – Iraq had WMDs (which they did not) and were planning to build nuclear bombs (which they were not), but truth never stops the demon organization and its army of sycophants. US intelligence reports have stated over and again that Iran does not possess nuclear weapons and does not plan to create them, yet kissing Israeli ass again the US makes a strawman enemy of Iran. And again kissing Israeli ass and never missing an opportunity to tweak Russia, the CIA and US policy attempt regime change over and over in Syria, going so far as to create and fund terrorist militias and move them into Syria (the Taliban all over again).

Barack Obama led more untamed missile strikes than any President, and expanded the secrecy of the state while claiming he stood for open government. Like other Presidents he complained of Israeli influence yet kissed their ass and bent over to take it up his. Donald Trump, willing to do anything for money and praise perfumed himself for the Israelis as they fucked him in psychopathic rape fashion. The amount of lies he told will never be fully counted – those who sought to count gave up under the onslaught of *thousands* of lies. The fear of Trump is not his legislative agenda, but the fact that he is a lover of fascism, and

249

under such an idiot the US may see its last vestiges of democracy destroyed.

The US has placed so much money and so many weapons into terrorist hands that the vision of perpetual war of the Dulles brothers has become the reality. Allen Dulles convinced Dwight Eisenhower that covert regime change was the way to go, and Eisenhower, thinking that a bloodless coup was better than war, agreed to authorize covert operations. How a man like Eisenhower could be so fooled by such a sociopath as Allen Dulles is sad. The CIA as we know it is the Frankenstein monster created by Allen Dulles. He and his brother thought that no amount of death and killing was over the line in the furtherance of capitalism. The covert operations role has expanded exponentially to become the major activity of the CIA. The law authorizing the CIA is a ceding of the Constitutional powers of Congress to make and declare war to the CIA, at least as long as no one finds out. Secretly, clandestinely, the CIA funds student groups in "enemy" countries, stirs up the capitalist forces in politics, supports candidates who are willing to kiss US ass, and provides money and weapons to right-wing terrorists. These covert operations have expanded from bloodless coups (if ever a thing actually existed) to full scale military operations, sanctioned by their mandate under the law interpreted broadly. The CIA has authorization to call forth US military forces (special forces, WMDs, gunships, etc...) anywhere around the globe, and no amount of killing and slaughter is distasteful or enough.

The ignorance of the American people is astounding. Either they remain ignorant for lack of information for which there is no excuse; or, they remain ignorant for ignorance' sake even after knowing the truth. Recently it has been repeatedly documented that US special forces are running the CIA war in Syria, funding and providing weapons to terrorists labeled terrorists by the US State Department. There have been multiple news articles regarding US special forces active in Africa (all over Africa). One story within the last few years was a special forces group of Army Rangers in active combat in Africa, and there were injuries and death. Does anyone stop to ask, when there is no declared conflict for the US in Africa, why the fuck are Army Rangers involved in active combat there and why are they dying? The fact is, according to former CIA intelligence analysts, the US has special forces active in ~85% of the countries around the world.

Sometimes it becomes difficult to fund all these things. The CIA figured out the solution to this problem years ago – weapon smuggling and drug smuggling and sales. Just like the British who wanted the opium trade to continue, the CIA wants the drug trade to continue. The lucrative importation of cocaine and heroin into the US, whether by Cessna or military transport (the latter I personally witnessed), provides the CIA with an unlimited slush fund from which to provide weapons where and when it likes. They helped Reagan weaponize his Contras, and they've helped Israel destabilize the Middle East.

This, in a nutshell, is the history of US global fascism. Pointing to the strawman of socialism, we (US and other colonial powers) have started war after war pretending to be fighting that which we created via imperialism, with the real purpose being protecting rich and powerful money interests. The documentation is everywhere, the sense to deal with it is not. US forces kill and cause destabilization around the globe on a daily basis. Every American, ignorant or choosing ignorance, is guilty of participating in this slaughter for nothing more than profits and power. Every knife I put into a brain, throat, heart, kidney, or liver; every bullet I put into the body of a human being; every strangled and mangled corpse... *you are all equally guilty*. The failure of Americans to reign in the CIA and the Presidents, and the failure to force elected representatives to place the check upon

251

this behavior makes every American guilty of murder and accessory to murder.

Trumpussolini

Il Ducebag

"Thus a sophistical distortion of the constitutional spirit wrecked constitutional freedom in Italy, setting an example for the Germany of Hindenburg and Hitler ten years later to follow; and under a Pharisaic pretence of fidelity that he had sworn to his people when ascending the throne the honest king became a perjurer...

"The Duce of Fascism, still residing in Milan, was bidden to Rome for constitutional consultation with the king...

"But now, for the first time in his life, he had known the taste of gain by bluff, of victory by threat. He repeated the stroke, which he was to repeat so many times in the years following. He declared unswervingly that he would not go to Rome, neither would he demobilize his army, unless the king pledged himself to entrust him with premiership...

"This was unconstitutional, unmistakably..."

"A 'Doctrine of Its Own'"

"Holy is the State and the State alone. Religion, in the particular case 'that particular positive religion that is [Evangelicalism]', is a valuable asset of the State and must be protected and fostered as such. The State, in its turn, is not at all the embodiment of a natural necessity, nor does it coincide with the natural facts of race and nation; in which case its expanding power would be limited within the narrowness of objective

253

bounds. The State is a creation of the Spirit, or of the Will of History. But where and how does this Spirit or Will visibly appear? Not in the God of the believer, since God, the God of [Evangelicalism], is merely an asset of the State, which definitely 'has no theology'. Nor does it appear in the Nature of the anthropologist or geographer. Nor, finally, in the demos of the democrat or in the mass of Marx. The Spirit or Will, otherwise called State, embodies itself 'in the few, nay, in the One'. In other words it is the despot, and the despot alone, who is the Holy."

Goliath: The March of Fascism – G A Borgese
(1938, New York, The Viking Press)
embedded quotes of Benito Mussolini

In the end the Little Prince, *Il Duce*, was caught attempting escape from the chaos, wreckage, and ruin he unleashed upon Italy and the world, after thoroughly infecting US corporate and power elite. He was caught by partisans who never believed him; but he was also caught by Vicars of Bray who changed with the new tide of the wind; he was also caught by his beloved Blackshirts who now were thoroughly demoralized. They hung his naked body on a meat hook from a lamppost on the street. As his fat ass and fatter head moldered in the sun, his own sycophants of the time, his Marjorie Taylor Greens, his Lauren Boeberts, his Mike Pences, his Mitch McConnells, his Ted Cruzes, *et al*… None of them were there kneeling at his body praying for the salvation of their messiah. They were gone, in hiding from their own deaths that would follow. For the fascist, once the power is gone the made up reasoning is gone.

Aging With Julie

If Love is not worth loving,
then Life is not worth living,
   Nor aught is worth remembering,
    but well forgot;
For store is not worth storing
and gifts are not worth giving,
   If Love is not...

As thy days, so shall thy strength be
– Christina Rossetti

Julie is only a few years younger than me, but she has always aged slower than me. She's always had beautiful long hair, mostly dark brown to black, yet with gold and copper infused throughout. When silver strands started to appear, she wasn't excited about it like I was. I told her I had been waiting years for those silver strands to make their appearance, and I love them.

We look after each other's aches and pains, and watch each other's health like hawks. We make each other breakfast and supper. We've never had much money, but we go out for breakfast every now and again. Sometimes we go for her favorite, Chinese food. The kids are teenage to 32, menopause and andropause have hit us, and the former relieves much of the stress related to sex.

Julie has shared with me regarding her traumas. I'm not the best person to help with some of this, because my anger tends

255

to get in the way. She has done so much internal work to not be destroyed by those experiences, and we both have benefited tremendously from what she has done and accomplished.

Sex and love are life, even when you get older. Julie has gained stretch marks from pregnancy and milk production. I have great respect for these marks. They show how much she gave of herself out of love to grow fine children and make sure they had the best nutritional start in life. She enjoyed her breasts, even in pregnancy and milk production in pleasant sexual ways. She enjoyed squirting her hot milk on my cock and licking it off. We rubbed her milk on both our bodies, and I think of this with reverence every time I suck her nipples.

As I push my hard cock into her and it touches her cervix, and I shoot hot cum into her, I'm reminded of fucking while she was pregnant, especially in the last few weeks to help the cervix along, and we laugh thinking how the kids don't know this (well, maybe now). I fuck her anally and her eyes role back in her head, she loses all sense of time and place, and cums with uncontrollable shudders. She fucks me anally with her strap-on and I whine like her little bitch as she forces my prostate to unload. We 69 and suck and rub until we both explode, and she kisses me deep with a mouth full of cum.

We both need this. Sex is life. Sex shares life. Sex makes life. Sex makes the bonding of love deeper and more meaningful. To sleep every night with a naked goddess, feeling her skin with my hands and body, is life sustaining. When I run my hands along her ass, when I feel the muscles in her legs, when I feel the hard and defined muscles in her back, it is an ecstatic experience. When she feels my hard cock, squeezes my balls, and moans with delight, I know she feels home.

256

We sit together in the living room on a love seat. She still puts her legs up on mine, and still gives me raging boners. If she's at the sink, I press into her and put my hands in her pants and rub her clit to distraction. If I bend over anywhere she reaches between my legs, squeezes my balls, and reaches around to feel my cock grow hard, and she moans.

To live with the same person, in deep love, for decades requires give and take, sharing, sometimes arguments, and sex – lots of sex – lots of horny un-judged sex. You can't be afraid to explore your limits with the one you love [Enigma]. Julie has overcome deep trauma and learned to live, love, and make love. She has overcome her initial feelings of bisexuality in me, and my not telling her sooner. I am grateful that she trusts me enough to touch her and love her, emotionally and physically. I love her so much I am overcome. I need her like Food, Water, Shelter...

Memorial Day

& 4 July & Veterans Day, et al

"**Memorial Day** (originally known as **Decoration Day**) is a federal holiday in the United States for honoring and mourning the U.S. military personnel who died while serving in the United States Armed Forces. From 1868 to 1970, it was observed on May 30. Since 1970, it is observed on the last Monday of May." (Wikipedia)

While a US holiday, we're sure many countries have remembrances that are effectively the same, so let's widen the expanse of this to include them, because *militaries in all countries tend to overreach into society*. While some form of this writing was always meant to be another book chapter, we were reticent because non-combat pretenders (NCP) can be quite stupid and vitriolic. But today, because my (Sean's) daughter was in a marching band, I once again had to go and witness this disgusting display, and get triggered.

First, let me describe the event in this city. The starting line is set up by two fire department ladder trucks raising a giant flag over the street. The first participants are a motorcycle club, yet dressed as a motorcycle gang. Why they're here, I don't know. But of course, in this country, nothing speaks more of Remembrance, morals, and ethics than a motorcycle gang. Next came a police cruiser... ditto. Then marching bands playing military anthems; and while I enjoy hearing them play... ditto.

258

Then the "veterans" come in waves. Some of you may think we're cruel here, but we are combat veterans, and we know what we're speaking of; and we have the right to call this out. These days it's almost exclusively VVA and Vietnam & Korean War VFW personnel who participate. There's a noticeable absence of combat veterans *extant*, and Gulf War combat veterans and above; and of those that are participating, they are almost exclusively Non-Combat Pretenders. Some of them are 100lbs+ heavier than they were when they were in the military, but they wear VFW costumes expressing that their identity is military and fake, and many participants have gone and bought fatigues in their new size, and emblazoned them with patches and even medals that have never existed. A military personnel truck comes along pulling an artillery piece. On the front of this truck the idiots have tied a rubber hand emblazoned with bloody gore… and they're proud of this. Another truck pulls a trailer full of these "veterans", and a single black man, obviously a true veteran of a recent (90's or above) conflict, who has lost the use of his legs, is made to follow behind this trailer on his scooter – he truly just wants to be a part of something, to make sense of losing his ability to walk. The "veterans" in the trailer suck down cold water and ignore him, and don't offer him water. My wife and I (Sean) give him water. There are decorated garbage trucks, which makes me think how totally appropriate they are; and they remind me of the movie Idiocracy. Another police cruiser ends the parade. While this is just a tiny fraction of say, a Soviet May Day parade, it is no different except in the idiocy.

In previous chapters, Rubicon's and my feelings regarding some of these things pertain:

"Thank you for your service" won't cut it, won't even satisfy a basic need for these combat vets; primarily because *you* haven't got a clue as to what "service" *you* are referring. It's a statement you would make to your food server, gas station mechanic, etc… Military personnel such as swim instructors, clerks, generals, cooks, officers off the battlefield, etc… all love this attention, but they don't deserve it, and every combat veteran knows this."

And,

"To this day I feel the guilt and responsibility of these actions. It astounds me that I went so long with such a *laissez-faire* attitude about killing. When people say "Thank you for your service" it makes me cringe. While other people rise and sing the National Anthem, I feel disgust and pain. When at meetings where people rise to "Pledge Allegiance", I can't make myself say it, and I want to stop my kids from saying it."

I include these quotes here because of those Non-Combat Pretenders (NCP). Combat veterans tend to avoid these parade displays of orgiastic patriotism, because they are fraudulent and highly triggering. NO combat veteran (unless he's a psychopath) would do these things, let alone decorate a truck with a bloody hand; that's how we know these participants are NCP.

"My neighbor is younger than I am. He spent time in Germany in the Army and praises it. He pretends to have been in Vietnam (not possible by his age). He's for slaughtering all over the globe, praises conservative "values", rants about government spending, and wears his 9mm in his butt-crack as he does his gardening. Yet, never having been in war, he proclaims himself a "disabled veteran" and had the VA install a ramp on his house and got them to give him a scooter,

260

and he's never used either one – he's too busy
chopping wood behind his fence where he thinks
no one sees. I had another 20-something neighbor
who believes in the military way of life, yet he too
is a virgin talking about sex. He wears his 9mm
stuck in the back of his pants as he washes his
truck – we don't live in a violent neighborhood – it
has never been violent. They follow the teachings
of Clint Eastwood (military swim instructor),
another virgin talking about sex who seems to be
in love with Antebellum slavery times. These are
all NCP, Non-Combat Pretenders."

X Rubicon – Boys And Men

But these NCPs are not just fraudulent "veterans", they are
the fraudulent civilian population as well. I noticed one of the
firemen carrying a 9mm – no firemen in this city have ever been
shot or even threatened… and why is he wearing this to a parade?
As we went back to the car, we passed 3 young men jogging with
flags, and a 4th jogging wearing body armor and an American flag
as a cape (and I wanted to run him over). So, WTF is going on
here?

Much of this is due to government propaganda, and yes, it
IS propaganda. The VA, DoD, veteran "help" programs from
WWP to Rush, with major funding from corporations, have ALL
started calling ALL vets (of whatever experience) "Warriors". A
military psychiatrist (VA) has written she is a "warrior" just like
her patients (men who have actually been in combat and have
ALL the mental gifts that come along with it). A military
psychologist has self-described himself as an in-the-know
"warrior" because he completed Ranger training (yet he's
NEVER been in combat!). I know that many men have
completed SEAL training, and then quit, just so they could say

they did it, like they're somehow special, as though it's like an obstacle course; and, sooner or later, they start describing themselves as combat veterans.

One of the "warriors" I sent a book to in 2022, an officer in the VFW, posted a trashing review on Amazon. When I looked at his bio, I understood. He's a member of the VFW, but he's NEVER been in combat, let alone a foreign war. He enlisted in peacetime, was stationed in S Korea attending a gun emplacement, filled a military career with no war or combat, joined the Reserves where for some reason they made him an honorary Lt; yet, he has never placed his life or mind on the line. This is a failure of the VFW (quasi-NGO) to respect combat veterans; and it says something about their criteria inviting and elevating "veterans" just because they were stationed or went temporary duty in another country. We've known many combat veterans, including ourselves, who were triggered by their VFW invitation, because, as our fathers-in-law (WW2 combat veterans) used to say, "It's full of a bunch of drunks and pretenders who never served in combat."

These people (men AND women) pretend because civilians are in love with the military, and these people love their accolades, and they enable the Presidents, Congress, and the military to spend more and more on imperialism. The frauds and their lovers are Virgins Talking About Sex. The egos of the frauds and their lovers have swollen out of proportion to all reality. Do these people have any clue what this patriotic Bullshit does to combat veterans? We think not!

What *should* we be doing on Memorial Day?

Memorial, *In Memoriam*, Remembering. If you *truly* want to show respect for combat veterans, those who have died and those still alive, get off your knees and stop sucking military cock. Start remembering history and how we got in all those wars, conflicts, and actions in the first place. Learn. Educate yourself. Become present and aware. Take your own responsibility as citizens seriously. *Every time you blindly praise war, its pain, and its costs, you blindly disrespect ALL those who have lived it.* Stop draping yourselves in flags. Stop saying your Republican is not a war monger. Stop saying your Democrat is not a war monger. Stop letting Zionists (Psychopaths, Terrorists, & war mongers) commit the US to war and war mongering. **Stop expecting other men to do your fighting for you.** Stop insisting that you're not a fascist, supporting *lebensraum*, when the fact is that you ARE. Stop bathing in the blood of infants & children, young men, men & women, old people, and those with different religion, beliefs, or melanin than you. Stop being psychopaths!

Learn to express Love. Learn to embrace Truth and accept it. Teach your children how to love, and how to love Truth. Teach your children and grandchildren to seek wisdom. Teach them to discern falsehoods, obfuscations, and lies. Teach them to build and not to destroy. Teach them to embrace humanity and put away the childish nonsense of superiority.

But the ONLY way you can do this is through learning and putting away propaganda and patriotism. You MUST read, especially history! You MUST be honest with yourself and accept that your country, just like EVERY country in the world, has committed numerous atrocities. We are supposed to be making ourselves better than we have been.

It's time for you to grow up and become a man or a woman, with a conscience!

4 July

And the Striving for Democracy

[The hypocrisy of America is borne out, first and
foremost, by its love of slavery...]

Thomas Moore, Irish poet

Once upon a time... the US (the Colonies) sought to
become independent of the British King. For years the Colonists
had fought war at the King's side, mostly against the French and
Hurons (Iroquois nations) for control of North America. The
French and Spanish also wanted control of the western continents.
But we, being loyal British subjects, at the time, fought to defeat
them. Defeat of **any** monarch, despot, or monarchical system is a
laudable goal (whether church related and/or political), and so we
moved on to defeating the British monarch as well. Having done
so, we celebrated, and continue to celebrate this victory and
independence with pomp and spectacle. As far as the British
King, or any royalty goes, fuck all kings and their aristocratic ilk,
always and forever.

But we need to be aware of, and accept responsibility for,
the atrocities we have caused and continue to cause, even if we
choose to call our King the "President" (whether Republican or
Democrat). At the time, we really weren't aware or sensible of
our own faults (are we ever?) in building an empire upon the
backs of slaves and wage slaves (a system based in greed and

fanciful notions of superiority, and that's a sign of mental illness), and driven by false notions of destiny, and authority to thievery, preached by Kingly deities, priests, pastors, and Reverend Doctors since the Dark Ages. (Read here (https://seangriobhtha.substack.com/p/the-polyglot-of-evil) to understand the transmogrification of Jesus into a blood soaked abuser and marauder). This doctrine, Manifest Destiny, allowed Europeans (Americans) to justify theft of property, wholesale lands, and the lives of natives. Yes, we stole, raped, pillaged, slaved, and slaughtered our way to prosperity and power. The natives, who did greet us warmly at first, turned against us as we continued stealing their land, raping them, slaughtering them, and driving them out (just like Zionists). We've never apologized, and we haughtily believe we had the right, because Americans to this day believe in their superiority and that "might makes right". What applies to Zionists, also applies to us, being "little concerned for human blood if it is not [our] own." (Morris Ernst, FDR's international envoy for refugees)

We have gone from a people who were told by their leaders that a standing army is an evil thing, and we should "stay out of foreign entanglements", to the largest military machine the world has ever known, to the tune of >1 TRILLION dollars per year, with hundreds of weaponized bases and mobile nuclear weapons around the globe.

This is NOT a new or recent thing. We started immediately after we celebrated that first victory. Clergy and politicians supported slavery and aristocracy, then and now, and the South *still* receives pity based upon those preachings of superiority, nevermind that they started a war where over 600,000 men lost their lives; and for what?... the abomination of slavery. Circa 1900 we sent US Marines and "volunteers" to the Philippines to crush what the Marine Corps and the Pentagon call the "Philippine Uprising". Those Filipinos were fighting to get

265

their land back from capitalist theft, and they didn't want to be used as slaves to collect coconuts for imperial powers (US). Thousands of Filipinos were slaughtered, raped, and tortured. Spain had felt they owned the Philippines, and when the US defeated their fleet, the US decided *we* owned the Philippines (and many Pacific islands), and we took violent control of all for the sake of greed and building another base of power operations (we learned so much from the abuses of the English throne, didn't we?). Earlier, we pulled this same force on Japan to force them to open their doors to capitalistic greed.

We forced Pacific islanders to stand still while we dropped nuclear test bombs around the Pacific (we also made US soldiers guinea pigs for these experiments).

We made best buddies of Japan, because they bowed to our power, and we grew them a protective shield, even after they had raped, pillaged, and murdered their way through east Asia and the Pacific, and tortured and slaughtered American servicemen. We decided to hate the Chinese for the sake of the British, and their losses of drug profits and control. Is it any wonder the Chinese drove the British out? We decided to hate the Vietnamese for the sake of the French and British. Is it any wonder that China and N Korea despise capitalists, especially since capitalists love their most violently aggressive torturer, Japan?

We invaded, yes invaded, Vietnam, Laos, Cambodia, etc... for the sole purpose of helping the French and English hold on to their stolen goods. If your home was invaded so others could steal your property, rape your women, torture you and/or take your lives, would you still agree with "might makes right"?

We have invaded Iraq, Afghanistan, encroached into Pakistan, all based on our own lies and Zionist lies, all while

supporting Zionist violence (rape, torture, murder), and
supporting Saudi murder; and we continue our insane ideas about
invading Iran. The British are still looking to take over the "sick
man of Europe", Turkey. The British have long memories, as
does the US. We toppled the the democratically elected President
of Iran, and with the British installed a puppet dictator (the Shah).
Arabs, who once trusted us and cooperated with us, *we* have lined
up in front of us and stuck knives deep into their backs by kissing
the Zionists' ass.

We have much to be sorry for. While we celebrate our
"independence" we come further under the control of foreign
influences, majorly the British and Zionists (who practically
control the British now). Will we ever be satisfied with enough?
Will we ever take our responsibilities as humans as seriously as
we take our greed and lust for more? Will we ever listen to our
combat veterans who continually tell us we are egregiously wrong
in what we're doing? Will we stop supporting Zionist
psychopaths in their *lebensraum*?

"Joe Biden is not the 'new FDR', he's the old Harry
Truman, and that's a serious problem." Biden has supported
every war, even though, or because, he's never had to fight in one.
If you think Barack Obama is a "good" man, you are seriously
wrong (the meme of his wife pontificating that her House was
built by slaves, and the Afghan child sitting in rubble below says,
"You have a house?!? Your husband blew mine up" pretty much
says it all. If you think Donald Trump is a "good" man in search
of peace and prosperity for you, you must be living with a
lobotomy, or you're stuck in deep denial. If you think George
Bush was a "good" President, then pull your head out of your ass
and reread the lies he told (based on Israeli lies) to drag the US
into war. This same analysis goes for almost every President
we've ever had, Republican AND Democrat; lies, corruption,
psychopathology of power, and much, much more. If you think

even one member of Congress is untouched by corruption, you
are deluded beyond belief.

This IS what we have become, a nation of war mongers &
thieves, psychopaths, and sociopaths. Stop listening to the
Church and political hierarchies. Stop listening to ecclesiastical
and political propaganda. Start getting yourself educated. Have
some pride man! Embrace the power you have as a Citizen and
slap the shit out of these people. Embrace humanity and send
everyone's god and greed packing.

> "It is the fate of many abstract words to be
> used in two senses, one good and the other bad.
> Morality means the will to righteousness, or it
> means Anthony Comstock; democracy means the
> rule of the people, or it means Tammany Hall.
> And so it is with the word "Religion". In its true
> sense Religion is the most fundamental of the
> soul's impulses, the impassioned love of life, the
> feeling of its preciousness, the desire to foster and
> further it. In that sense every thinking man must
> be religious; in that sense Religion is a perpetual
> self-renewing force, the very nature of our being.
> In that sense I would make no thought of assailing
> it, I would make clear that I hold it beyond
> assailment.
> "But we are denied the pleasure of using
> the word in that honest sense, because of another
> which has been given to it. To the ordinary man
> "Religion" means, not the soul's longing for
> growth, the "hunger and thirst after righteousness",
> but certain forms in which this hunger has
> manifested itself in history, and prevails today
> throughout the world; that is to say, institutions
> have fixed dogmas and "revelations", creeds and

rituals, with an administering caste which claims supernatural sanction. By such institutions the moral strivings of the race, the affections of childhood and the aspirations of youth are made the prerogatives and stock in trade of ecclesiastical hierarchies. It is the thesis of this book that "Religion" in this sense is a source of income to parasites, and the natural ally of every form of oppression and exploitation."

The Profits Of Religion – Religion – Upton Sinclair

On 4 July, I beseech you to come to your senses which you have within you; to leave the man-made non-sense behind, to embrace your humanity and that of all the humanity of the Earth. **Everyone**, *not just you*, wants independence.

Guilt, Repentance, & Change
Why Guilt is Important and Can't be "Forgotten"

Come all you young Rebels,
And list' while I sing;
For the love of one's country,
Is a terrible thing;
It banishes fear with
The speed of a flame;
And it makes us all part of
The Patriot Game.

Patriot Game – Dominic Behan

I was moved to write this after reading *15 Useful Facts…* by Caitlin Johnstone (Substack: @caitlinjohnstone), specifically in regard to Guilt. I enjoy her writing, attitude, and sentimentalities; but I don't always agree. This isn't really a disagreement, just an expansion of the meaning of Guilt, and its *necessary* place in humanity. I understand her use of the word in the context of her experience. At a young age she was brutally raped. My wife was also brutally raped at a young age. In that context, Guilt for a rape victim is misplaced… it shouldn't be in their mind, even though it is one of the first thoughts that occurs to them. No matter what mistakes or misjudgments they may, or may not have made, rape is theft of life and spirit, and no one has the right to do that to another. She wrote that Guilt has no place or purpose, and again in the context of her and my wife's experience, I completely agree. However, in the context of the

270

perpetrator, Guilt is required. The rapist or physical murderer must come to terms with what they have done; and in this context Guilt is a very valuable tool of our nature to bring justice and repentance to the perpetrator, even though this doesn't often happen because humans can be trained to ignore guilt, or cover it up… In some cases it means a psychopath has been grown; rape is always the act of a psychopath, and as I grow older psychopaths become easier to spot, and their population is expanding – from Presidents to rapists, and sometimes they are one and the same.

Jim Gaffigan has a great routine regarding cats. They kill indiscriminately, sometimes torturing and playing with their prey in the process. Yet they never repent of this torture or killing (even when they don't need the food); they never get teary eyed and regretful; they never go around crying that "I've killed something… I feel terrible". But humans do have that capacity, and they have it for a reason. Combat veterans (unless they're born sociopaths or they've turned into psychopaths) do become riddled with Guilt, and not many of them would say they don't deserve this Guilt. While many would say, "It's not your fault… you have to let that go", these are just not possible; and the first of those statements isn't completely true. Even rape victims don't "let it go", rather, just like the traumas of combat veterans, it comes back in triggers, dreams, and waves for their entire life; and while it's important not to live in the past, it's as sure as anything known that the past informs the present and the future in order to cause change in humanity. Silence and burying traumas hurt humanity; the populace not being in full communication with traumas hurts humanity. These traumas must be discussed, and I applaud my wife and Caitlin Johnstone for saying out loud and in writing what has happened, and how they feel about it, and how they've struggled to cope.

271

This also applies to combat veterans. We are perpetrators. We have killed upon the orders and demands of others; and it doesn't matter whether we are personally responsible for 1 death, or >300 with participation in thousands of deaths; we as humanity and a people must talk about it, otherwise the same psychopaths, mistakes, and atrocities continue again, and again, and again, and again... *ad infinitum*. Many combat veterans are unable to talk about it because it may cause a mental breakdown (very few can even discuss their experiences without breaking into tears); many *can* talk about it yet choose not to – they believe they shouldn't express these things out loud, or they should protect others from the horrific pain they feel for the rest of their lives; and many choose to divert their attention to self-medication of whatever kind; and some go so far into denial they never return. But combat veterans, who despise what they have done, should be encouraged to tell their tales (minus patriotic vainglorious bullshit) to all the people, and the people should be encouraged to *listen*, because that is the only way we, the people, will make progress to stopping wars and atrocities.

I have Guilt for what I've committed, and you should feel it, because being a Citizen in a democracy *requires* you to shoulder that kind of responsibility. If you don't educate yourself and if you fail to come down hard on your elected representatives (Democrat, Republican, Labor, Tory, Liberal, Conservative, or whatever) you are as Guilty as any GI. You may think a veteran's voluntary service contract absolves you, but it does not! WW2 vets, fighting what has been considered to be a righteous war, didn't feel absolution, and the same applies to the volunteer force. Lies and propaganda are fed to veterans and the people, and these must be addressed and change enacted.

I never wanted to become a killer. But you'll understand that lies and propaganda in lieu of reason cause a steering onto paths that you never thought, in your wildest dreams, that you'd be walking on – especially when this happens at a young age, before your mental braking system has fully developed. Once it's happened, Guilt is your saving grace to stay human. Guilt leads to repentance. I'm an atheist, and I don't mean repentance in a religious sense (unless you follow Upton Sinclair's sense of Religion), but in a truly human sense. I could have *only* blamed others, but that wouldn't be honest.

The details of what I did -- even if I was led, coaxed, coached, and ordered into doing it – infuse this book. As I stated, it's a *mea culpa*, an admittance of Guilt; and I've lived with that Guilt for over four decades. Sean's notes of my babbling inform you further:

> I'VE BEEN ASKED... why November and December bother me so deeply, when the time of year is for Thanks and Love. But the time of year is also for reflection. In November 1980, while Americans prepared to give Thanks for being alive and well, at the beginning of the month I was in the Guatemalan jungle taking the lives of four men by knife strikes, because the God Capitalism demanded it. At the end of the month, while Americans were in earnest to give Thanks and feel warm and cozy with family, I was in El Salvador killing and helping to kill several hundred men and women, and I put a bullet in the brain of man for whom I had, and still have, respect, because the God Capitalism demanded it. In the first third of December 1980, I was in Central America again, while Americans were snug in their beds, with visions of power, glory, and sugarplums in their heads, and I was executing a plan to kill ~1000 people, and once again I was killing guards with knife strikes and being soaked in blood. I did this

for ALL Americans and their God, Capitalism.
THIS is what I reflect on every November and
December (and every other month has its own
reflections). Within 30 days I had killed and
helped kill ~1400 humans. THIS is what you ask
young men without developed frontal lobes to do
for you... your Dirty Work for false Gods...

Rubicon (Notes for <u>X Rubicon</u>)

You will obviously sense the pointing of my finger, and I
truly believe you are as Guilty as I am; but this chapter is
specifically about my own Guilt, how it came about, and how it
constantly resurfaces. As stated, many things in life are rubicons.
For combat veterans, like myself and Sean, a permanent shift
happens and the pathway back and the destination are obliterated.
Once you've taken a life, who you were before is dissolved and
you must remake yourself in the best way you can manage. Some
men never get that far. Suicide among combat veterans far
outpaces the civilian population, especially as they age, which
exposes another problem – men living for decades in silent Guilt
until they just can't live with it anymore in silence. This book
provides you a better understanding of the seriousness and
magnitude of the problem. Don't waste what is offered to you.
PTSD and Guilt are the forgone conclusions.

Prior to my military separation the Guilt ate away at me,
but I still had a protective shell going, so it ate away at the edges
and ate toward my heart. As the Guilt ate deeper, it allowed me to
finally say no to continuing as I had been, and saying no to the
propaganda and lies. But make no mistake, the changes within
are permanent and painful. Without Guilt, repentance and change
will not come. I've had people and therapists, with no experience
in these matters, tell me Guilt serves no purpose, and I should
simply, "let it go". But that's really asinine *because* these

changes are permanent. You can learn to live with it, and control it somewhat, but it never goes away; but this living and control can only be achieved through repentance.

At first, the Guilt was overwhelming and I couldn't see any solution but suicide to stop the pain. At the time(s), I hadn't fully accepted my responsibility, and so there was no repentance. As your frontal lobe brakes develop and come into their own, it's like an adult with wisdom finally walks into the room and shouts at you, "What the fuck have you done?!?" Your brain and your heart have a Herculean task. Self-preservation is part of your base programming, and it fights mightily against the pain, yet it embraces the Guilt to try to get you to think, to understand what you've done. No one wants to be blamed, not even by their own brain and heart, nevertheless, it's a grief that you must go through in order to accept your own responsibility. Different people have different timelines. For me, it took 25-30 years of pain and remembrance to get that far.

Your brain's greatest weapon against your own intransigence is dreams/nightmares. They start almost immediately after the trauma and gain strength. Dreams with the kind of power we're talking about force adrenaline output. This adrenaline doesn't bring you out of sleep mode, but it alters your body's natural function of curbing movement during this supposed sleep cycle, and you begin running, shooting, stabbing… and when you do wake up, you are exhausted, and w/o medication the dreams stick with you throughout the day. Alpha and beta adrenaline blockers can help with this, but there are still breakthrough dreams.

These dreams, and the many manifestations of trauma that occur throughout the day, are the main reasons you can't "forget"; and I truly believe that we are not supposed to forget, otherwise, how can evolutionary changes come about? My experience with others informs that many of them would like not to know about these things, or they would like these things to be forgotten, or they would like to forget them, or just have them go away. This attitude is what allows atrocities to keep taking place. But the combat veteran will never be able to forget, so you should listen to them if you really want to see a better world come into being.

Some of the manifestations are from triggers. By far, the greatest triggering comes from Virgins Talking About Sex; and within this category are the Rolfs (named after the Nazi youth in the Sound Of Music). None of these people know anything about war and pain, yet they pontificate freely about these being necessary, glorifying, "to the victor go the spoils", etc... and the Rolfs' dream of killing for the fatherland in an insane psychopathic orgasm becomes propaganda. Also, "patriots" and control freaks are highly triggering to combat veterans, as it's these kind of people who make atrocities probable and possible. The military is full of all these categories; and Presidents are the epitome of the types. And then there are the idiots in Congress who deny that PTSD exists even as they send more men to die, and they play with proxy wars with the lives of others (even in the millions) paying the price; but of course, never being in harm's way... Virgins Talking About Sex.

The reminders are constant. Within months after leaving the military, my brain gifted me with another permanent manifestation. My main area of slaughter was in Central America, and the slaughter produced plenty of blood. When the weather turns hot and humid, I look at my hands and they appear to be covered in blood, and I can smell it. When this first occurred I almost lost it. After quite a while I knew there was no blood, but it still appeared and I could smell it; and it continues to this day.

276

I love babies. They're so joyful and they spread that to those around them. But for me, babies also are a stark reminder of a particular baby no longer with a mother to love and care for it and watch it grow, which is the essence of motherhood. The past informs me that I took the life of a pregnant rebel, and that baby never got to see life, and its mother and father never got to see it grow.

My right arm, hand and wrist, as I grow older have become racked with pain directly related to over 40 years ago. This was the arm and hand that plunged knives into other humans, and twisted a wide-blade knife in their bodies to make death as swift as possible.

My back, legs, and hips have pain informed by multiple parachute drops, and being yanked off the ground by Fulton Recovery System pick-ups. My right ankle gives me pain, informed by the memory of twisting it and being tracked by FARC guerrillas. My brain and heart have permanent memories of heads full of holes, bodies torn to shreds and pulverized into mist by my actions:

> You get used to the variety of explosions rained down by these gunships, especially when you're not receiving the death from above. But when a dry road has been turned into mud by the blood of humans; when you see bodies with burn holes that may have started as small shrapnel wounds, yet burned out to holes the size of grapefruits to basketballs from exploding tracer rounds (red phosphorus) or exploding 105mm rounds that contained white phosphorus (yes, it's illegal); when you see bodies half to almost fully vaporized by 105mm rounds; when you see bodies missing their top, or their bottom, or their leg, or their arm,

or their head... Sooner or later your brain, heart, and soul must pay the price for participating in this. That time came for me a few months later, and I no longer wanted to live.

X Rubicon – Guatemalan Swamp Convoy

There are so many memories, mental and physical, of pain and violence. How could those possibly be "forgotten" when they've altered your DNA? Your brain, heart, and your cells are not a computer. Humans have no delete function. Whatever goes in, you are required to face head-on. The Guilt is what stops a combat veteran, or a rapist, from continuing; that is why combat veterans rarely stay in the military; and that is also why the military desperately wants men below 25, before their brakes are developed.

Guilt is what can inform change for humanity. Please don't disparage and throw away the tools Nature gives you because you find it uncomfortable. Show respect for those who can admit their Guilt and allow their experience to inform change within you; their Guilt is not just for them, it's for humanity to do better.

Forgiveness

Some showed me Life as 'twere a royal game,
Shining in every colour of the sun,
With prizes to be played for, one by one,
Love, riches, fame.

Some showed me Life as 'twere a terrible fight,
A ceaseless striving 'gainst unnumbered foes,
A battle ever harder to the close,
Ending in night.

Thou – Thou dids't make of Life a vision deep
Of the deep happiness the spirit feels
When heavenly music Heaven itself reveals
And passions sleep.

Three Aspects – Mary Coleridge
Opus 176, No 1 – HH Parry
Performed by John McCormack

    The first of these stanzas I experienced when still a boy. The only thing that mattered was money, making money, and obtaining possessions, fame, and power. Even though my greatest interests were music and sex, my father and my siblings (save one) made it clear that nothing mattered but money.

    The second stanza occurred when I joined the military – the fight against our evil foes was a never ending battle that could only end in total destruction. But to the religious zealots of the US, this never seemed to matter. To many zealots, Israel must be maintained in order to bring on the Apocalypse. Some would love to hurry that along, and when idiots feel killing is ordained by God, how are you supposed to argue? This also allows Israel to commit atrocities non-stop and hide behind US, religious, and Holocaust skirts. When idiots lie and say God told them, or told them to do it, what response can there be to such an insane mind?

Julie brought me in from the cold. Julie made me feel and see love. Julie saved me from myself and has stayed by my side through extremely difficult times. At times I hated myself so deeply I couldn't understand her love for me. I knew what I had done, and she didn't, and I was so afraid to tell her who I was and what I had done. She patiently waited until "the time was right".

I'm slow to figure out some things, but the perpetration of needless and unjust death threw me down hard. As I've said, for years I couldn't accept what I had done. Then I refused to accept it even though I knew better. I tried completely blaming others for some of my own choices. I even tried denying that I had done anything at all, yet at the same time, working against that notion to try and find details and answers.

Becoming a killer happened in a relatively short time span, but it didn't happen overnight and it didn't happen without help – serious programmed conditioning. The 2-1/2 years involved in dealing out death took at least 40 years of my life, and nearly 40 years of Julie's life. It took me 38 years to tell Julie, the fear was so great. How do you tell a person that you were a volunteer killer? How do you tell the person you love that you've cut off a man's head, shoved knives into throats, hearts, kidneys, livers, and souls? How do you describe such a thing to those you love? Holding it in all those years was excruciating, but letting it out was just as excruciating. Writing these events down has drained me.

Yet Julie still stands by my side encouraging me and loving me, hoping for me to find peace. She wants nothing more than for me to be able to relax with her and enjoy what is left of life. That is quite difficult for me, because I can't forgive myself for being so naive and stupid. Every night the dead visit me in my sleep. The woman whose life, baby, and husband I took away is the most frequent. After telling Julie about these things, Julie started appearing in the dreams with the woman and her mates attempting to kill her.

For years Julie had to put up with my kicking, running, punching, and stabbing in my sleep. Listening to my calling out attack vectors. I would wake up so exhausted like I had been in the field the entire night. The dreams would stick with me throughout the day because they were able to engage my entire brain in the conflict, and I would feel the original traumas all over again.

While still in the military, PTSD was listed in the 1980 DSM under anxiety disorders; yet the psychiatrist who interviewed me in 1981, with all information available to him, completely ignored this. Subsequent treatment throughout the '80s ignored this diagnosis. It wasn't until the early 2000s that a psychiatrist diagnosed me with PTSD without even knowing the details. The truth is that PTSD was generally ignored as a diagnoses for veterans until Gulf War veterans demanded to be treated in the '90s. The VA had to be shamed and forced into utilizing and treating PTSD in the '90s. One of the fortuitous breakthroughs for PTSD nightmares came when a VA doctor treating vets for urinary problems associated with prostate issues gave his patients prazosin, an alpha receptor adrenaline blocker, and many of those patients reported it helping with PTSD dreams.

My dreams had increased dramatically again in the last few years. They had caused such a huge loss in sleep over the years. At one point I would drink coffee into the middle of the night to avoid sleeping and the dreams. With my full brain and body being activated, trying to sleep at times became like trying to sleep during combat or in a loud movie theater. Last year I began therapy with prazosin. At 1mg my movements (stabbing, kicking, punching, etc...) dropped in half. At 2mg my body movements stopped. At 3mg the vast majority of my brain was locked out of the dream viewing room, and restful sleep started to come. At 4, then 6mg the viewing room is locked and other brain functions are not allowed to participate. While the dreams still exist, the rest of my brain is not allowed to activate in response to the dreams, and sleep is generally deep and rejuvenating, and I want more. This is a wonderful turn for me, but I can't help wonder what it would have been like to have this medicine 40 years ago. Prazosin was developed in the '70s to treat high blood pressure, so it was there, just not prescribed for my purpose. But there it was, in my world. How might my life and Julie's life have been different?

I find that my view of the mental health profession is skewed negatively. First there's the psychiatrist who obviously ignored the warning signs in order to support a predetermined diagnosis made for the sake of command expediency. Therapists have followed general medicine and most only look at the foremost problem of the day or week, and ignore the whole person. Psychologists have been documented being involved in torture in cahoots with the CIA, politicians, and the military. The VA is still dragging its feet on PTSD treatment regardless of what it says publicly. The majority of vets with PTSD are driven away by the VA, either by outright opposition to treating them, making them jump through hoops for treatment, or by leaving them on wait lists FOREVER. In the early 2000s the VA was castigated for not moving fast enough with PTSD treatment still. Congress ordered something to be done, and the process sped up a little. Then Vietnam vets and those before 9/11 were demanding PTSD treatment, and the VA and Republicans whined about its budget. The backstabbing Congress without fanfare declared new VA

282

policy which required that for the VA to treat a vet for PTSD, the event which caused the trauma must have occurred within the last 10 years. In one fell swoop those not already in the system were turned away. The system which screens the vets has a redoubled purpose for turning soldiers away from treatment. To make matters worse, recent research shows that the VA is no more successful at treating PTSD than private practice – in other words, they fail most of the time; and of their successes (PTSD diagnoses removed after such and such a period of time), many of those removed from treatment after having been considered "cured" have their symptoms return months to years later. Why is this important?

Anyone who's gone through the trauma of combat knows that there is no cure. The guilt, shame, and sadness that occur are a life-long struggle. This is true for all PTSD victims. My father-in-law was a WW2 infantryman. He came back from Europe and held a steady job and had a family, had a heart attack in his 40's, and when he got old he was sure he was going to Hell for what he had done. For those soldiers, like myself, who are perpetrators, there's a special pain to deal with. But if the government and its Agency refuse to deal with what they have wrought, where does a veteran turn?

Many turn to work and family, have heart attacks, and die. Many turn to drugs and/or alcohol, and die. Many turn to angry violence, and die. Many turn to a gun and blow their brains out. Many turn to the streets and become homeless, and perhaps die. Many turn to justifications based on the propaganda that got them in the mess in the first place; and many turn to religion, seeking justification in the Father, Son, and "Holy Hand Grenade of Jerusalem" (*The Holy Grail* – Monty Python), seeking a higher power to provide blank check forgiveness.

Some have SOs and spouses who struggle so hard to help this person they love so dearly. My best advice for them is listen without judgment – they didn't choose to make this journey. Take them to a GP to have prazosin or propranolol prescribed – the more sleep they get the better. *Take an active interest in the journey that got them where they are.* Not many choose to become killers, yet programming in lieu of just reasoning makes it happen.

If you have children, DO NOT ALLOW RECRUITERS TO TALK WITH THEM. Be honest with your kids and tell them the truth when they're old enough. Recruiters are nothing but lying car salesmen – "What do I have to do to put you with this M-16 or body bag today?" Be honest with yourself about what your government does. Boys and men are expendable to governments and war – they have been since the beginning of time. Life means nothing to a power hungry politician, ruler, or ideological or religious fanatic; or, at least no life matters but their own.

If you want to help a veteran with this type of PTSD, show them respect and love. Participate with them in grounding, and I don't mean touching the floor in a therapist's office, but the ground, nature, sex, and elements of the Earth – From the Earth we came and to the Earth we will return. They could talk to other vets if they're still around, but what they need is for their loved ones to understand them and their predicament. This will take a fair bit of mind opening. Most people don't have a clue what combat really is, or how damaging to the psyche it can be. A spouse and family must be willing to expand their knowledge. *Every American needs to expand their knowledge, and take responsibility for what they ask young men to do in their name.*

The men I knew then, at least the ones I wanted to know, are dead. There are no vets of similar experience lining up to

284

talk, other than patriotic vainglorious bullshit. The work to understand how 2-1/2 years became an all consuming 40 years, segueing into a lifetime, has fallen on myself, alone, and then my wife. At great sacrifice to herself she has kept me alive out of love, to help come to an understanding.

Charlie Rangle used to insist that all Americans serve, not because he loved war, but because he felt that mothers, fathers, voters would pay more attention to what their government gets involved in if they had a personal stake, a life, in the process – they wouldn't be so quick to support war and destruction. A volunteer force for colonial power is unsustainable without lies and unemployment. The head of the Michigan VFW stated not too long ago that what bothers the volunteer veterans most is that while they joined based on unknown lies, and thought all Americans were in this together, they found out that most Americans are ignorant spoiled bitches that don't pay attention, especially not paying attention to the damage done to veterans. And then there are the Americans I call *Rolf*, praising war and destruction and calling out the need to kill for the fatherland while having no experience in such – virgins talking about sex. Many vets feel abandoned by a spoiled population, and this is the most damaging part of PTSD, the abandonment and lies. Joe Biden has never gotten his comeuppance from his years of meddling, not even after his support of a war in Iraq based on nothing but lies – he's a putrid Machiavelli who can't even apologize. He continues looking for his next "splendid war" – and this also contributes to PTSD, the lack of justice and retribution for those who cause the problems. If only they had the honor to fall on their swords.

PTSD almost accomplished what thousands of rebels and Iranian soldiers couldn't. Julie saved me from death multiple times. Without her love, without the expansion of her fine mind, I wouldn't be able to fully adapt. She has realized things of which she was unaware. She continues to work with me and stay with

285

me. I will always have to live with the guilt, shame, sadness, and anger, but Julie is here to help me. What I, what all veterans, and veterans with PTSD, also desperately need is for Americans to wake the fuck up and join reality and the human race.

PTSD is multifaceted. While its true that a PTSD veteran must do hard work to get into treatment and participate, either by himself or through others, a veteran finds it difficult to impossible to forgive treachery and lies by their government and commanders, especially as they never express guilt and shame for what they have wrought. A veteran finds it difficult to impossible to forgive the propaganda and programming that turned him into what he never wanted to be. A veteran finds it difficult to impossible to forgive the chicken hawks and virgins talking about sex who have no clue what the fuck they are praising or talking about. A veteran finds it difficult to impossible to forgive the lying accounts of officers writing books seeking glory and hero status for themselves, and writing justifications for wars and policies that destroy life for ideological and unjust reasons, especially when it is civilians, enlisted men, and NCOs who do the majority of killing, dying, getting wounded and scarred, and living with guilt, shame, and sadness for life. There are definitely worse things than dying.

A veteran may be able to forgive himself for being young, naive, programmed, etc…, but he will always kick himself for not having been smarter and wiser in discernment – even if that were not possible at the time. He may forgive himself if he is drafted and literally has no choice but death by battle or the firing squad. He will not be so ready or willing to forgive himself when he is a volunteer in an all volunteer force. Regardless of whether drafted or not, and of being able to spread fault around, he will be unable to forgive himself for the throats he cut, the brains he splattered, the livers he tore open, the hearts he stopped beating, the decapitations, or the targets he destroyed that later overwhelm him by the realization of the humanity he destroyed when the programming wears away. Forgiveness, for self and others, is as multifaceted as PTSD and is not always possible.

When Vietnam soldiers returned and were spat upon, they were the wrong targets of wrath, mostly berated by the same virgins talking about sex that have always existed. The anti-war movement targeted the wrong people. Overcorrecting, the population at large – still virgins talking about sex – came up with "Thank you for your service", regardless of how the veteran feels about that service or how it affects them when you say it – because you have no idea what that veteran has gone through or done *in your name*. It's a phrase that makes the virgin feel better, not the veteran. In doing so the speakers absolve themselves of their own part in the killing and destruction. The targets of wrath should have been themselves for allowing their government to go too far. The targets of anti-war wrath should be the Congressmen and women who fail to hold their government accountable to their Constitutional duties, and who fail to provide a check upon secret and Presidential power. They should be castigated for signing away their duties to secret agencies and Presidents who have nothing but gain from war.

Responsibility

Gravedigger
When you dig my grave
Could you make it shallow
So that I can feel the rain

Gravedigger – Dave Matthews

I want to make this as clear as possible. Every citizen in a democracy is responsible for what their government does. That means every American, every last one of you, is responsible for the atrocities, killing, and destruction performed in your name. You cede your power to Congress, and they cede it to secret agencies and Presidential power grabs. The whole premise of the Constitution is the control of the government by the citizens, specifically control of the Executive. The President is supposed to preside, not control; they are supposed to execute *your* wishes, not make them up.

Every last one of you is a killer, the same as me. You were there when I stabbed those men and women. You were there when I cut those throats. You were there when I drove the knife up into the brain of the Nicaraguan guard. You were there when I decapitated the cartel guard. You were there when I put bullets in so many heads they can't be properly counted. You were there when we killed unarmed nuns. You were there when I dug the grave and buried the husband, wife, and unborn baby. You helped me perform all these kills. You are responsible as responsible can get, and yet you can't seem to fathom why so many people round the world hate you, or at least see your guilt.

Ironically, because of your orders, which I defied, you were not there to save the baby. You were also not there to save the girl from getting raped; on the contrary, you were with the troopers providing them weapons and equipment to perform rape and murder (you seem to enjoy it). The bullets that blew out the troopers brains were also meant for you.

You supported corruption, torture, rape, and murder in apartheid South Africa for years. For decades you have supported and still support corruption, torture, rape, and murder in Palestine

288

(apartheid Israel). You supported and still support corruption, torture, rape, and murder in the Philippines, throughout Central and South America, Africa, and across lower Asia. You created the drug war and cartels including the corruption, torture, rape, and murder fomented by their growth. You play the ignorant dupe as Biden continues to play his *Rolf* games with the CIA in Ukraine. YOU are ultimately responsible.

> Cold wet stone,
> Deep river bed,
> Once so clean and clear now runs red.
> You know too well
> Was me that called you here.
> Trouble get behind me now,
> Trouble let me be.

> *Trouble* – Dave Matthews

Boys And Men

Some folks are born made to wave the flag,
Ooh, they're red, white and blue,
And when the band plays "Hail To The Chief"
Ooh, they point the cannon at you, Lord…

Some folks are born silver spoon in hand,
Lord, don't they help themselves, oh
But when the taxman comes to the door,
Lord, the house looks like a rummage sale…

Some folks inherit star spangled eyes,
Ooh, they send you down to war, Lord;
And when you ask them, "How much should we give?"
Ooh, they only answer, "More! More! More! More!"

Fortunate Son – Creedence Clearwater Revival

Most men and boys are ready, willing, and able to step up and fight to protect their family and their country, and to fight for real reasons of justice. There are just causes for war and conflict, regardless of blind pacifists' rantings. Most men and boys are unwilling to fight for injustice, lies and deceit, corporate profits, or others' privilege, political power, and gains. Women don't *really* enter this equation, regardless of the hypocritical nonsense NOW or feminists scream from every angle (virgins talking about sex). Although many women may be willing, the vast overwhelming majority of women are unwilling and unable to fight in combat, and… they suck at it. Women make excellent assassins in the social context of war (single kill via poison or knife), but they are not made or meant for the battlefield. Women *are not* expected to participate by either majority sex… Men and boys *are* expected to participate in this function by both sexes.

Men are expendable. Your government expects you to die to protect them and their corruption and deceit. Women expect you to die protecting them. Feminists expect you to die protecting them, and then to just die; or, submit yourself to castration for docile slavery. Capitalists expect you to die protecting profits. Religious zealots expect you to die protecting the "correct" religion, and to slaughter all those in the "incorrect" religions. War mongers expect you to die protecting war and war profiteering. Humans of both sexes with no honor or experience expect you to die for the vainglory of family and country.

Rudyard Kipling liked to praise the glories of war… until he lost his son to war. Achilles thought there was glory in war, until his best friend Patroclus was lost to battle… then it just became an exercise in madness in which he lost his own life. Socrates, himself a veteran, knew there was no glory in war, only death, but like any man he was willing to fight to save his city. What he also knew was that listening to rulers and oracles pretend that war was predestined or ordained from above was asinine. He paid for his teaching against this foolishness with his life. I'm familiar with parents who believe the propaganda concerning Arabs and that we're fighting for democracy everywhere; and regardless of the documented facts, they are only too willing to sacrifice their son(s) for false reasons in order to kill all brown and black "towel heads" out of xenophobic fear. I am familiar with "Christians" who believe the entire world depends upon Christianity destroying other religions and socialism, and are willing and able to force the never ending deaths of boys and men, yet fail to realize the fact that Jesus, as portrayed, was a socialist and would not have raised a finger against other religions. In fact, the only persons Jesus raised his fingers against were corrupt money interests – you remember, turning over tables

291

and flinging epitaphs – the self-aggrandized rich, and the false
and corrupt theologians of his own religion. I am familiar with
Zionists attempting to "cleanse" their Nazi purity of non-white
and Goyim blood. I am familiar with rich persons, ready and
willing to sacrifice the lives of any amount of boys and men to
further their religion, capitalism; yet, just like rich persons from
the beginning of time, they won't be willing to sacrifice
themselves or their progeny for their cause – they'll buy their way
out of any draft or violence while continuing to cause and support
violence for the sake of money.

I've known men and women to praise war and ignore its
destruction and pain, simply because they are virgins talking
about sex – they don't know the first thing about it. George Bush
Jr made sure to join a National Guard squadron (in a state he
didn't even live in) in order to avoid deployment to Vietnam, yet
started a global war on terror based upon his own and US lies and
Israeli lies. Ronald Reagan only acted in war movies (like John
Wayne, Sylvester Stallone, Arnold Schwarzenegger, and on and
on and on – all virgins talking about sex), yet was ready to
sacrifice any amount of lives in war. Jimmy Stewart was a
decorated bomber pilot, yet starred in a movie afterward praising
the southern purity over the terrible Yankee marauders (a
Hollywood favorite topic). Barack Obama never served, yet
joined right in with the secret proxy wars and assassinations and
asserted more powers of secrecy than any other President even as
he promised open government. Donald Trump never served
(military school doesn't count) and found a foot problem to avoid
Vietnam, yet he too was more than willing to sacrifice life and
liberty, and is still willing to sacrifice life and liberty, except his
own fat ass. Kid Rock, a major Republican mouth, never served
(virgin talking about sex) – even with his "homies in cellblock 6".
Ted Nugent, a large Republican war mouth (virgin talking about
sex), avoided Vietnam by shitting his pants on purpose at the
enlistment center (he admitted it like he was smart), but he's more

than willing for *you* to sacrifice. Joe Biden (virgin talking about sex) never served and somehow avoided Vietnam, yet has worked tirelessly since the early '70s supporting every war the US has been involved in, willing to even sacrifice his own son(s) for the vainglory of war; Biden doesn't even have shame over the lies of Central and South America, Afghanistan, and Iraq, insisting he'd do it again. These are not the type of people who should have control over lives or making war. Conflicts were meant to be debated in Congress openly, not secretly started by proxy.

In all of American history, only four conflicts have any basis in reason and justice. The Revolution shed the English throne. The War of 1812 stopped the return of the English throne. The Civil War ended the most egregious hypocrisy and human rights violation of slavery – yet, the English again attempted to interfere supporting the south in its "way of life" for profits. WW2 halted progress of the scourge of fascism, yet we, before and after, continued being addicted to the power of fascism for corporate interests. The first two of these were fought by militias with men volunteering to fight for their country. The Civil War instituted a draft but many men were still volunteers. WW2 had a draft, and many volunteered to fight an obvious evil. Korea was mostly a draft affair, and many men had no idea why they were there. When Vietnam rolled around, the draft was heavy and there were serious attempts to avoid it. Why? Because Vietnam was an attempt to force men to fight for a false action – a secret action – an unjust action. And yet, TV showed Gomer Pyle spending four years as a Marine at a base in sunny southern California as though no war existed – being a soldier is all fun and games!

For decades the Israelis have been committing genocide and establishing an apartheid regime aimed at reestablishing the ancient kingdom. This land does not belong to them regardless of the zealotry arguments. The basis of their claim is "God gave us the land"… well, *Dixit*! End of discussion, eh? – "God" told them to enter a land that didn't belong to them, in which they didn't live, and *slaughter* every last inhabitant (men, women, children) "lest they be a thorn in the side forever". Israelis are attempting since pre-1947 to pick up where they failed centuries ago. Their Chief Rabbi, who advises the Zionist government, has stated on the record that "Hitler had it right, he just chose the wrong people." The US supplies them with weapons and money, **billions** from US taxpayers to commit genocide and apartheid. The US makes love to this opportunistic whore and allows them to destabilize the entire Middle East – *and you American boys and men* will be called upon to slaughter and be slaughtered for the kingdom. The whore comes to Washington, and for serious cash the Congress and President bend over and take it up the ass in a gleeful rape, and then allow Israeli lobbyists to write legislation federally and in the states.

The US kisses royal Saudi ass allowing them to destabilize even more, and to produce terrorists that move adroitly around the world. We supply them with weapons to commit genocide and violations of human rights, for the sake of British whining and oil, royalty, and money. The US has allowed the British to drag the US into every conflict in the Middle East which affects their profits, after the British so royally screwed the world with their own fallen empire. British and French politicians are as corrupt as any who ever existed, and will stop at nothing to bring home the imperial profits, now more than ever by selling weapons. The US allows major corporations and the financial system to drag the US into conflict around the globe.

When I was a boy, veterans of 4 major wars (WW1 through Vietnam) were everywhere; and many more men were dead. An older boy who lived close by to me (and many others) was drafted for Vietnam, and he was dead within months. At this time, the draft is not being used, but with the US creating major

conflicts around the globe on a non-stop basis in order to feed
Lockheed and General Dynamics (the largest contributors to
legislative and world corruption), at some point the money
interests will require *your* sacrifice. The voluntary force cannot
be maintained to support this never-ending war making, and a
draft will come again. If you are a boy becoming a man, STAY
AWAY FROM RECRUITERS. You mean nothing to the military
but a body to fill a bag. Once you are in you will lose all rights to
challenge deployment and you simply become an enabler. The
voluntary force requires poor and ignorant kids to sign up.
Donald Trump, an asshole of phenomenal proportions, was
correct in his assertion that soldiers are "suckers", suckers in that
they enable assholes like Trump and Biden (virgins talking about
sex) to avoid fighting in the wars and conflicts they so love to
create. Recruiters will tell you that you will gain experience,
education, yada, yada, yada... They don't tell you that you may
become fodder for bombs and missiles, that you will kill for the
sake of money. Ask yourself – How much is my sight worth?
How much is my arm worth? How much are my legs worth?
How much is my life worth? How much is my lifelong sanity
worth? How many men, women, and children am I willing to kill
or allow to be killed before I'm overwhelmed by the magnitude of
what I've done?

The military WILL ruin your life. Still, you will hear from
some, virgins talking about sex, that the military (name your
favorite branch) "took care of me" and "gave me a good life".
These are non-combat pretenders – virgins talking about sex – in
love with the provider of free food and a place to live. Others just
look kindly upon a system that may provide them with a death
akin to suicide (You've heard of suicide by cop – this is no
different).

My neighbor is younger than I am. He spent time in
Germany in the Army and praises it. He pretends to have been in

Vietnam (not possible by his age). He's for slaughtering all over the globe, praises conservative "values", rants about government spending, and wears his 9mm in his butt-crack as he does his gardening. Yet, never having been in war, he proclaims himself a "disabled veteran" and had the VA install a ramp on his house and got them to give him a scooter, and he's never used either one – he's too busy chopping wood behind his fence where he thinks no one sees. I had another 20-something neighbor who believes in the military way of life, yet he too is a virgin talking about sex. He wears his 9mm stuck in the back of his pants as he washes his truck – we don't live in a violent neighborhood – it has never been violent. They follow the teachings of Clint Eastwood (military swim instructor), another virgin talking about sex who seems to be in love with Antebellum slavery times. These are all NCP, Non-Combat Pretenders.

You must learn at an early age to distrust your government, to be suspicious of government activities and what they say their motivations are, especially in relation to war. Cowards, men and women, virgins talking about sex, will lie and propagandize in order to get you to serve and fight – to save *their* way of life. Seeing that the US has been involved in war and conflict almost non-stop since its founding, and only four conflicts have any real justification, you must become wise quickly and not let yourself be dragged into unjust actions.

Sex and Love are in preservation of life. Women who give birth naturally receive chemical rewards and incentives from nature. Giving birth and raising children is the hardest positive task a woman will ever take part in. Natural childbirth is excruciating and painful, yet the woman is rewarded by nature twice: 1) with the bonding love of her child which continues on again in nursing; 2) nature provides a chemical softening of the excruciating physical and psychic pain in the fact of remembrance – the bonding and love are elevated and the physical pain, while

296

not forgotten, is chemically softened in the brain memory system, otherwise, no children would be born after the first. This demonstrates the importance of Sex and Love in life, and that children are necessary to sustaining life.

There is no such memory softening for trauma – rape, incest, murder, and killing for your government. This also demonstrates the fact that nature doesn't allow you to forget those traumas; nature wants correction of deviance, an *advancement* of the species. Remembering the deviance from continuing life is important to the species, and is supposed to be communicated and passed on as knowledge. The pain remains in full force in order to wake humans up to the need to care and share rather than take and kill. There is no cure for PTSD. There is no softening of pain and effect in PTSD.

Killing for your government will start to destabilize your life at some point. The first kill or kills may be disturbing, less so from a distance, but the kills become easier for a time, at least until you see their faces, eyes, and breath. You may get through several conflicts and even perform flawlessly through many deployments, but at some point it will hit you with force that you have ended human life, that you killed for no other reason than you were ordered into a situation that you would never have become involved in if left to your own learning and conscience. You will see their faces in your dreams, and you will perform these kills over and over in your "sleep", *ad nauseam*. Your spouse may never understand your anger, pain, and depression.

If you are already in the system, you must educate yourself about the conflict, and you must remove yourself from that influence and environment as soon as practicable. You must remember that you are never required to follow an illegal order, and orders that violate international law and the Geneva Conventions are illegal orders. You may feel that you are doing

297

your part, that what you're doing is acceptable, but if it's based upon lies and deception, your part is most certainly unacceptable. You must never remain quiet or accept situations like a zombie.

If you've already gotten out of the system, and you've been in combat, you most likely have PTSD from your participation. Some get caught in the dregs of depression from PTSD and cannot get out or forgive themselves. Many have secret kills involving civilians or retribution, and the burden of carrying those memories is a struggle to say the least. And seeing that the VA is no better at treating PTSD than than anyone else (and may even be worse because they are a false war apologist, and they label *everyone* in uniform a "warrior" – which propaganda opiate gets repeated in third party "help" programs), and you may have trust issues and anger regarding the failure of the VA and their apologist stance, then you must gather your wits and place the burden upon the civilian mental health system. They are not all that great either dealing with PTSD because many of the therapists and doctors, just like those in the VA, are virgins talking about sex, and many practitioners prefer to direct vets to the VA which has failed them, however, that must not be allowed because ALL are responsible to vets for what has been wrought in the country's and citizens' names. Make your GP participate and prescribe an alpha- or beta- blocker so at least you can regain some sleep. Take THC gummies to stay calm. Seek out psychoactive solutions to expand your own thinking, like LSD or Magic Mushrooms. Tell your politician that they are as responsible as you for what has been wrought and they should be paying for these things. Make the civilian system step up and provide combat trauma specialists, especially for perpetrators – if they can do it for cops, then they certainly can do it for vets. You must be honest and open with anyone about what you've done. *Civilians have no right to be protected from the details of what they have helped make happen.* Younger men and boys must be made to understand the consequences to themselves and the society regarding war and conflicts, especially secret proxy wars and conflicts started by the CIA. *Virgins talking about sex must be corrected.* But most importantly, you must throw yourself into sex and love, not with prostitutes, but with someone you will commit to and who will commit to you. You must stay engaged in the life-giving and sharing properties of sex and love in order to stay human, and not just become a self-hating and angry retributive animal. You must allow yourself to love and be loved.

Responsibility

There are laws in many states allowing that a home owned by a couple cannot be taken for debt owed by one spouse. Creditors hate these laws. They argue that how can a house be owned 100% by each person? While failing the blind math test, it makes total sense and it completely satisfies the social test. Guilt and responsibility for war and secret proxy wars is much like this. I am 100% responsible for what I've done, yet, YOU are also 100% responsible for what I've done; the government is 100% responsible for what I've done; capitalists are 100% responsible; chicken hawks are 100% responsible; anti-communists are 100% responsible; Zionists and Christians are 100% responsible; virgins talking about sex are 100% responsible; etc... **You simply can't call for war, slaughter, and destruction like you're calling a dog**; you can't allow these things to be done in *your* name and then just turn your head away when you find it uncomfortable. "With great power comes great responsibility", which in turn requires thought and discussion, especially when the consequences are so great.

There have been many theories espoused concerning the fall of Rome (and these same theories could apply to any imperial government); but the fact of the matter is Rome and other imperial governments fail for a few basic reasons. First, you

299

cannot steal (peace, land, property, lives) from the rest of the world and expect respect – only hate and anger. If the legislative power (Representatives and Senate) is too weak and relinquishes its authority to kings, emperors, presidents, and executive agency then all decision making is done in secret with power and perpetuation of the status quo in mind. What is that status quo? In a word, Corruption. All governments fail from Corruption because they fail to defeat it, rather they choose to appease it for personal gain. Legislators' and party pockets are lined with corporate and foreign cash. Presidents lose their better sensibilities (if they ever had any – yes *you* Obama) and seek power through foreign interventions and stealing. Understanding history will spell out in detail that Corruption killed Rome, and it will kill the US.

Everyone must make their representatives and senators respond and force change upon a runaway system of secret undeclared conflicts and actions. Regime change as a tool must be taken away from the CIA, and the Dulles CIA must be converted into something better, healthier, and incorruptible. The US must cede authority to the United Nations to control death and destruction, and commit to making a better conflict free world environment, which must start first and foremost with stopping support for the fascist apartheid regimes like Israel. The Presidents need to be reigned in to original Constitutional powers only – the imperial presidencies must end. The US needs to support and help expand the United Nations and the International Criminal Court, and if they want to indict George Bush, Donald Trump, Joe Biden, Benjamin Netanyahu, etc… let them take them, and we should support it. Send them all for retirement at the "Fletcher Memorial Home for Colonial Wasters of Life and Limb" (Pink Floyd). The world will not become a safer or more livable place until all Americans commit to removing corporate, religious, gender, and secret power in politics, and making politicians responsible for the decisions they make and participate in. Secrecy should not prevail in a democracy, and a democracy cannot prevail if it allows secrecy.

YOU – <u>every single last fucking one of you</u> – are responsible and owe every veteran, those who have lost their lives, and those who must continue to live with what they've done in *your* name. It's time for YOU to step up. Those who remain silent give consent.

> Being a witness applies to the individual and the people of [America]. If we individual [Americans] are witnesses to the people, then there will be a people [America]. If we individual [Americans] fail to be witnesses, there will be no people. To be a witness means to be involved, to accept responsibility. Upon the involvement in the responsibility of the individual [Americans] the very existence of the people depends. To witness man's cruelty to man and remain indifferent is an act of betrayal of the legacy of [America]; it would be a grave sin for the [Americans] of our day to go on enjoying the prosperity and comforts of this age and to remain deaf to the sufferings of our brethren, not to care when they are oppressed, not to feel hurt when they are molested.
>
> The Insecurity Of Freedom – *A Declaration Of Conscience*
> – Abraham Joshua Heschel

– Life Begets Life – Sophia Rose – 2020

We Are Not Your Soldiers

I invite all of you to support and participate with a well-respected national organization, <u>We Are Not Your Soldiers</u> (wearenotyoursoldiers.org). They provide volunteers/vets to speak with students, in participating school systems, in order to educate them on the realities of military "service". You may also gain insight from another well respected organization, <u>Veterans For Peace</u> (veteransforpeace.org), with chapters across the US, Australia, Japan, Vietnam, and more. They provide the same service of educating students on the realities of war and the military. Recruiters, ROTC, and JrROTC interacting with students are a violation of trust. ROTC and JrROTC down into middle school is morally bankrupt and morally criminal. The military indoctrinates children at 10 years of age and below (<u>https://youtu.be/FUJRDxf5jLQ</u>). The military does NOT belong in schools, because war and killing is NOT an opportunity.

****

Please consider reviewing and/or rating this work where you purchased it from.

Sean Griobhtha (gree-O-tah) is a combat veteran. You can find him mostly on SubStack.

Printed in Great Britain
by Amazon

44953928R00169